Managing Technology in Financial Institutions

Managing Technology in Financial Institutions

JAMES ESSINGER

FINANCIAL TIMES

PITMAN PUBLISHING

For Sandy

Pitman Publishing
128 Long Acre, London WC2E 9AN

A Division of Longman Group UK Limited

First published in 1993

© James Essinger, 1993

A CIP catalogue record for this book can be obtained from the British Library.

ISBN 0 273 60023 0

Phototypeset in Linotron Times Roman
by Northern Phototypesetting Co. Ltd, Bolton
Printed and bound in Great Britain by
Biddles Ltd, Guildford and King's Lynn

CONTENTS

ACKNOWLEDGEMENTS

It was inevitable, given the wide scope of this book, that many of the ideas and procedures covered in the book have been suggested to me by other people. I am particularly grateful to the following for their kind assistance: Ian Clowes (Logica Cambridge), David Duggett (NatWest Stockbrokers), Chris Elliott (Siemens-Nixdorf), my brother Rupert Essinger, Paul Foll (ACT Financial Systems), Rob Farbrother (Nexus Payment Systems), Julian Goldsmith (Sector Public Relations), Bill Potter (Vista Concepts), Mark Vargo (Memorex Telex) and Jane Watts (AIT).

Philip Kerr's excellent novel *A Philosophical Investigation* provides exciting speculation on how virtual reality might develop in the future, and I have drawn on some of Mr Kerr's ideas for Chapter Four. I am also most grateful to David Crosby of Pitman Publishing for his commitment to this project and the energy with which he helped steer it home.

My warmest thanks go to Joseph Rosen, chief information officer of New York-based Dubin & Swieca Capital Management, who has been an enduring and enthusiastic fellow researcher in financial technology for many years, as well as a good friend. Joe read through an earlier draft of this book, and made many incisive suggestions to improve it.

James Essinger
Canterbury

Note: In the text, I have used 'he', 'him' and 'his' when referring to a hypothetical user or supplier of financial technology only because 'he or she', 'him or her' and 'his or hers' is horrible to write and even worse to read. I hope that my female readers will merely regard my restrictive choice of pronouns as a literary convention and not as indicating any lack of respect on my part towards them.

1 DEFINITIONS AND DESTINATIONS

Introduction

This chapter has three objectives:

- to provide an overview of the role which financial technology is playing in today's world
- to define the key concepts used in the book, and state the overall attitude which will be taken towards terminology
- to examine the most fundamental reason why financial institutions deploy financial technology: the need to gain a competitive advantage over their rivals.

FINANCIAL TECHNOLOGY IN THE WORLD TODAY

This book gives practical guidance on the deployment of one of the most important and exciting types of technology in the world: financial technology.

Financial technology is rapidly creating a world which makes the jargonistic and overused term 'global village' actually have a meaning as: depicting an international environment where electronic links connect bankers, securities traders, fund managers and their consultants in fractions of seconds, wherever the participants may be located.

A good case could be made for maintaining that applications of technology within the financial sector are the most important type of technological applications in today's world. Financial technology draws the countries of the world closer together, locking them into mutually beneficial trading and negotiating networks which, it could reasonably be argued, have already helped to make the world a more peaceful place by showing nations that their inhabitants are happier and more prosperous if they are doing business with the inhabitants of other nations rather than fighting them. The national and international networks which financial technology creates have already played their part in ending the Cold War – Russia, after all, has stock exchanges now – and in time to come international networks between the developed and developing worlds may prove a more potent means of increasing Third World prosperity and health than any number of relief shipments.

It is not possible to obtain precise figures, worldwide, of expenditure on different types of technology. However, it is likely that more money is spent on military technology than on any other form of technology. Financial technology would come a close second. Yet military technology – whether actually deployed or held in reserve – is a stark embodiment of the divisions in politics, religion and creed between nations. Financial technology, on the other hand, does indeed provide the practical means which enables nations to trade with each other, co-operate economically with each other, invest across each other's borders, and help each other in a variety of different ways. During the past thirty years, financial technology has been one of the great unsung heroes of the world; facilitating a level of efficiency and international co-operation in finance and business that has never before been seen by mankind.

All the same, the relationship between military technology and financial technology is less antagonistic than might be supposed. The unavoidable fact is that many of the most brilliant types of applications of financial technology have been foreshadowed by similar developments in military technology, a few years before. An example of this was the rapid pro-liferation during the late 1980s, of computer programs, based around large numbers of logical *rules* (or heuristics). These programs sought to imitate human judgemental reasoning by providing a tool for making informed subjective judgements on which course of action a user ought to follow when confronted by large volumes of rapidly changing data.

It will come as no surprise that these systems were first developed to cope with battlefield conditions, with many of the lessons also being learned within the famous 'Strategic Defense Initiative' (SDI) or 'Star Wars' pro-gramme. What may be more surprising for many readers to learn is that the designers of many of these so-called 'artificial intelligence' systems left their military projects in the mid to late 1980s (particularly when 'Star Wars' fell out of political favour) and joined commercial systems houses designing computer tools for financial institutions. As this book explains (see pages 48–50) the greatly overhyped artificial intelligence bubble of the 1980s has now burst, but the tendency for many former military technologists to seek profits from the financial sector continues, even though the general recession in the world's financial sectors during the early 1990s tended to slow the process down.

I make no apologies for starting this book with a fullsome tribute to financial technology. Not only is the financial technology industry an extremely innovative, fast-moving and exciting industry, but the challenge presented by harnessing the power of technology to the domestic and international activities of financial institutions continues to attract some of the world's most resourceful and enterprising minds. No one can work within this industry for long without feeling profoundly privileged to be involved in it.

WHY THIS BOOK WAS WRITTEN

I wanted to write this book because there is no reliable, single source of information about how to *manage* the deployment of financial technology. There are some books which look at specific types of financial applications and suggest how technology can be used to deal with these applications – indeed, I have written some such books myself. However, there is nothing available which draws together current thinking and best practice in deploying financial technology into a strategic guide. It is precisely this gap which this book is designed to fill.

Did your heart sink just now when you saw the word 'strategic'? Did this make you begin to suspect that this book will be full of 'management waffle'? Do you fear being subjected to the sort of verbiage which is aired every day in financial technology-related conferences in London, New York, Tokyo; anywhere indeed, where conference organisers are confident of making a profit? You know what I mean: those horrible words and expressions which are used not because they actually mean anything, but because they give the user an air of superficial authority while relieving him from the responsibility of thinking. Words and terms such as 'empower', 'strategic' (sorry), 'strategic management', 'horses for courses', 'significant changes'; the list is, regrettably, almost endless.

In this book I have made every effort to keep my language straightforward and direct. I do not subscribe to the notion – common, I am afraid to say, among the more expensive types of management consultants – that the higher the fee being charged, the longer the words ought to be. Nor do I believe that polysyllables indicate complexity and depth of thought.

MY OWN EXPERIENCE IN FINANCIAL TECHNOLOGY

I have been writing about financial technology since 1986, when I was fortunate enough to work as public relations consultant to a consortium that was busily creating Britain's first shared network of automated teller machines (ATMs). Between 1986 and 1988 I spent about half my time working as a writer and researcher within the financial technology industry, and in 1988, when I was commissioned to write my first full-length publication on the industry (a study of the role which computerised trading systems played – or didn't play – in the 1987 Crash), I began working within the financial technology industry on a full-time basis, and have done so ever since.

I give these brief autobiographical details because I believe that anyone who claims to provide authoritative information – as I am unashamedly claiming to provide in this book – ought to make clear to his readers the basis for his claim to be an authority. In my case my claim is founded upon an acquaintance with applications of technology covering a wide range of financial functions, including:

- administration (back office)
- commercial (wholesale) banking
- data communications
- data storage
- financial information vending
- foreign exchange
- global custody
- hardware
- insurance
- investment management
- retail banking
- securities trading
- software design.

I should add, however, that I have surveyed these and other types of applications of financial technology as an *observer*, first and foremost. I have never worked directly as an employee of a bank or software house. Instead, I have found out how literally hundreds of banks and other financial institutions use technology, and how a similar number of hardware, software and systems houses meet their financial customers' practical requirements. Many readers will have a justifiable claim to be more expert than me in several of the *individual* areas listed above (with the possible exception of global custody and investment management technology) but I can reasonably claim to be in the unusual position of having a wide knowledge of technological deployment across all the above areas of the financial sector.

Whereas a consultant, software designer or the end-user in the financial institution will have a greater, more detailed knowledge of a particular technology application than an observer and researcher could hope to have, a sufficiently experienced observer and researcher will be able to provide an overview not only of the entire range of technological applications in the financial industry, but – more to the point – will be able to identify certain key themes and important procedures which are common to all these applications. This is precisely what I seek to do in this book, where possible illustrating the principles with case studies drawn from the real world and showing how specific financial institutions (although I am not always at liberty to name them) have sought to deal with the challenges that face them.

DEFINITIONS

In order that the areas of discussion can be clear from the outset, it is necessary for certain terms to defined here, with these definitions being adhered to rigorously throughout the book. An undoubted problem facing anyone who writes about financial technology is the lack of agreement within the industry of the definitions of many fundamental terms, with the result that much industry discussion appearing in journals and even books is of little practical assistance to anybody, since the precise matters under discussion are insufficiently clear to the reader.

I first encountered this problem when researching my first book. After talking to sources in the UK and the US about 'program trading', I began to realise that the term was being used by various people to denote three completely different things, namely: a basket trade; a trade which is carried out using a computer; and a trade which involves arbitrage between different markets or market indices. It was particularly alarming to discover that the New York Stock Exchange defined the term 'program trading' in a significantly different way to the experts who wrote the Brady Commission report: the well-known report, ordered by former President Ronald Reagan, into the causes of the 1987 Crash. This use of the term 'program trading' to define three different concepts would not have been a problem had everyone agreed that the term had three distinct meanings, but unfortunately this was not the case. Some people interpreted the term to mean one of the three concepts, others regarded it as meaning two of the concepts, and some – including myself – came to believe that it meant all three.

It seems to me, therefore, that it is essential to define terms of reference precisely at the outset.

In this book, *financial institution* (which is often abbreviated simply to 'institution' in the text) means any private or public organisation which derives the greater part of its revenue from handling, managing or investing money, either on its own behalf or on behalf of its customers. This book steers away from excessive use of the term 'bank', partly because many financial institutions are not banks, and also because in many regulatory frameworks (eg in the UK) the term 'bank' has a legal meaning, relating to status and a proven track record of successful and solvent trading, which many financial institutions *already* carrying out banking-type functions have not yet attained, and are therefore not allowed to call themselves banks.

The term *technology* is used throughout the book to denote information technology: that is, any freestanding or networked computer or computer system which has as its main objective the storage, processing, handling and relaying of digitised (ie electronic) information. Note that, where computers are used in the financial industry, the information that is stored, processed, handled and relayed by computers can be of great immediate value, if it is a message governing the transfer of funds from one account to another, whether within a branch, in an institution or even across a national border. As Chapter Six on computer security makes clear, the immense potential value of financial information held within a computer system requires a legal and regulatory structure which recognises the value of this information, and statutory and professional regulatory frameworks have in many cases been slow to recognise this need. There is, however, little to be gained for discursive purposes from distinguishing between funds transfer information and other types of financial information. In practice, the secure storage, rapid retrieval and accurate transmission of all types of financial information should be regarded as equally important.

The term *technology* is a friendlier and more concise term than information technology, and both are better than the acronym 'IT', which not only is too easily seen as a two-letter word if the full stops are removed, but introduces a note of harshness and – as with all acronyms – truncated communication that is inappropriate for a book, such as this, which seeks to advance understanding rather than bewilderment. Where, as is occasionally the case, the term technology refers to other types of technology which are not information technology, this is clearly indicated in the text. Similarly, other computer-related terms are explained as they occur.

FINANCIAL INSTITUTIONS' ATTITUDES TOWARDS TECHNOLOGY

To say that financial institutions' attitudes towards technology are in a state of profound change sounds like – and is – the worst kind of banal platitude, but the fact is that since computers were first installed by financial institutions, great changes in attitude towards technology have occurred. These changes so condition the current nature of the financial technology industry that it seems essential to set them down here, before proceeding with the main material of the book. As might be expected, some of these changes in attitude mirror developments in public attitudes towards technology in a wider sense. Among the most important changes in this context are the following.

1 *Institutions are no longer in awe of technology.*
When technology first began to be deployed to a great extent in institutions during the 1970s, both management and junior staff were often in awe of the system. If it went wrong, or if they found it impossible to use, they tended to blame themselves rather than the computer.

It is natural for people to be in awe of – and even to fear – technology when they do not understand it. However, it is equally natural – and certainly healthy – for people to become used to working with the technology within a fairly short time, and eventually to become sceptical of its effectiveness, blaming it not only when it genuinely does malfunction, but also when they themselves make an error and the computer works perfectly. One of the first lessons which technology vendors who begin working within the financial industry learn is never to expect gratitude from the institutions to whom they sell their systems. This is particularly true of users who rely heavily on decisions which may be based on information provided by the computer skills. Usually, where a decision turns out wrong, the user will if possible blame the machine, but take all the credit himself or herself if the decision turns out right, even if the computer obviously played an important role in the decision, either by providing the basic information, or by making a specific prompt.

It should be noted that a situation where users are in awe of technology generally indicates that the technology is not being used to its full efficiency and potential. A very good way of regarding computers is to see them simply as sophisticated tools, and people have every right to expect to be master of the tools they use, not vice versa. It is no more logical for a user to blame himself if he cannot understand how to use a computer than it would be for him to blame himself if he cannot workout how to open a glass door with no handle. Human impatience with a tool usually at least indicates that the tool is playing a key role in the person's life, given the need to rectify the problem that is causing the impatience. Generally speaking, people have evolved to expect more, not less, from the tools that they use, and never to be entirely satisfied with them. This is a fact which designers of technology for financial institutions would do well to bear in mind from the outset.

In the case of financial technology, the period when users were in awe of the technology finished around the end of the 1980s, and nowadays the only people likely to be in awe of financial technology are either junior staff who have not yet been trained in its use, and members of the public – particularly the elderly – who have never mastered computers, and are now not likely to. Financial technology vendors who imagine that their users will make any-thing more than the smallest of allowances for technology that does not do what it is supposed to do are in for a shock.

⊀   2 *Institutions no longer expect technology to be difficult to use.* ⊁
This change in attitude is directly connected with the first, above; indeed it might said to be an extension of it. The more familiar a new tool becomes to people, the more they expect to be able to use it 'seamlessly' (a jargonistic term, but a useful one here), that is, without noticing it. Similarly, people quickly forget that they ought to consider themselves fortunate to have access to a particular tool at all, and demand that the technology becomes more convenient and more easy to use, the more convenient and easy to use it actually is.

When aeroplanes were first developed, passengers were quite happy to wear goggles, get buffeted by the wind and the rain, and lie in an uncom-fortable – not to say, dangerous – position on the plane. For them, the thrill of flying was enough. Now that most people have some experience of flying, airlines are – if they want to stay in business – obliged to design the interiors of their aircraft to be as homely and comfortable as is compatible with flight.

The technology can never be entirely unnoticeable and seamless; sheer practical considerations dictate that a traveller must first go to an airport and must then submit to the actual process of flying, but a jet flight today is probably about as seamless a way of travelling that is possible until some other form of travel – instant teleportation, perhaps – is invented. And seasoned travellers may, like all experienced users of technology, develop an ability to avoid noticing the intrusive elements of the technology which prevent it from being entirely seamless. For them, travelling as it were by their own internal automatic pilot, a flight may well amount to much the same as stepping out of their front door at home and finding themselves at their destination.

There are two main reasons why financial institutions must deploy technology that is easy to use. Firstly, ease of use is essential if staff (who will of course include dealing and investing personnel as well as administrative staff) are to get the full benefit of the institution's technological investment. Secondly, even if staff are content with the technology, the institution cannot afford to rest on its laurels, since it must also maximise the useability – that is user convenience and ease – of its technological systems which are used by the general public. Deploying technology which is not only easy to use but which customers *positively enjoy* using is, in today's highly technologically streamlined climate, an important way for an institution to gain a competitive advantage, especially for those institutions which have a substantial degree of retail business. Which leads us on to the final change in financial institutions' attitude towards computers.

3 *Institutions have recognised the need to use technology as a competitive weapon.*

This is unquestionably the most important of the three trends. Winning a competitive edge has become of fundamental importance within national and international financial sectors where, for many financial institutions, the prime emphasis of activity now rests on providing an ever-improving level of service to existing clients and customers, and winning new business through the sheer quality of service provided and the ingenuity of marketing activity. Ultimately, it is only through establishing a competitive advantage over rival institutions that an institution can hope to maximise profitability.

In financial sectors where establishing a competitive advantage has become so important, it is necessary for institutions to pay particular attention to the role which technology plays in offering them an opportunity to gain this advantage. The rationale for this emphasis on technology is the general consensus that the future progress of the banking business will be dictated by three principal driving forces, namely:

- increased competition
- increased deregulation
- opportunities offered by new and existing technology.

Increased competition is caused by the gradual breakdown, over the past twenty years or so, of the notion that the provision of financial services is something remote, elegantly secretive, and distant from the normal hubbub of business activity. The great opportunities (not necessarily always realised, of course) which financial services have for generating profitability has attracted many organisations into the financial services arena. The public, in turn, perceiving the greater level of competitiveness in the marketplace, have instinctively responded by becoming more demanding, and more prepared to switch their account or custom from one institution to another: something which was almost unheard of twenty years ago. Seeing the willingness with which the public are prepared to switch their accounts, more organisations have moved into the financial services sector, and the process has been repeated and reinforced, until the level of competitiveness in the marketplace has become very high.

Increased deregulation, that is, the breakdown of regulatory barriers which formerly restricted entry into the financial services sector as a whole and into particular niche markets within the sector, has gone hand-in-hand with increased competition. There is a definite relationship between the two, although the precise nature of the relationship is by no means clear, since, as is often the case, it is difficult to tell whether changes in regulatory frameworks are a cause of, or a result of, changes in the environments that they govern. However, there is little doubt that the election in the UK and the US, at the beginning of the 1980s, of relatively right-wing governments, spurred on a process of deregulation throughout the commercial environments in these countries which has persisted to this day, and could scarcely be reversed.

The formerly existing demarcation barriers between different financial services niche sectors have been weakened or erased completely, and although in many cases (eg following the introduction of the Financial Services Act 1986 in the UK) the regulatory requirements for organisations or individuals wishing to operate in certain niche markets have actually increased, the new requirements have been installed primarily for the purposes of investor protection. Indeed, any financial institution which meets the niche regulatory requirements can operate in whichever niche sector it pleases. In most national regulatory frameworks today, there are no longer restrictions on an institution operating in one niche sector if it is already operating in another. This single fact alone has immensely important implications for competitiveness within the financial sector.

The opportunities offered by new and existing technology consist of all the new initiatives – administrative, procedural, marketing-oriented, strategic or relating to other areas of the institution's business – which can be furthered by the introduction of new and existing technology.

It should be clear that out of these three driving forces the one which provides the greatest opportunity for a financial institution's executives to exert a level of *control* on the pace of change is unquestionably the opportunities offered by new and existing technology. The factors of increased competition and increased deregulation are essentially macrocosmic factors: an individual institution can expect to do little to alter the pace of change in these two areas and to a considerable extent must be content with reacting to change here, rather than influencing it.

This, however, is not at all the case with technological deployment, since the extent to which technology is deployed within a financial institution is clearly a matter of managerial policy and budgetary allowance.

Most studies of the future of banking and financial services pay attention to the role of technology, but usually reveal little in terms of what a banker should actually do in order to ensure that his bank is making the most of the opportunities offered by technology. This book, however, focuses entirely on this subject, and constantly refers to the role which technology plays in assisting financial institutions to gain a competitive advantage. One can even go so far as to argue that the *prime function* of technological deployment is to assist an institution to gain a competitive advantage. This last point has such momentous implications for financial technologists that it requires elaboration here.

The first point to make is that the notion that technology should above all help financial institutions to outcompete their rivals is a relatively new one. Until even the mid-1980s, many institutions saw technology as primarily offering them the opportunity to undertake routine chores faster than was previously possible and freeing staff for more interesting and profitable work. While applying technology for these reasons has brought great benefits to institutions, the idea that technology should principally be installed by an institution in order to help it process data is now outmoded. It ignores the huge impact which technology can have on an institution's competitive position by enabling the bank to offer its customers both a better service and a wider range of services. Financial institutions the world over are now becoming alive to this very point, with the result that at most institutions the term 'data processing (DP) manager' is becoming, or has become, obsolete. Today's technology managers who work within financial institutions take it for granted that the systems they deploy will provide efficient data processing and storage. However, they are normally more concerned with the system's impact on their bank's competitive position.

In addition to making improvements in operational efficiencies, institutions have the potential to achieve a competitive advantage over their rivals from any aspect of their technological deployment, from the use of hardware through to specific applications programs designed for niche market areas.

This book aims to cover the widest range of technological applications which can offer a competitive advantage to banks, as well as many of the niche market areas themselves.

Finally, in which specific areas of their activity can institutions gain a competitive advantage through the use of technology? The best way to analyse this is to identify the problem and consider the role that technology plays in solving the problem. This analysis, in turn, will depend on whether the institution (or department within an institution) is primarily carrying out a retail function (ie providing financial services to the general public, which includes both private individuals and businesses) or a wholesale function (ie providing financial services to other institutions, or to large corporate customers). Some problems will be common to both types of institutions.

HOW FINANCIAL INSTITUTIONS CAN ESTABLISH A COMPETITIVE EDGE

1 RETAIL FINANCIAL INSTITUTIONS

The problem: retaining existing customers and winning new ones

The role which technology can play in solving the problem: this role consists of providing customers with attractive and convenient means of obtaining banking services and making payments. There is a particular advantage in using technology here, in that it is especially appealing to younger customers, who will often be attracted to an institution because of the technology that it deploys and stay with the institution for the rest of their lives.

The greatest single advantage which technology offers institutions from the point of view of serving customers is that it allows them to provide a wide range of banking services round the clock and without requiring customers to queue for long periods. Financial institutions providing these services may reasonably expect to keep existing customers happier, and win more new customers, than institutions which do not provide these services.

The main means by which technology achieves these objectives is via the automated teller machine (ATM). This is a mechanised banking service provider which may equally well be installed in the branch (a lobby ATM) where its main role is to offer convenience and speed of service, in the wall of the branch (a through-the-wall [TTW] ATM) or in an alcove inside the building but not necessarily in the branch. Alcove installation – which usually requires the user to open the alcove door with his plastic card – is particularly popular in cold countries (eg Canada) or in locations (eg the US) where the user's safety and security is a paramount concern.

Any retail financial institution wishing to compete successfully in today's retail financial services marketplace must offer its customers a range of ATM facilities, particularly TTW ATM facilities. One particularly important benefit provided by ATMs is that, where the institution in question is part of a shared ATM network, its customers can obtain banking services through other institutions' ATMs, thus dramatically boosting the number of ATMs to which a particular customer has access.

Since the beginning of the 1990s, one necessary rider to the doctrine of the all-pervading importance of ATMs has started to emerge. This is the somewhat ironic point that, having been so successful at developing ATM-based service channels to customers who, using the ATMs, do not even need to step into the branch, institutions have begun to realise that they make a far higher percentage profit from providing such services as mortgages, loans, insurance and buying and selling stocks and shares on customers' behalf than they make from providing everyday account-handling services such as cash withdrawal facilities and payment facilities. This being the case, institutions have naturally started to look very hard at ways to bring their customers back into the branch, where they can be sold these more lucrative (from the institution's point of view) products.

Which is not to say that institutions no longer want their customers to use ATMs; they do, particularly since no major financial institution would nowadays be able to provide an adequate service to its customers without the assistance of ATMs. However, the need to bring customers back into the branch remains. Here again, however, technology has a crucial role to play, with useful practical applications being as follows.

Use of dedicated multifunction customer access terminals in the branch
Such terminals are in effect specialised ATMs, providing one or two specific services and in many cases making full use of user-friendly interfaces, colour (which cannot usually be used in TTW ATMs because current technology cannot easily provide an economical colour screen capable of being read in the glare of natural light, although considerable progress is being made on this problem in the US) and even specialised interactive devices such as touch-screen facilities. By providing such terminals, institutions hope not only to attract customers back into the branch, but also to use the terminals themselves to sell the more profitable products.

Use of advanced cash handling equipment to create a friendlier appearing branch

An important, if fairly unglamorous, use of technology in this respect has been the deployment of electromechanical (ie not information technology-based) devices which allow cash to be dispensed from human tellers who do not require arrays of bars and glass windows around them. The usual procedure is for a branch to deploy a number of 'friendly' tellers who can deal with fairly small retail transactions (eg up to about £200 in value) from open workstations which are served by tills where each cash withdrawal (or paying in) transaction is handled separately, with the banknotes being paid in (or arriving) via an automated device which rapidly carries them to and from a remote and secure location in the branch. Other tellers, who will deal with larger retail transactions, would be situated behind the familiar protective glass and metal panels.

Providing electronic payment services

Another major aspect of how financial institutions use technology to attempt to gain a competitive advantage in the provision of retail services is in the area of providing electronic payment services to customers. There is, in fact, a surprising lack of practical research into how customers feel about technology-related payment methods, with institutions generally making the assumption that customers invariably enjoy the convenience and speed of being able to pay for goods at the point of sale by the use of a card which activates an electronic funds transfer at the point of sale (EFTPOS) system. There is, however, a growing body of evidence supporting the belief that offering such electronic payment facilities to customers provides retail financial institutions with a definite competitive advantage.

Branch automation

Branch automation (ie the automating of an entire branch) has a key role to play in making the branch's services more attractive to customers. This is particularly the case with those high profit-generating services discussed above. In an ideal automated branch scenario of the future, not only would a branch contain a variety of dedicated terminals which can be used to dispense a variety of specialised products such as loans, share buying and selling, and even mortgages, but online computer terminals would be available to counter staff to allow rapid access to funds and customer information. However, at present the front-counter computer systems of even the most technologically advanced retail bank still offers human tellers access to far too little information about customers, even given the need to guard against indiscriminate use of data to comply with national data protection regulations. This is an area in which all retail institutions can improve their performance.

The problem: freeing staff for personal interaction with customers

The role which technology can play in solving the problem: although dedicated branch-based terminals have a key role to play in attracting customers into a branch and acting as the media for selling various profitable products and services, retail institutions wishing to gain a competitive advantage must recognise the importance of technology's role in freeing staff from mundane, routine administrative functions. This releases them into areas where they will interact more actively with customers, and in most cases thereby generate a higher profit for the institution than simply by providing the more mundane account-based services.

The problem: handling customers' accounts more efficiently and cost-effectively

The role which technology can play in solving the problem: ever since computers were first used by financial institutions in the 1960s to replace the drudgery of the manual handling of customers' accounts, the scale of the account-handling task facing retail institutions has induced them to use large mainframe computers and to orientate the account-handling process around the customer's account number. This approach, while permitting rapid access to a very large number of accounts, has the major disadvantage that only straightforward types of information is summoned up by the system, relating to the customer's account.

Since it seems obvious that successful retail banking increasingly depends on an institution building a closer relationship with its customers, there is a clear need for institutions to develop methods of handling clients' accounts which facilitate the nurturing of these relationships. To date retail financial institutions around the world have a great deal to do in this respect. What is needed is an account-handling system which will still allow large numbers of accounts to be accessed on a day-to-day basis, but which will facilitate the creation of a relationship between institution and customers which centres on the institution handling a wide range of the customer's needs, such as current and savings accounts, mortgages, loans, insurance and investment portfolios.

Fortunately, the means which would facilitate this process has already been developed. *Relational databases* are databases which allow users to store and retrieve data in a wide variety of configurations relating to the user's requirements, rather than simply according to an alphabetical or numerical listing. Using a relational database, a user could, for example, retrieve the names of all customers earning more than a certain specified sum, the names of customers living in a certain geographical locality, or indeed any of a wide range of other parameters.

Retail financial institutions are already making use of relational databases for marketing and related purposes, but these applications are still a long way from a situation where, when a customer comes into the branch, he can give his name to an assistant and, on keying in the details to a terminal, the assistant can retrieve an entire range of data relating to the customer. There would, of course, be a need here to observe data protection legislation, but there can be no doubt that a retail financial institution which developed a comprehensive system for retrieving information on customers would soon establish an important competitive advantage over one which had not.

The problem: developing more effective data communications, both within the bank and to counterparties

The role which technology can play in solving the problem: maximising the effectiveness of data communications is an important priority for retail institutions. There are two types of applications of data communications which are of importance here.

1 Data communications facilities used by customers
Customers will quickly grow impatient if they experience any inconvenience or even slight delay in using the institution's electronic payment services (such as ATMs, EFTPOS or telephone banking) all of which will inevitably rely heavily on data communications. There is a distinct need for retail financial institutions to deploy 'fault-tolerant' systems which operate by incorporating redundant features – either contained within the hardware or the software – which ensure that if one component or piece of software fails to operate, the communications process will be maintained without the user even being aware of what has happened, and with no information being lost. Placing an absolute priority on the integrity of data communications is essential for a retail financial institution.

2 Data communications relating to administration
Clearly, the financial institution will only be efficient if these data communi-

cations are working at maximum efficiency, and indeed if they are as comprehensive as budgetary provisions permit.

2 WHOLESALE FINANCIAL INSTITUTIONS

The problem: providing staff with better sources of decision support information

The role which technology can play in solving the problem: for any wholesale (ie business to business) financial institution operating teams of financial traders or investment managers, providing these teams with the latest in decision support information is perhaps the most important way in which the institution can use technology as a means of gaining a competitive advantage. Although traders and investment managers use a wide range of information on which to base trading and investment decisions, the type of information under consideration here is that which reaches them via a screen. This information can usefully be categorised under the following three headings. Financial institutions wishing to deploy decision support technology to maximum competitive advantage should ensure that in each of these three areas they have provided their staff with the greatest breadth and depth of information, to allow staff to reach trading and investment decisions based on news of all the factors to which they can reasonably expect access.

1 Real-time information
This relates to prevailing, current prices in financial markets around the world, with the price information constantly being updated on a simultaneous basis if the market is still open, and the closing prices (and corresponding volumes) being quoted if the market has closed.

2 Historical information
This relates to prices which have prevailed in the past. Many systems offer a wide range of historical parameters, with the most popular parameters being prices prevailing over the past seven to ninety days. Note that graphical displays are particularly important with historical information, as they allow the information to be displayed in an easily recognisable and highly accessible form.

3 'Value-added' (analytic) information
The potential for gaining a competitive advantage is greatest here since

there is no practical limit to the number of possibilities that exist. Institutions can use a variety of analytic techniques and screen-based services to analyse, reconfigure or re-present real-time or historical information in such a way as to be of maximum utility to traders or investment managers. New types and theories of financial market analysis are literally being invented every week, and it can be seen as proof of the rapid expansion of value-added information facilities that it is difficult to tell whether the application is driving the technology here, or the technology driving the expansion.

The problem: maximising the efficiency of administrative support

The role which technology can play in solving the problem: the mid to late 1980s saw a great emphasis being placed on how technology could make wholesale banks more competitive in the front office, and in particular relating to decision support information. However, the Crash of 1987 and the worldwide recession of the early 1990s drew attention away from the front office and to the back office (ie the administrative department), where it was being increasingly felt that considerable opportunities for increased efficiency and cost savings (the two often going hand in hand) existed.

It is sufficient at this stage to say that technology plays an essential role in the back office of wholesale banks in streamlining operations, reducing staffing costs, and introducing higher accuracy and greater speed. Any wholesale bank which seeks to gain a competitive advantage over its rivals must deploy technology which meets all of these objectives.

The problem: handling customers' accounts more efficiently and cost-effectively

The role which technology can play in solving the problem: just as retail financial institutions can gain a high degree of potential competitive advantage by deploying technology for this purpose, similar competitive advantages will accrue to wholesale financial institutions which maximise the efficiency of their account-handling facilities and the degree of personalisation of service which the facilities permit.

The problem: developing more effective data communications, both within the bank and to counterparties

The role which technology can play in solving the problem: maximising the effectiveness of data communications is as important for wholesale institutions as it is for retail institutions. Not only do wholesale banks communicate with their customers via data communications, but they also send trading, negotiation and funds transfer messages, the integrity and security of which it is essential to maintain.

INTERVIEW
with Bill Potter, Vista Concepts Inc.

Finally, to conclude this chapter, is an interview with one of the brightest young stars in the world's financial technology firmament. Bill Potter, managing director of New York-based international securities industry system house Vista Concepts, has overseen the successful development of a company which has managed a high rate of growth even during the hard times of the early 1990s: times which have brought many other financial technology vendors to their knees. I interviewed Bill during September 1992 regarding his thoughts on the direction of financial technology in the future, and what principal concepts were going to be important. The result was fascinating, with implications for financial technology applications well beyond the scope of Vista Concepts' own areas of application.

Vista Concepts is one of the world's leading vendors of packaged accounting and clearing systems for participants in the global securities industry. Vista Concepts is the vendor which won the contract from the London Stock Exchange to develop the much-delayed TAURUS securities settlement system. Vista Concepts was originally founded in 1979 by three individuals as a privately held company providing consulting services, primarily to the financial community of banking and brokerage firms on Wall Street. The organisation now has a staff of more than 160. Vista Concepts' growth is principally the result of the development of a series of software products, which have attracted an international client list.

JE: How did Vista Concepts come to be associated with the Taurus project?

POTTER: A tender for provision of software and services for Taurus went out from the London Stock Exchange in 1990 to a number of software houses in the US and UK. The London Stock Exchange narrowed bidders down to two or three preferred vendors and began to hold detailed discussions with those few selected. At the time we had just installed an enhanced version of our Vista software in Midland Bank in the UK. We had delivered an online, real-time, multicurrency securities movement and control system to perform UK custody, clearing and settling. This same software is the base for Taurus. As one of the four primary UK clearing banks, Midland was an ideal showcase for Vista's skill and securities expertise. Vista was selected by the London Stock Exchange late in 1990.

JE: What do you think the role of technology within the US financial sector is likely to be during the following five years?

POTTER: Within the US financial sector, and increasingly throughout the international financial sector, technology has developed as a means of providing for highly automated operations in high-volume, transaction processing and account-handling environments. The requirement for technology to continue to fulfil this role will persist, as financial institutions – whether retail or wholesale – realise that they must compete intensively with each other if they wish to retain and maximise market share, and that they are going to need high-volume transaction processing systems if they are to succeed in the competitive battle. The only way for them to deploy the most efficient high-volume transaction processing system is to make sure that they have the right technology.

JE: Talking specifically about the securities industry, what demands does technology have to meet at present?

POTTER: There are two sides of this coin. First, to take the case of the banks which handle and manage the holding of securities investments – that is, global custodians and subcustodians – the technology which they use will need to respond to the needs of custodians' own clients for value-added services. Within the custody industry, as in so many niche market areas of the financial sector, change is happening at a very rapid rate. The fast acceptance within most national custody arenas of the recommendations of the Group of Thirty [an international think tank which makes recommendations on economic policy and is highly influential within the international securities industry], the new depository institutions that are coming online, the need for multicurrency and multilingual back-office systems, and the changing number and types of instruments that are occurring in the world all require that custodian banks have systems which allow them not only to keep up with the changing pace of their business but to anticipate this change and profit from it.

Above all, custody technology needs to be easily maintainable, and should continue to offer a track record of high-volume capability.

On the other side of the coin you have securities traders and investment managers. Following the mid-1980s, during which most securities traders of any size installed state-of-the-art dealing systems and information reception systems, the degree of automation at most securities dealers is very high, even though they cannot always afford to update and enhance their systems as often as they would like. After all, a system installed in the mid-1980s is probably approaching the time when it cries out to be replaced, even if is still working properly, which it may not be.

On the other hand, the level of automation within investment management organisations remains smaller than it ought to be for all but the largest organisation. Few investment management organisations are as well automated as they will be required to be in the near future in order to compete within increasingly competitive national investment management industries. There are many PC and small hardware-based packages for investment managers, but I don't think any of these really meet the investment management industry's needs for a package that facilitates the handling and management of an entire portfolio. I think that in an increasing number of cases the trend here is for investment management organisations to 'do their own thing' as regards technology. Some of these home-made products will be branded and marketed to fellow investment managers.

The expected result, which is in fact exactly what one sees, is a proliferation of investment management, portfolio management and performance measurement analysis products across the board, but few clear leaders in terms of technology in that area. I think this will change over time. In particular, I think that there will be far more integration of technology used by custodians and investment managers. I also foresee increasing use of downloading of portfolio data to PCs so that investment and portfolio managers can retrieve their own information from their local PC and client servers. Investment managers will go to a central depository for some standard types of investment and portfolio reporting. However, the investment manager will need the capability to load data on an *ad hoc* basis for his own local and *ad hoc* reporting. I definitely think that this is the direction in which the technology is moving.

JE: Do you believe that, in the financial technology industry, the application drives the technology or that the technology drives the application? Please give your reasons.

POTTER: I think that technology has been driving the application. In all honesty I think that it ought to be the other way round, but the reason why it is the way it is stems from how the financial technology industry has developed. Within the industry the technology has usually come first, and then the application has been designed to fit in with the technology. This is fine as far as it goes; the trouble is that sometimes you get a blinkered view developing within the financial technology industry because people come from cultures where the technological solution to an application is almost habitual; such as back office – IBM, and front office – DEC or Tandem. I don't think this necessarily always makes for the most creative solutions to a particular application-related problem. What is needed is unquestionably an awareness of the fundamental, and the widest, demands of the application functionality, even before anyone starts to think about applying technology to handle a particular application.

Similarly, within certain application areas such as securities processing, demand deposit or brokerage you will tend to see a certain combination of hardware technology going in a rather blinkered way with a particular type of software. Again, I think these hardware-software linkages exist because these linkages were first devised about twenty years ago and have become habitual for many people, with a point being reached where people assume that the old way is the only way to do it. Again, this is not necessarily the path to the most efficient, or the most effective, solution.

The point is that there is nothing inherently wrong, in themselves, with the more familiar hardware-software linkages or the mental connections which people often make between a particular vendor and a particular application, as long as the linkage does not stifle creativity and the possibility of reaching more efficient solutions. And the possibility of more efficient solutions exists today as it has never existed before, due to the increasingly wide use of open systems and more compact, powerful and less expensive hardware. It will soon be the case that any technology can be run on any hardware platform and that technologies which were once different are becoming more and more standardised. Admittedly, the full impact of open systems on the financial technology industry has yet to be made and until it does people are going to be cagey about abandoning the types of actual or mental linkages which may have been at the backbone of their careers. However, the revolution of open systems is already happening and in the future I believe we'll see the application functionality making technology take the back seat to the application. This is certainly where we need to be as an industry. We're not there yet.

JE: What are the principal differences which you have noticed in the way that financial technology is specified, designed and implemented in the US and the way that this happens in the UK?

POTTER: We've done a lot of development in the US and in the UK at a number of different sites and, frankly, I don't see many differences. It's interesting because when I talk to many of the large banks in these areas, they think there is a difference. Having built systems now for ten years in different countries, I think there are a lot more similarities between the way in which systems are designed and implemented than there are differences, and I often find it difficult to find the differences. There are some financial institutions which, for instance, might spend more time testing, more time documenting and more time undertaking one part of the systems development life cycle than another, but I don't believe that the differences in approach relate to different countries. For example, in Canada we encountered some institutions that spent a good deal of time on documentation and methodology and also some which just put the system in place and ran it to production. I think similar things could be said about the UK and other countries.

JE: What role do you think data communications will be playing, globally, in the financial sector in five years' time?

POTTER: The role of data communications in the financial sector is clearly becoming more extensive every day. Perhaps the most significant development is that the sheer cost of data communications is going down. I think we are going to see a good deal more video conferencing in the future, just as I expect there to be a good deal more remote data processing. Local data processing centres communicating back to centralised data processing centres will, I think, be the future trend. I think that the development of software and the communciation of transactions between different systems all around the world will use more data communications, because it is becoming so much cheaper and easier to use. You can go pretty much into any country now with a PC and dial in on their local line and go at 9600 baud inexpensively, and with very few difficulties, turn the PC into a terminal communicating directly with the mainframe. If that isn't significant progress, what is?

2 THE FUNDAMENTALS OF FINANCIAL TECHNOLOGY

Introduction

The previous chapter discussed the main terms of reference of this book, and introduced the essential concept that financial institutions have increasingly come to understand that their prime motive for deploying financial technology should be to gain a competitive advantage over rival institutions.

This chapter examines the fundamental elements of financial technology: appraising the primacy of data storage and retrieval systems; looking at the basic nature of financial technology; surveying the building blocks of financial technology – the principal computer, the data communications method, the terminal and programming techniques. The chapter concludes with an examination of the different methods of constructing a financial system.

THE PRIMACY OF DATA STORAGE AND RETRIEVAL

This book is primarily concerned with leading-edge applications of financial technology. Inevitably, this means that it mainly focuses on applications where technology is playing an extensive role in making the application succeed. Although in theory some of the applications documented here could be carried out manually, in most cases this would not even be theoretically possible. In such applications – which in practice means the vast majority of uses of technology within the financial services sector – the technology does more than make the task more efficient; it makes it possible.

None the less, it is essential to bear in mind that the reason why computer systems were first deployed in financial institutions was to provide a means of automating the immense and tedious drudgery of handling the details of numerous accounts and transactions. This role of computers in handling *data storage and retrieval* remains the prime application of computers in the financial sector, for all that the data storage and retrieval process is technologically relatively straightforward compared with the more complex technological applications discussed later. However, all these more complex applications rely on the efficiency and reliability of the institution's data storage and retrieval systems.

The justification for focusing on more complex applications is that the ability of a financial institution's computer system to store and retrieve data is usually taken for granted by members of staff and by customers nowadays. However, as is always the case within the financial sector, it is necessary to ensure that the somewhat mundane operational fundamentals are in place before looking at more sophisticated applications. Furthermore, even though it is indeed usually taken for granted that a financial institution will have an efficient data storage and retrieval system, there are certainly ways in which an institution can seek to maximise this efficiency, and even hope to establish a competitive advantage from these operations.

It is therefore appropriate to begin this chapter by examining how an institution can aim to maximise the efficiency of its data processing facilities.

MAXIMISING EFFICIENCY AND GAINING A COMPETITIVE ADVANTAGE

Many technology managers will be surprised at the notion that their data storage facilities offer them the opportunity to gain a competitive advantage. They regard storage facilities as an essential part of their institution's computer resources, and are well aware of the need to maximise the efficiency, speed and cost-effectiveness of handling data. But gain *a competitive advantage from data storage?* How can that be possible? Saying this, the technology manager in question may return to developing or refining a specialised back- or front-office application from which the institution does indeed expect to gain a measure of competitive advantage.

In today's financial technology industry, there has never been such a wide range of packaged software and customised systems deployed within financial institutions. Technology managers are often tempted to take for granted their organisation's data storage facilities, and come to regard these facilities as something which should simply be allowed to run smoothly while the technology department investigates specific applications which respond to customer and staff requirements, whether actual or perceived.

No doubt technology managers are often influenced in this thinking by the feeling that while specialised and application-oriented front- and back-office technology projects are both challenging and exciting, data storage is fairly mundane, requiring minimal planning and playing no role in establishing competitive advantage. Not only is this far from being the case, but a technology manager who concludes that data storage has no crucial role in establishing competitive advantage is rather like an architect who takes a great deal of trouble to design a beautiful building, but only spends a few moments on designing the foundations, or indeed forgets to incorporate any at all.

The truth is that specialised front- and back-office applications are refinements – albeit very important ones – of a computer system which has as its primary function the efficient management and storage of data.

Data storage demands placed upon computer systems are increasing at a high rate across almost all commercial and industrial sectors, with most industry analysts in the computing sector estimating the average annual increase in the amount of data being stored from between 40 to 60 per cent.

The annual figure for the average increase in data storage demands within the financial industry is certainly closer to 60 per cent than 40 per cent. At a 60 per cent annual increase, an institution would need to more than double the capacity of its data storage facilities in two years, and quadruple them after three years, merely to cope with the expected increase, let alone in order to provide a boost in competitive advantage.

In what specific areas can a financial institution typically hope to gain this all-important edge by means of better management of its data storage facilities? It is reasonable to identify three areas where this can happen, as follows.

1 Increased administrative efficiency

Effective management of data storage is an essential element in the smooth running of an institution, but it can also establish a positive competitive advantage.

For example, greater availability of access to a wide range of account information can often improve cash flow and profits, whilst high-quality administrative information plays a key role in the ultimate effectiveness of management planning, which is geared, almost by definition, to the winning of a competitive edge.

An institution's access to good-quality archive information plays a particularly important role, allowing planners to have clear information, regarding which areas of business have proved historically most profitable and suggesting areas for effective expansion in the future.

2 Increased data integrity and security

Ensuring that stored data is adequately backed-up and protected against external interference will always be a question of maintaining a balance between the back-up and security facilities required and the budget available.

What is incontestable is that investment in back-up facilities and computer security measures is essential for an institution which wishes to gain competitive advantage through avoiding the expensive loss of critical data, and by securing storage installations against malicious interference by a third party, which can again lead to heavy financial loss as well as attracting negative publicity.

3 Better handling of customer information

The extremely competitive trading environment within which institutions are currently operating has put a premium on the need to win new customers, and success here naturally leads to increased demands being placed upon data storage facilities.

However, the need to accommodate details of new customers is only part of the burden that is being placed on financial institutions. The entire emphasis of today's retail or commercial financial industry is on providing a better level of service, and this inevitably means installing facilities for storing and retrieving an ever-increasing amount of data about individual customers.

Even the largest retail banks in the UK are still very limited in terms of their ability to cross-reference customer information and to target their marketing activities around customers' specific needs. What is ideally required is a system whereby once a customer is in the branch, face to face with a personal banker, the banker can gain screen-based access to a wide range of financial parameters relating to that individual, thereby assisting the customer in the most effective way.

In order to have the best chance of establishing a competitive advantage in the three areas discussed above, a financial institution must not only maximise the speed, capacity and the efficiency of the back-up facilities of its data storage installations, but also do its utmost to ensure that opportunities for cost-effective increase of storage capacity are available now, and will continue to become available. Installing and maintaining a complete storage system which meets these objectives is the key to good data storage management.

There is no doubt that the financial industry, and particularly the retail side of the industry, has a long way to go before it is close to exploiting the full potential which technology offers for using data storage as a *prime element* in the struggle to gain market share, rather than as an ancillary facility.

It is now necessary to consider what measures a financial institution can take in order to improve its data storage management along lines that maximise the likelihood of it gaining a competitive advantage. Naturally enough, before this question can be addressed, it is important to consider how most financial institutions' data storage facilities are currently configured. A schematic configuration of a typical storage facility used by a financial institution is shown in Figure 2:1.

It is convenient to depict the standard storage configuration as a pyramid, with the cost of the different types of storage media, and the performance of those media, increasing the higher that medium is located in the pyramid. The pyramid does in fact show a hierarchy, with the movement from the

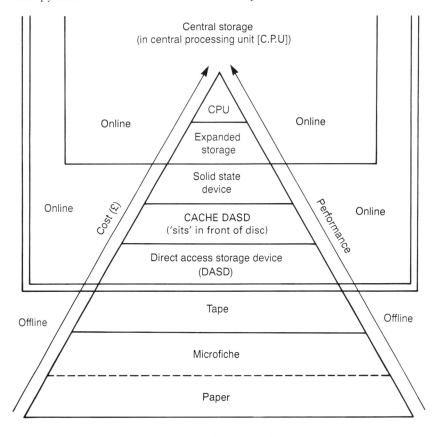

Figure 2:1   The data storage hierarchy

bottom of the pyramid (paper) to the top of the pyramid (central processing unit, or, CPU) representing not only a progression in terms of storage speed and convenience, but also an increase in cost of the storage medium. The notion of 'convenience' here assumes that a great deal of data is being processed within very short time frames; clearly data can only be stored on and retrieved from paper and microfiche very slowly compared with electronic media.

Another important preliminary observation is that two types of storage medium must be identified at the outset: *online* media (those media which are permanently connected to the computer system) and *offline* media (those media which are not permanently connected to the computer system).

As Figure 2:1 makes clear, tape, microfiche and paper are all offline media.

Paper, at the foot of the pyramid, is the simplest and cheapest form of storage media, but is inconvenient and cumbersome.

Microfiche storage is more convenient, but, like paper, suffers from the serious disadvantage that it depends on a cumbersome process of making marks on a surface in order to store the information. Paper and microfiche are of course not electronic storage media, but can usefully be included on the pyramid as representing older technologies.

Tape occupies the lowest position in the hierarchy of any electronic storage medium. Nowadays the considerable handling and storage advantages which fully enclosed cartridge tapes provided over old-style reel-to-reel tapes has been recognised in all industrial and commercial sectors, and particularly in the financial sector.

Being an offline medium, however, tape suffers from the serious drawback that the tape must be physically connected to a computer system before the information can be accessed. This is a particular problem for medium to large financial institutions, whose sheer volume of storage may require many hundreds of tapes to be available for accessing at any moment, with the system often only needing to be connected to the computer system for a few seconds at a time.

This requirement has led to the development of the Automated Tape Library (ATL), which is in essence a robot that is able to select the correct tape from the tape library, insert it into the relevant tape drive and remove the tape when the system has finished with it.

Pioneering work which leading hardware vendors have completed in assessing costs of ATLs suggests that they can be profitably deployed in all storage applications ranging from Midrange to mainframe ('Enterprise system', in IBM parlance) and thereby free staff to be used more efficiently.

Moving up the hierarchy, the first online medium encountered is the Direct Access Storage Device (DASD and usually pronounced 'dazdee' within the storage fraternity). The DASD unit is a disc drive which, while usually connected within the computer system, can be detached if necessary. Access times to DASD will typically be of the order of 10 milliseconds – on the face of it fast enough, but actually relatively slow where high performance is at a premium.

The next stage is the Solid State Device (SSD). SSD is a memory device consisting of many integrated chips, which is attached to the central processor on a purely electronic basis. The SSD sits between DASD and the processor in the storage hierarchy, and its speed and accuracy of the SSD makes it the ideal storage location for data outside the central processor. However, the inevitable space restriction in SSD means that the storage system must restrict SSD storage to the most important data if the system is to perform efficiently.

The demarcation line between SSD and DASD is extremely important, since it represents the line between purely electronic (SSD) storage and storage which involves both electronic and mechanical processing (DASD). The difference between an access time for DASD of about 10 milliseconds and an access time for SSD of perhaps 10 nanoseconds may not seem very significant, but where a large storage task is running – such as one involving a large number of inputs and outputs (I/O) – the difference between using SSD and DASD can mean the job running in a matter of seconds rather than several hours.

It is possible to get round this problem by 'caching' the DASD. A DASD cache is a small amount of electronic storage, set in front of the main DASD discs. The cache is used to store data which will be required more often than that data stored on the principal DASD discs, and which therefore requires a much faster access time.

Finally, we move on to central storage, which is the computer's central memory. Information stored here can be accessed instantly by the system, but the relative lack of space within central storage means that only the mission critical data which is required *constantly* can be stored here. Even within central storage there is a hierarchy. In most computer systems today there is an additional storage location within central storage. This is generally referred to as 'expanded storage' and is an area of storage place where the CPU can hold data which will be needed imminently but not immediately while avoiding the delay of holding it on DASD.

As Figure 2:1 shows, a central principle to the efficient and cost-effective use of storage is that the further up the hierarchy one proceeds, the more expensive the storage medium becomes. There is thus a simple trade-off between performance and cost in data storage: the faster the storage and retrieval speeds, the more expensive the medium becomes.

Any programmer who wishes his institution to make the most efficient and cost-effective use of data storage must first of all understand the nature of the storage hierarchy and the essential relationship between performance and cost. Once this is all understood, the next stage is for the technology manager to accept that the way to maximise the efficiency, cost-effectiveness and competitive advantage of various methods of data storage is *to ensure that data is always stored at the correct level within the hierarchy*.

One drawback of using off-the-shelf packages for storage and memory is that they can often embody a storage and retrieval policy which is out of the user's control and takes away from the user the ability to choose between different options eg whether to save data in a location well up the hierarchy and thereby gaining the most rapid access to the information; whether to compute computationally intensive information anew whenever this is required rather than taking up storage space by saving the results of previous calculations; or choosing exactly what data is required at a particular moment in order that the requisite application and/or display can be met.

Storing data at an unnecessarily high level wastes money because expensive, high-performance storage capacity is being used when a less expensive and lower-performance storage medium would be more appropriate.

Conversely, storing data at too low a level in the hierarchy is ultimately a false economy because the overall performance of the computer system (which naturally depends to a great extent on its data storage and retrieval performance) will be impaired.

Technology managers wishing to maximise the competitive advantages accruing from the institution's data storage facilities really need to know where to store each particular type of data. For example, should a nation-wide bank of new business information relating to the specific needs of many thousands of new business prospects all be stored in the same storage medium, or should, say, details of customers with specific profiles be stored at a higher level in the hierarchy?

There is of course no single answer to such questions. The correct positioning of particular data will depend on a wide range of factors relating to the nature of the data, the number of occasions on which it will be used, and the purpose of storing the data.

Only specialists – which in practice means technology consultants and storage systems engineers employed, the leading vendors of storage hard-ware and peripheral systems – can answer the all-important questions relating to the correct location of data. The answer will vary from case to case. However, understanding the data storage hierarchy and the opportunity that exists for gaining a competitive advantage in the data storage arena are crucially important steps on the way to formulating a correct strategic and tactical approach to data storage.

THE BUILDING BLOCKS OF FINANCIAL TECHNOLOGY

Having suggested the primacy of the role of data storage and retrieval in even the most technologically advanced financial technology implementa-tion, it is appropriate to focus on what financial technology actually is. The best way to do this is to examine the different 'building blocks' which will feature in most, if not all, applications of financial technology.

The following analysis looks at the building blocks, and gives specific analysis regarding how they should be implemented most efficiently and effectively.

THE PRINCIPAL COMPUTER

There is no better example of the speed at which the financial technology industry is changing than in the apparently ever-increasing power and compactness of the principal computer which powers a system. This computer, which is often known as the 'host' computer, was until the late 1970s a large, cumbersome and inevitably expensive mainframe. However, the introduction and widespread use of the microchip in the early 1980s paved the way for a whole generation of computers which carried out the functions of the mainframe (and soon began to go well beyond the main-frames of the 1970s in terms of speed and power) but cost significantly less and were much more convenient to handle; requiring less room, less human intervention and having no need for an expensive controlled environment (eg with special dust extraction facilities, air conditioning and watercooling systems). This generation of 'Midrange' computers (or 'minicomputers') nowadays includes such highly popular models as the IBM Application System (AS)/400, the DEC VAX and the Stratus machines.

The power of Midrange computers is such that 'downsizing' (ie switching from a mainframe to a Midrange computer or even to a powerful micro-computer) has become a major issue within the computer industry, with

Midrange and microcomputer vendors taking great pains to point out to users the cost savings of downsizing.

The financial business is one where an ability to handle a large volume of data is of great importance for many institutions. Because of this, the largest institutions have stuck with mainframes even though the ability of Midrange computers to handle all but the very largest and most demanding data storage applications has been proven for several years. However, such is the power of Midrange systems that all institutions which are able to downsize are seeking this option.

Midrange systems are not yet suitable for applications where millions of customers need to access a particular function (such as a retail institution's automated teller machine [ATM] or electronic funds transfer at point of sale [EFTPOS] system. Similarly, wholesale institutions usually feel more confident with a mainframe to handle their applications – such as a trading system involving large numbers of dealers and perhaps many thousands of counterparties – which are most demanding in terms of data storage and retrieval, linked with transaction processing. However, this scenario is itself changing, as Midrange computers become more powerful. By the end of the 1990s it is quite possible that Midrange computers will be able to act as the principal computers for every type of application within the financial sector.

The reason why computers have become more powerful, less expensive and more compact is that the technology behind the central processor of computers has to date remained on a constant path towards greater miniaturisation and greater power.

The first central processors – used in the cumbersome pioneering computers which were built in the 1930s and early 1940s – were not electronic at all, but made use of electric relays. The use of relays – a purely mechanical device – was so restrictive that these machines were not much better than the cogwheel calculating devices that they were supposed to replace. Computers only became truly useful devices with the introduction during the 1940s (and widespread use during the 1950s) of the electronic valve as the hub of the processor. This increased the speed and power of machines enormously, which could now, for the first time, be seen as significant assets to mankind rather than mere intriguing oddities. Electronic valve technology is nowadays so outmoded that it bears little relation to the computers of the 1990s.

It is interesting, however, to mention in passing that a moth which found its way into a valve in one of the electronic circuits in an early American computer was immortalised when a computer scientist, who found the deceased moth, announced that there was a 'bug' in the system. The name has stuck, and come to indicate glitches of an entirely non-insect nature.

Electronic valves were replaced in turn by the transistor, which made possible the development of the compact printed circuit board. Today's microprocessors themselves contain transistors, but transistors so greatly miniaturised that it is no exaggeration to say that a circuit board the size of a fingernail contains more processing power than the largest mainframe computer of the 1970s.

The drive towards less expensive and more compact and powerful micro-processors continues, with new types of materials – such as gallium arsenide – often replacing the familiar silicon and research focusing on new ways of miniaturising processors further. Some of the more interesting research looks at how the need for conductive surfaces (which inevitably put a physical limitation on how far miniaturisation can be taken) could be removed by designing microprocessors that work with light impulses. These are becoming known as optical computers.

A great increase in the opportunities for downsizing from mainframe to Midrange is, however, only one major consequence of continuing improvements in the speed and compactness of microprocessors. The other consequence – at least as important and arguably even more so – is that personal computers (PCs, also known as 'microcomputers'), which were first feasible in the late 1970s as a direct result of the development of the microchip, have greatly increased in power. Indeed, some of the largest PCs – such as the Sun and HP workstations – have acquired a level of processing power which makes them comparable with Midrange computers.

There are two principal results of the PCs increasing their processing power. The first is that the old concept of the 'dumb' terminal – that is, a terminal which, rather like a television screen, is used merely to display information and contains no onboard processing power – has become outdated, since PCs with processing power are relatively inexpensive. The second is that the strength of PCs is nowadays such that many office-based computer systems are nowadays being powered by a PC rather than a Midrange or mainframe computer. For the most demanding office applications a dedicated PC with no display screen (this device is often known as a 'server' or 'superserver') is frequently used, with the server or superserver being in effect a small Midrange computer.

In the light of the information above, it will not come as a surprise to discover that the 'traditional' boundaries between mainframe, Midrange and PCs are becoming blurred. Such is the processing power of today's microprocessors that an increasing number of applications within financial institutions can be met by Midrange computers and PCs, with the power of the three types of computer appearing to be moving increasingly towards a scenario where processing power is easy and inexpensive to add, and where only the largest and most powerful mainframes stand significantly above the most advanced Midrange machines and PCs in terms of processing power.

These developments have been hastened by the introduction of 'parallel processing' whereby individual computers contain more than one processor. In practice computers featuring parallel processing contain about thirty processors, although some of the latest US computers contain as many as one thousand processors.

Managing the principal computer

As with successful and efficient data storage and retrieval, the key to successful implementation and management of the principal computer is to make as close a match as possible between the needs of the application and the power of the computer. Unfortunately, this is easier said than done, for two reasons.

1 The needs of the application are subject to change
Although it should be fairly straightforward – with expert assistance – to decide what kind of principal computer is most relevant for a particular application at any one time, the needs of the application will inevitably change; which almost invariably means that more transaction processing power, storage capacity and overall speed will be needed in the future.

This problem can be solved superficially by ensuring that the computer chosen has ample spare capacity. However, the larger the amount of unused capacity, the less efficient the fit between the application and the computer, and efficiency in this respect is exactly what is required.

2 The technology behind the principal computer is continually improving
Most cases of downsizing occur not because a user organisation made an initial mismatch between the needs of the application and the power of the computer, but because increases in the power of a less expensive computer made downsizing a feasible option. Any assessment involving matching the needs of an application to a computer must accommodate the inevitability of technological improvement and change.

It follows from the above that the way to manage efficient use of a principal computer is to pay particular attention to two factors.

Firstly, the computer that is chosen should contain sufficient spare capacity to meet the foreseeable needs of the financial institution for at least two years.

Secondly, the computer that is chosen should if at all possible feature modular enhancement, allowing capacity to be enhanced to meet needs beyond those which can be foreseen during the next two years. There is a strong case for purchasing the computer from a large vendor who will offer favourable terms for downsizing, should this be necessary. It is as well to discuss the possibility of downsizing when first buying the computer, and presenting the vendor with a variety of hypothetical scenarios centred around the user's need for greater speed and capacity, and finding out how the vendor would respond to these.

Finally, a financial institution should give strong consideration to the possibility of deploying a principal computer which features a degree of 'fault-tolerance' in its hardware or software. Fault-tolerance is a form of design incorporating built-in redundancy, and thereby ensuring that if a particular component fails, the principal computer – and the system which it powers – continues to operate. This is a particularly useful feature in any system which involves the processing of transactions. The following section discusses this in more detail.

THE DATA COMMUNICATIONS MEDIUM

Continuing this survey of the building blocks of financial technology, we move on to the data communications medium, that is, the method by which data communications is maintained within the system.

Any system used by a financial institution will inevitably involve communications between the principal computer and the terminal which is being used by a staff member, counterparty or customer.

There are two major types of communications method, the Wide Area Network (WAN) and the Local Area Network (LAN). As the names suggest, they differ in their scope, a WAN being used when the application calls for communications being maintained outside the building where the principal computer is located (and which can, of course, involve international and intercontinental communications), with a LAN being used where the application calls for the communications process taking place entirely within the building (or complex of buildings) where the principal computer is located.

The technology used by a WAN or a LAN often differs, too, with WANs generally employing leased or proprietary telephone lines and for communications covering large distances satellite communications, and LANs usually employing internal computer networks, although LANs often use leased telephone lines, also. Apart from this, the WAN or LAN communications process is remarkably similar. Since the speed of electrons through wire is about one-sixth of the speed of light and therefore about one circumnavigation of the globe per second, communications across WANs or LANs are effectively instantaneous unless the communications process involves links across several thousand miles, in which case there can be a slight delay if land cables are used.

Data communications are only instantaneous if the communications process takes place in *real-time*: that is, if the principal computer is sending and receiving messages over the network as soon as the messages are available for despatch. In most financial institutions, this real-time data communications process is the most frequently used type of communications process. The reason for this is that transactions are best processed in real-time, where the relevant accounts can be updated at once, accounts modified in the light of the new information, and customers and clients served better since the institution knows exactly what transaction they last initiated. However, the alternative method of *batch processing* bundles groups of transaction-related messages together and sends them over the network during periods when communications are inexpensive, such as at night.

Real-time communications are often known as *online* communications. Note, too, that as real-time communications are so important for transaction processing, real-time systems which handle transactions are often referred to as online transaction processing (OLTP) systems.

Fault-tolerance should be considered an essential element of an OLTP system.

Managing data communications

Efficient management of data communications is of great importance for any financial institution. For most institutions, communications failure would be catastrophic, resulting in lost transactions, lost (and probably permanently lost) data, loss of customer goodwill and lost revenue. Many of these problems can be avoided by building fault-tolerance into the principal computer. There are also numerous methods to build fault-tolerance into data communications, whether in terms of designing redundancy into the communications hardware, or into the software which controls the process.

Equally important is the need to install real-time rather than batch processing communications systems wherever the budget allows this. Not only do batch processing systems have the severe drawback that they compromise the institution's ability to provide up-to-date customer service, but there are distinct security problems with batch processing. These are:

- a batch processing system cannot verify the user's bona fides in real-time, and so runs a higher risk of providing a service to an unauthorised user
- a batch processing system cannot check in real-time whether house limits have been reached by a particular customer for a particular time period, and thereby runs the risk of accommodating a transaction which goes beyond the house limit
- most serious of all, a deliberately fraudulent transaction is less likely to be spotted quickly when batch processing is used than when real-time communications are used. When a financial institution has been the victim of a deliberately fraudulent transaction, it is essential that the institution raise the alarm as soon as possible if there is to be any chance of catching the perpetrator of the fraud, and/or retrieving the stolen funds.

Apart from the need to ensure that real-time processing is in place wherever possible, another important management issue relating to data communications is to ensure that the communications process is used effectively. This is a particular problem with LANs, which are frequently not used by staff as they ought to be. All too often, LANs that were built to act as state-of-the-art communications devices between members of staff are merely deployed to link, for example, a workstation with a printer.

The remedy for this problem is that all staff whose workstations interface with a LAN must learn to regard the LAN as an invaluable tool for internal communications and for streamlining the flow of information. Information that has been gathered at considerable expense of time and money should be available instantly to interested parties via the LAN. This leads to greater efficiency in all aspects of the financial institution's activity. Above all, managers should guard against the syndrome whereby, instead of the LAN being used as a real-time device for making the institution's information widely available among staff, staff become jealous of their own information and are reluctant to share it. Another problem which often occurs is that staff are unable to understand all the functions of the LAN or are not convinced that these features will lead to greater efficiency or fail to find the LAN user-friendly.

The result is that staff might, for example, use their workstation to prepare a report which they then circulate to colleagues as a written report. This is a slow, cumbersome and inefficient way of communicating compared with using a LAN. Similarly, the full potential benefits of using LANs to relay electronic mail are rarely used as widely as they should be. Instead of using electronic mail, institutions often rely on slow and old-fashioned methods using paper.

An interesting innovation in LAN technology which will probably play an important role in the financial sector in time to come is the concept of the 'wireless LAN'. The first tentative application of which has been in certain US open outcry commodities trading markets, where it is usual to end each trading day with paper order confirmation forms strewn across the trading floors. The new idea is that instead of the old paper-based order entry and confirmation system, hand-held wireless terminals, which would create what was essentially a wireless LAN in the commodity trading exchange, could further speed up the trading process, minimise errors and save the labours of the exchanges' clearers. Although it may be some years before the use of wireless LANs becomes extensive within open outcry financial markets (the most logical location for such LANs) they are an important possibility for financial technology managers to bear in mind. Wireless LANs have already been tested in Chicago commodity and futures markets operated by the Chicago Board of Trade and the Chicago Mercantile Exchange.

THE TERMINAL

The computer terminal is the third element in most financial systems used by institutions today. It is linked to the principal computer by the communications method (which, as we have seen, may be a WAN or a LAN) and will typically communicate with the principal computer in real-time.

Terminals carry out an extremely wide range of applications in today's financial technology industry. These applications are examined in detail later in this chapter. For the moment, it is useful to group the applications to which terminals are put into three main classifications.

1 Decision-making
This covers all tasks which involve the institution's own managers obtaining information which helps them to make a decision relating to how the institution is run. It also includes the preparation and enactment of decisions by traders or investment managers, and similar persons employed in money-making tasks.

2 Transaction initiation
This means any action which initiates a transaction which will pass through

the institution's books. Examples of such actions are use of an automated teller machine (ATM) or electronic funds transfer at point of sale (EFTPOS) service, when the terminal will communicate (in real-time or via a batch processing system) with a retail financial institution; any kind of trade initiation process within an institution to institution setting, when the terminal will communicate between two wholesale financial institutions; or any kind of front-office task carried out by a cashier, which could apply equally within a retail or wholesale institution.

3 Administrative activities

These cover the entire range of tasks which are necessary for the smooth running of the institution and customer and client accounts. Such tasks would include all the accounting functions and the maintenance of the bought and sold ledger, as well as all activities which involve consulting or creating customer or staff records.

The most fundamental point to make about terminals is that, with most terminals nowadays having an onboard processor, they are much more than simply recipients of information, but will typically have considerable processing power themselves. In fact, such is the processing power of today's terminals that they are often known as 'workstations': implying that although certainly one of their main functions is to communicate with a principal computer, they are selfcontained computers in their own right. Even terminals for specialised retail banking functions (such as ATM transactions or EFTPOS) usually contain a good deal of processing power which is not used for the specific functions that they were built to undertake.

Financial institutions also sometimes use 'X Terminals': that is, terminals which are a sort of hybrid between a PC and a dumb terminal; being more powerful than a dumb terminal but less powerful than a PC.

Managing deployment of terminals

As with all aspects of the deployment of the three fundamental building blocks of financial technology (ie the principal computer, the data communications medium and the terminal), the key to success is to match the technology to the application as closely as possible. Taking into consideration, also, the need for surplus capacity to be built into the system to accommodate future increases in data storage capacity and processing power, as well as the related need to ensure that the system can be swiftly and cost-effectively enhanced to take advantage of improvements in technology, which usually means improvements in processing power.

As for terminals, where a *specialised* terminal is being used the institution will, generally speaking, have to opt for whatever is on the market, although extensive opportunities usually exist for negotiating deals with vendors that give the institution the opportunity to update the terminal in the future. Where workstation-type terminals are being deployed, the market for these terminals is extremely competitive (a point proven by glancing through any PC magazine) and vendors ought to offer extremely competitive deals in return for a large contract and, perhaps, an additional service contract.

IBM OR NOT IBM?

We have now examined the three building blocks of financial technology that relate to the physical hardware of the system. Before moving on to the final building block which is discussed here, it is useful to address one question which any financial technology manager will have to address many times during his career: should he, or should he not, go for IBM?

IBM is by far the largest manufacturer of business computers and related hardware in the world. It is a truly international organisation, with offices, or representative agents, in every country of the world except the most undeveloped. IBM's overseas activities date back longer than many people realise. On a visit to Tokyo in 1989 I was surprised to discover that IBM had been located in Tokyo since the 1920s!

IBM pioneers many of the major developments in business computers that relate to improvements in hardware. It is a measure of IBM's enormous impact on the market that numerous multinational organisations have been founded on the basis of producing products that imitate just one area of IBM's activities. Many computer software companies (of which Microsoft is perhaps the best-known example) based their initial growth to prominence on having IBM as their client.

Faced with such a large, successful and reliable vendor, a financial technology manager can be forgiven for thinking that opting for IBM is the most rational, safe and sensible choice. For many managers, anxious to make an impact on their institution and with a mortgage and two children to think of back home, the familiar phrase 'no one ever got fired for buying IBM' will have a reverberation that is both compelling and convincing, even though the shedding of staff and fairly mediocre financial results that have been a feature of IBM in the early 1990s have dented the organisation's reputation as the absolutely safe choice.

However, managing financial technology is not necessarily about choosing options that are safe, solid and reliable. We have seen that managing financial technology is really about establishing a competitive advantage over rival institutions. Of course, some managers may wind up considering that opting for the reliability and reputation of IBM products is a good first step towards establishing a competitive advantage, and this viewpoint is certainly understandable. However, it should also be borne in mind that the 'IBM-compatible' industry is also a very large, reliable and solid industry, and that many vendors of IBM-compatible hardware have established a significant niche in the market because they provide something which IBM does not provide. Typically, the edge that IBM-compatible vendors seek to provide over IBM lies in one or more of the following areas:

- lower cost of hardware than IBM
- lower cost of computer servicing than IBM
- faster and more flexible reponse to customer needs than IBM provides
- product range that fills gaps which IBM does not fill.

Note that this is not to imply that any IBM-compatible vendor necessarily *will* outcompete IBM in any of these areas; the above is just to show the areas in which IBM-compatible vendors do seek to outcompete IBM. Clearly, it would not be appropriate in a book of this nature to recommend readers to opt either for IBM or for an IBM-compatible vendor. As always, the vendor that is most suitable for a financial institution can only be ascertained when the institution's specific needs are known. However, just as it is fair to point out the cast reputation which IBM has gained for producing reliable, innovative hardware backed by an international network of sales offices and engineer locations, it must also be said that many IBM-compatible vendors themselves have international networks and a client list that includes many of the world's largest financial institutions. Similarly, many of these IBM-compatible vendors have proved themselves able to supply hardware that does most, if not all, that which corresponding IBM hardware can do, and costs less. It should also be said that despite the range of hardware which IBM offers, there are certainly some gaps in its product range which have successfully been filled by IBM-compatible vendors. For example, in the summer of 1992 the IBM-compatible vendor Memorex Telex launched its 5100 Automated Tape Library (ATL) which was specifically designed for use with Midrange and smaller mainframe ('Enterprise system', in IBM parlance) applications. This ATL was priced considerably below any IBM ATL, and Memorex Telex claimed that the 5100 did in fact fill a gap in the market, since IBM offered no comparable ATL for the Midrange and smaller mainframe user. This claim to fill a gap is arguable, but what is indisputable is that Memorex Telex devoted considerable efforts to produce a product which would offer the user something exceptional. This kind of competitiveness is, of course, ultimately in the user's interests.

PROGRAMMING TECHNIQUES

The final building block of financial technology examined in this chapter relates to the invisible, but essential, element within any financial technology installation: the technique or techniques that are used to program the software which runs on the system.

The purpose of this section is to give the reader an overview of how financial systems typically operate. This section is not intended to be (nor, indeed, could it hope to be) a replacement for a computer manual, and even less a replacement for a particular professional's programming expertise.

More to the point, from the perspective of this book's title, rationale and scope, is that managing financial technology does not require a detailed knowledge of a particular computer language, any more than managing an airline requires a detailed knowledge of how to fly a Boeing 747. Indeed, the possession of a large body of technical knowledge may actually prove a handicap to the management task, which demands an overview of the entire process, rather than a body of specialised knowledge relating to one particular stage of the process.

The first point to make about computers – and one which is explored in more detail in Chapter Three – is that, for all their complexity, they are essentially nothing more than huge collections of on/off switches, with the individual switches flicking on and off at immense speed. These on/off switches, which are themselves electronic components that only allow electrons to pass one way (which is exactly what valves did and transistors do), are used within computers to manage the binary processing which is the basis of all computer functioning. This first level of computer operation is the initial, *electronics*, level.

The second level of operation, the *operating system*, is essentially a protocol for allowing the electronics of the computer to operate an application. What the operating system therefore does, in essence, is to instruct the electronics to add one stored register to another. When this process occurs many millions of times per second, the computer can perform useful work.

The past few years have seen a distinct trend for operating systems to become standardised. The reason for this is that if an institution buys a computer which operates on a standardised operating system, the institution can not only run a much wider variety of programs than would otherwise be possible but will also be able to run programs that will be developed in the future on the standardised operating system. In the financial sectors today (and, indeed, in many other industrial and commercial sectors) the advantages of standardised operating systems are regarded as so great that the UNIX operating system is rapidly becoming the most important standard within the financial industry, with Windows NT and the IBM OS/2 also gaining in importance. It seems likely that the polarisation around UNIX or DOS will persist, and that eventually one or the other may achieve supremacy. Note, incidentally, that IBM's own branded version of UNIX is AIX which is compatible with UNIX.

The third level of operation, the programming language, 'sits' on top of the operating system and is a way for the human operator (the programmer) to instruct the computer to do a useful task. The programmer's job is to interpret the requirements of the job in hand in such a way as to enable the computer to carry out a useful task. The most common programming languages used by financial institutions are Common Business Orientated Language (COBOL) – which was specifically designed for business activities involving numerous different accounts – and C: which has many applications in PC programming.

The fourth level, the applications language, does not feature in every banking application but is used where the application requires an additional level of programming complexity.

Popular programming techniques within the financial industry

It is useful for financial technology managers to have a knowledge of those types of programming techniques which are most popular within the financial industry today. Before launching into this discussion, however, an important preliminary point ought to be made.

Computers are not, and may never be, in any sense 'intelligent'. A fuller definition of what the term 'intelligent' means in a computer-related sense is given below, but it is essential to begin this discussion by emphasising that the computers which human ingenuity has developed to date do not in any sense think for themselves. This point needs making, because articles appear regularly in the quality and tabloid press alike which seem to suggest that some development at a laboratory somewhere has led, or is about to lead, to the production of a computer which is a true artificial brain. Even entire governments can be misled over this. For example, in the early 1980s the Japanese announced that they were about to start work on a 'fifth generation' of computers, which would be the first generation of computers to display onboard reasoning power and intelligence. This announcement inspired considerable unease in many national governments, and in particular the British and American Governments, who immediately responded by voting large sums of money to their own national programmes to examine the feasibility of intelligent, self-reasoning computers.

In fact, the Japanese expectations were soon revealed to have less substance than an overcooked piece of *sushi*. The UK and US programmes plodded on, costing both respective governments many millions of pounds or dollars, but these programmes, too, came nowhere near revealing methods for constructing computers that could in any sense be described as intelligent, although certainly there was interesting work done in discovering how computers could be programmed so as to simulate, in admittedly a very crude fashion, an intelligent reasoning or judgement-forming process. These findings are discussed in detail below.

The moral of this tale for financial technology managers is simple: *do not trust any expert, consultant, member of staff or journalist who tells you that he/she has developed, or knows about, an intelligent computer system.* More particularly, *do not give such people any money.*

The reader might well ask why I am so certain that intelligent computers neither exist nor are about to exist. At the most straightforward level this observation is based upon five years of practical experience researching financial technology worldwide, during which I have seen nothing that even vaguely approximates to an intelligent computer. At a somewhat more complex level my belief regarding the impossibility of designing an intelligent computer with current technology is grounded on the objection that it is inconceivable that an artifical intelligent system could be constructed until we understand more about the workings of the brain, whether this is the human brain – which is highly intelligent – or the brains of other mammals, who are also relatively intelligent, even if obviously less so than humans.

It seems deliberately provocative to state that our understanding of the workings of the human brain is not *significantly* greater now than it was at the beginning of this century, but such is indeed the case. The problem with our understanding of the brain is that it inevitably relies too heavily on experience derived from studying morbid cases: such as, say, people who have have lost a particular intellectual function due to brain damage. The brain is thus understood by omission only, so to speak, which is no way to understand a highly complex, living organism. It is not even known for certain at present whether the brain's complexity could, in theory, be analysed in terms of billions of isolated processes taking place all at once, or whether the brain's operations involve some different, additional, process coming into play which is not yet understood. This may sound farfetched, but the possibility that this 'additional' element of processing may take place in the human brain would seem to be suggested by the existence of consciousness, which seems to be a product of all the complexity in the brain but which does not appear to be located in a particular site in the brain (unlike, say, the mechanism that sends us to sleep when we are tired).

In fact, any attempt to compare the workings of even a rudimentary animal brain (say, that of a reptile) with a computer soon becomes faintly ludicrous, with the computer showing that it can do nothing at all except that which it has been programmed to do, while the animal can think for itself, make a wide range of decisions very quickly regarding how to react to a particular environmental or situational change, and may even indulge in various more or less complex reasoning processes, regarding which we have no information.

Having said all this, I have no doubt that *eventually* human beings will discover how to build artificial brains that not only display advanced reasoning and judgement-forming abilities but even have a consciousness. I do not, however, believe that electronic computers are the route to this goal, any more than hot air balloons proved to be the route towards international jet travel. I think it likely that an entirely new type of technology will have to be devised before artifical brains are constructed. In the meantime, we are stuck with computers.

It is useful to identify three different types of programming technique that are particularly popular in the financial technology arena. The motive for drawing a distinction between the three techniques is that it will help financial technology managers to understand how the software they are considering deploying actually works. However, the differences between the three techniques are fairly superficial, and all related to the objectives that the system has rather than to how it works. All computer programs used in today's financial sector work in the same fundamental manner: that is, they apply the computer's immense processing speed to a sequence of simple instructions (ie the program) which, when all the instructions are followed by the computer in the correct sequence and assuming that there are no errors or 'bugs' in the program, will allow the computer to carry out a useful task.

This explanation of how computers work should itself be sufficient to show how it is absurd to regard computers as being in any sense intelligent.

The only reason why computers have sometimes been mistakenly regarded in this light on occasion in the past is that they work by electronics, which is an invisible and sufficiently mysterious process for some people to speculate that humans may not fully understand the workings of the devices that they have created, or (in even more sinister fashion) may have created devices that will one day 'take over'. This premise, while both false and impossible, undeniably makes for good science fiction, and it is indeed the basis of many successful and popular novels and films. The two internationally successful 'Terminator' films are based on the premise that a computer system, known as 'Skynet', and used throughout the US to control and monitor military activity, one day got smart and decided to do its utmost to destroy humanity. This could not happen, but it is interesting to imagine that it could. However, financial technology managers should keep their feet firmly on the ground and cast a cold eye on reality, at least when they are at work.

Given that all computers work by the process of sequential programming described above, we can identify the three most popular programming techniques used within the financial sector as being the following. Note, incidentally, that it is usual to refer to a program as 'code' when a detailed application is the subject of the program.

1 Traditional responsive programming
This means programming which focuses on carrying out the application by in effect splitting the application into numerous small tasks, each one of which would form an individual line of code. 'Responsive' is my own term, and is used to suggest the idea of the close relationship between the needs of the application and the program itself.

Examples of applications ideally suited to this type of programming technique are: account handling, transaction processing, interactive computer-based negotiating and all types of administrative functions that involve storing and retrieving data.

2 Numerical analysis
Programs involving numerical analysis are designed for decision support applications where a human trader or fund manager wishes to make a considered decision regarding the likely future fluctuation in certain variables such as the prices of certain financial instruments on a financial market. There are many public domain and proprietary theories relating to how variables such as market prices are likely to behave in the future, given that fluctuations in variables in the past are known. Numerical analysis

programming techniques involve designing programs that apply a particular numerical theory to the variables.

Typical examples of applications of numerical analysis are in the trading of financial instruments, and in the management of a portfolio of such instruments.

3 Artificial intelligence

The remainder of this section focuses on the computer programming technique known as *artificial intelligence*.

The use of the word 'intelligent' to denote an artificial system which displays a high level of ability to self-adjust to changing circumstances and to make quasi-human reasoned decisions has been widespread since the proliferation of computers since the 1960s, but does in fact date back to the beginning of this century. Probably the first use of the word intelligent in this way was by the Anglo-Polish writer Joseph Conrad – a technically astute fellow – who as far back as 1907 had, in his novel *The Secret Agent*, a character who spoke of an explosion initiation device in the following terms:

> I am trying to invent a detonator that would adjust itself to all conditions of action, and even to unexpected changes of conditions. A variable and yet perfectly precise mechanism. A really intelligent detonator.

The key phrase 'artificial intelligence' was first used in the 1940s. It is usual to give the credit for the invention of the term to the British mathematician, Alan Turing (1912–54). In 1937, Turing published an article entitled 'On Computable Numbers', which is generally regarded as providing the theoretical basis for the introduction of the electromechanical digital computer in the 1940s.

Turing was probably influenced by the work undertaken in the 1830s by the brilliant British inventor Charles Babbage. At the dawn of the Industrial Revolution, one of the most pressing needs in applied mathematics was for the production of reliable logarithmic tables, which played an essential role in civil engineering. In the 1830s these tables could only be compiled through extremely laborious manual calculations, which inevitably involved numerous errors. Where measurements for use in civil engineering and construction generally were based on erroneous logarithm tables, the consequences could be extremely serious. Indeed, there are some historians who believe that the disastrous collapse of the Tay Bridge in the mid-nineteenth century was due to errors in the logarithms which were used to calculate the dimensions of the bridge.

Babbage resolved to deal with this problem once and for all, by constructing a machine which would embody the mathematical processes needed to compile the tables and which would eliminate human error. The machine that he proposed, designed and began to build was known as the 'Analytical Engine' and was a remarkably advanced device for its day. It even incorporated a primitive printing system, whereby the final calculation was printed on a paper by the relevant cogwheels being automatically inked and then pressed onto paper. Cogwheels, because Babbage naturally had no access to electronics and was forced to rely on the only technology of his own day which seemed to offer possibilities for the construction of his machine: the use of mechanical cogwheels and connecting rods. His design did, however, contain several features that anticipated modern computer design, including a memory – a set of cogs which could 'store' a partial calculation – and a program: in his case an initial manipulation of the cogs was necessary so that they could operate together in order to calculate whatever was required.

Babbage's machine was well known throughout the nineteenth century as a powerful calculating device. Charles Dickens, for example, refers to the machine in a letter to a friend. However, while parts of the Analytical Engine were indeed successful on an experimental basis, it was never completed to the degree of complexity that Babbage envisaged. The reason for this was primarily that the machining industry of his day was unable to produce cogwheels to the extremely close tolerances that his device required. However, the fact that the Analytical Engine was viable, and would have worked, was proven this century by a team at the Science Museum in London who constructed a fullsize working model of the device using precisely machined cogs. This modern version of Babbage's machine, along with the touchingly primitive original attempts to build the machine, can be seen today in an excellent permanent display at the Science Museum.

Even Babbage, however, would probably have laughed at the notion that his machine could have displayed any intelligence of its own, although he would probably have been less sure of this impossibility had he possessed any idea of how electronics would enable machines many millions of times more powerful than the Analytical Engine to be constructed to fit into a snuffbox.

The first of many problems which are encountered when examining the concept of artificial intelligence is that definitions of the word 'intelligence' are by no means clear. Most dictionary definitions of the term 'intelligence' revolve around reasoning capacity and an ability to understand, which is ultimately a circular type of definition. Dan Diaper, in his book *Knowledge*

Elicitation even argues that 'only the most foolish of undergraduates attempts anything more than an operational definition [of intelligence] (ie intelligence is what intelligence tests measure)', a circular definition if ever there was one. However, we clearly do need some kind of working definition of 'intelligence' if a discussion of the programming technique known as artificial intelligence is to be fruitful.

Perhaps the best way to achieve a working definition is not to attempt a banal and ultimately circular version but rather to list some of the fundamental attributes of intelligence, and base the definition upon the possession of those attributes. Such a definition is inevitably incomplete and not entirely satisfactory, but this is a practical book, and some definition of intelligence is better than none. The following, then, are some of the attributes of intelligence:

1 an ability to learn from experience
2 an ability to make rational judgements
3 an ability to provide a reasoned analysis of a problem
4 an ability to think creatively, which in its most fundamental sense can be said to mean original thinking which is only partly prompted by that which exists already.

Computers can do none of these four types of task for themselves. However, artificial intelligence programming does not seek to create a self-contained, artificial reasoning device. Its far more modest aim is to program a computer so that it provides a *simulation* of human intelligence. In fact, 'simulated intelligence' would be a much more accurate description of this programming technique than 'artificial intelligence', which is extremely misleading in its suggestion that the objective here is indeed to create an artificial system which is intelligent.

To date, two types of methods have been used to attempt to simulate human intelligence within a computer program. These methods are known as *rule-based* or *knowledge-based systems*, and *neural* or *neurone nets*. They are now examined in turn.

Rule-based systems

These systems, which are also known as knowledge-based systems, derive from the theory that one way to try to simulate human intelligence in a computer is to aim to program it with the 'rules' (or 'heuristics') which *supposedly* govern the thought processes of a human in a particular field of expertise. Supposedly is an important word here, for reasons which will be explained shortly.

The process of attempting to formulate these rules and then to instil them in a computer program is known as 'knowledge engineering'. The process of obtaining these rules in the first place – which involves a rule-based programming specialist observing an expert in the chosen field of expertise at work and persuading him verbally to articulate the thought processes that went through or are going through his mind when he made or is making a particular decision, is known as 'knowledge elicitation'.

Why should a financial institution want to create a rule-based system? The following are the most usual reasons:

- in order to provide a computerised resource which can, if necessary, operate round the clock and which never needs time off, and never gets ill
- in order to 'capture' the expert's skill and ensure that these skills 'stay' within the institution, even if the expert decides to leave
- in order to deal with far more problems during the day than the expert could himself be expected to deal with
- because of the exciting possibility that a rule-based system could be designed which captures the expertise of several experts
- because a successful rule-based system would offer the institution that deployed it an important level of competitive advantage.

Whether or not an institution has the right to capture an expert's expertise in this way is a moot point, although in fact the practical and conceptual difficulties of building a wholly successful rule-based system are so extensive, for reasons examined below, that the problem of whether capturing an expert's entire expertise is ethical or even legal does not usually arise. There is no doubt, however, that many experts are innately suspicious of knowledge elicitation, since they fear – unjustifiably, in most cases – that once their employer has done his best to capture their expertise, they will no longer be required. The result of this is that experts often avoid articulating all their skill to the knowledge elicitator, or may even deliberately mislead him. This, one need hardly add, severely hampers the work of the elicitor, who, as we shall see, is in any case greatly handicapped by fundamental practical difficulties, unrelated to an expert's co-operation, of gaining access to all the expert's expertise.

The principle behind rule-based systems holds that, in an ideal situation, the human expert's wisdom can be reduced to a series of interconnected generalised rules called the 'knowledge base'. A separate computer program called the 'inference engine' is then used to search the knowledge base and draw practical, commercially useful judgements when confronted with data from a particular, real-life case. A workable artificial intelligence system which experience has shown to be capable of being applied with some degree of success to a commercial problem is sometimes known as an *expert* system.

What is extremely interesting about the concept of rule-based systems is that it is by no means a new concept. In their book *Mind Over Machine*, Hubert and Stuart Dreyfus point out that more than 2000 years ago the great Athenian philosopher Socrates searched Athens for experts who could articulate their rules. As Dreyfus and Dreyfus comment:

In one of his earliest dialogues . . . Plato tells us of an encounter between Socrates and Euthyphro, a religious prophet and an accepted expert on pious behaviour. Socrates asks Euthyphro to tell him how to recognise piety. 'I want to know what is characteristic of piety . . . to use as a standard whereby to judge your actions and those of other men.' But instead of revealing his piety-recognising heuristic, Euthyphro does just what every expert does when cornered by a Socrates: he gives him examples from his field of expertise. Euthyphro cites situations in the past in which men and gods had done things everyone considered pious. Throughout the dialogues Socrates persists in interrogating Euthyphro about his rules, but although Euthyphro claims that he knows how to tell pious acts from impious acts, he cannot state the rules that generate his judgements. Socrates encountered the same problems with craftsmen, poets and even with statesmen. None could articulate the principles on which he acted. Socrates concluded that no one knew anything – including Socrates, who at least knew his own ignorance.

This discussion from antiquity is very important for our examination of rule-based systems, since it puts a finger on the principal problem with these systems. This problem is simply that even if an expert is extremely willing to articulate his knowledge and thereby help a knowledge elicitator to accumulate it in a form that could be embodied in a computer program, there are great limitations on the process. These limitations derive from the fact that *not even the most capable and verbally gifted expert can articulate all of his expertise*. Indeed, there is evidence that the more complex and advanced the level of expertise, the less able an expert is to articulate it.

Why should this be? Euthyphro, we notice, is extremely good at providing examples of pious behaviour, but he is not able to say exactly on what he bases his generation of examples. Socrates, for his part, mistakenly concludes that because none of the experts he meets in his researches is able to 'provide rules', that is, to articulate their expertise, none of the experts knows anything. But this is to assume, quite erroneously, that just because someone cannot say *why* they have arrived at a particular conclusion, the conclusion is of no value. We all know from day-to-day life that this is not at all the case.

In fact, Euthyphro could not articulate the rules behind his skill at determining someone's piety because this skill of his was largely or entirely a *tacit* skill. *Tacit knowledge* is a term used by cognitive scientists to describe that intuitive, inherent knowledge and expertise to which we have no conscious access. The term was first used by M. Polanyi in his book *The Tacit Dimension*.

How does the brain operate at a tacit level? Unfortunately, we know very little about this. What is clear, however, is that instant, intuitive thinking plays an extremely important role in human and animal thinking, and certainly comes before slower, problem-solving types of thought processes in the brain's development. As far as we know, animals rely wholly or almost wholly on tacit thinking to make the relatively simple decisions that they have to make in order to survive: decisions such as whether to eat a particular item or not; whether, on being confronted by another animal, to run away or give chase; whether to make a mating approach to a particular member of the opposite sex. Many of these thought processes appear to be instinctive in origin, but for the purposes of this discussion it does not really matter whether a particular thought process is instinctive, or simply formed very quickly through a deep acquaintance with the subject at hand.

In the financial sector, there seems little doubt that some of the most important human skills and judgement-forming thinking are not carried out according to the kind of logical, sequential thinking that makes ideal fodder for the knowledge elicitator, but rather are tacit skills. Examples of tacit skills within the financial sector are:

- decisions regarding whether to trust somebody or some organisation
- decisions regarding whether to buy or sell a particular financial instrument
- decisions regarding how seriously to take a particular piece of research information (such as a news story in a newspaper, a recommendation by a broker, or even a conversation with a colleague).

The last skill mentioned here is so much a tacit one that it is difficult to see how a rule-based program could be of much assistance in simulating the skill. However, the first two skills clearly do provide some scope to the knowledge elicitator. After all, while the final decision may well be a 'gut decision' – that is, an instinctive, intuitive, tacit decision – the expert will probably have based much of his decision on a logical assessment of certain parameters. In the first case – the decision regarding whether to trust somebody or some organisation – these parameters might include the candidate's trading record, details of cash reserves, any evidence of criminal activity, details of future business plans and similar matters. In the second case – the decision whether or not to buy or sell a particular financial instrument – these parameters might include an assessment of quantitative data such as yield, return (and risk, which is usually calculated as the standard deviation of historical returns), general results of similar instruments (eg if the instrument is an equity, other equities in the same industrial or commercial sector) and other data. Where an expert's decision is at least partly based upon quantifiable parameters, a rule-based system at least has a chance of simulating some of that expertise.

Even so, rule-based systems would be much more effective simulators of human skills and/or judgement-forming thought processes if more was understood about how the brain functions at a tacit level. Little is understood about this at present, which is of course not to say that human understanding of the brain will not greatly increase in time to come.

One interesting clue as to how tacit knowledge functions relates to the process of learning. When a new skill is learned, the learning process often takes place mechanically, according to a system of rote that might be seen as being in some way akin to a computer's sequential reasoning. However, once the skill has been learnt – by which we usually mean that the skill has been mastered with such thoroughness that the skill can be practised almost intuitively (itself, in a sense, a definition of tacit knowledge) – the brain appears to 'shift' the elements of the skill to another location; where intuitive learning resides. Anyone who has mastered a particular skill – whether learning to drive, learning a new foreign language or understanding a complex task in the financial sector – will be aware of this process. There seems little doubt that the existence of tacit knowledge is an evolutionary necessity. A Stone Age child no doubt learnt from its mother that bears were dangerous because they tended to chase you, kill you and eat you; but when the child was confronted by a bear he would be unlikely to survive very long if he carefully went through in his mind the reasons why a bear was dangerous. His tacit knowledge would cause him, once he had recognised a bear, to either play dead or dash for the nearest tree.

Similarly, where more advanced skills are concerned, it is interesting to note that an attempt to explain (ie articulate) why you do what you do would, if you were carrying out the task at the same time, probably render you incapable of carrying it out. An obvious example of this is the difficulty of driving a car when you are explaining every detail of your actions to someone sitting beside you.

Practical applications of rule-based systems in the financial sector

Despite all that has been said above regarding the apparent impossibility of embodying tacit knowledge in a rule-based system and the practical problems of persuading an expert to articulate that knowledge, rule-based systems have demonstrated a real and practical usefulness within the financial sector.

The heyday of these systems within the financial industry was in the years from around 1984–9. This was the period of 'artificial intelligence hype', when many of the best rule-based systems designers left their posts where they had designed rule-based systems for battlefield and 'Star Wars' applications and set out to make their fortunes selling rule-based systems to Wall Street. Before the bubble burst, which it began to do in the late 1980s, many of these rule-based systems designers did indeed make their fortunes. Whether their banking clients did is another matter, however. Almost from the very beginning, financial institutions – entirely ignorant of such concepts as tacit knowledge and almost equally ignorant of the practical difficulties of knowledge elictation – had almost absurdly high expectations from rule-based systems, which they saw as the ultimate means of obtaining a competitive advantage over their rivals. For example, one large Wall Street investment bank – whose name I know but which I had better not mention – spent more than one million dollars on a rule-based system for spotting arbitrage opportunities, then had to scrap the entire system for reasons that have never been made public, but which no doubt related to the system's failure to perform as expected. Meanwhile, the designers of this and other systems pocketed their fees, and bought themselves limousines.

The bubble first began to burst in October 1987, when the global Crash suddenly brought the boom years of the 1980s to an abrupt halt. Investment banks, hitherto the main customers for rule-based systems in the financial sector, were obliged drastically to cut their expenditure on technology in general and advanced programming techniques such as rule-based systems in particular. The fortunes of rule-based system organisations began to ebb, staff were laid off, and the days of hype were, within a year or so, a mere nostalgic memory.

However, the usefulness of rule-based systems within certain types of financial application is still recognised, and deservedly so, although nowadays it is fairly rare to find a rule-based system being used exclusively in a crucial investment bank decision support application such as trading or investment management. What is more usually seen is the decision support system being based around a numerical analysis program – which provides a reliable level of basic decision support – but with a rule-based system being incorporated into the system to provide an additional level of decision-making which the institution hopes will enable it to obtain a competitive advantage. In such cases the rule-based element will probably be completely invisible to the user.

Note, too, that during the days of rule-based system hype, financial institutions exercised great secrecy in regard to the rule-based systems that they were developing. I confronted this secrecy myself in 1989, when I visited New York to research applications of rule-based systems in Wall Street and found that my visit took on the dimensions of a detective story. However, what I have seen since then confirms what I suspected at the time: that much of the secrecy was to disguise failure rather than to avoid disclosing success. Eventually, if a system is successful, the user will want to talk about it, because he knows that the positive benefits of attracting talented staff and profitable business to his institution generally outweigh the disadvantages of letting the competition know what he is doing.

The following two case studies are representative of the most usual applications of rule-based systems in the financial sector and focus on credit authorisation and investment portfolio compilation – two areas of application where rule-based systems have been conspicuously successful. Before we examine the two case histories in detail, it is useful to mention how rule-based systems actually work. In essence, a rule contained within a rule-based system is a *logical IF/THEN statement with a probability attached*. The statement connects one consequence with a recommended action, but usually only offers a *probability* that the action should be followed.

Even though the rules imply a logical connection between the consequence and the recommended action, the rule will in most cases be grounded upon a subjective opinion rather than on some objective fact. It is in this that the rule-based system's claim to be a simulation of intelligence is founded, compared with a traditional type of computer program which is based upon quantifiable variables and upon lines of code which say things like 'If X is greater than 100 go to line 56'.

A rule in a rule-based program, however, would take the form of a proposition centred around the matter at hand. For example, a rule-based program which was aiming to assist with the decision-making process relating to the purchase of shares might contain a rule which was based on the hypothesis (inevitably only a matter of opinion) that an increase in general economic prosperity should increase the value of leisure shares. So, for example, a rule embodying this might say:

'IF average incomes during the past year have increased by more than 5 per cent THEN there is a 70 per cent probablity that 10 per cent of your equity portfolio should consist of leisure stocks.'

This admittedly crude rule is only given as an example; I take no responsibility for anyone following this advice.

When many such rules are assembled in a program the different probabilities (which are inevitably somewhat arbitrary and based on the opinion of one or many people) make sense as they enable the program to function as an accumulation of different rules which can be used to govern a specific decision.

Case study
THE AMERICAN EXPRESS 'AUTHORISERS' ASSISTANT

A major part of the activities of American Express (Amex) is the operation of its charge card: the American Express card, which comes in four brands – green, gold, platinum and black. Cardholders (referred to by Amex as 'card members' must settle their bills in full within thirty days.

Amex's card business revenue stems principally from the annual subscription fee which cardholders pay for the card and the percentage commission which Amex receives from retailers (merchants) who have accepted the card as payment for a particular transaction. The American Express card is a *charge* card rather than a *credit* card: that is, cardholders do not receive credit but must pay their bills within thirty days, although credit is in effect extended to cardholders who for some reason are having trouble repaying their account. American Expess is notoriously tough with cardholders; they are likely to have transactions disallowed if they are late paying in a particular month.

Despite this policy of being tough with cardholders who do not pay their bills promptly, the fact remains that Amex only makes money when a transaction is allowed, or authorised. On the other hand, Amex does not want a cardholder to run up debts which the organisation will be unable to recover. Besides, there will also be instances where a cardholder has a very good reason for paying late (eg he has been travelling in somewhere out of the way) and Amex would not want to upset him by declining what could be a crucial transaction. Although credit and charge card companies alike insist on advertising their cards as being the means of paying for expensive luxuries in exotic settings, the fact remains that one of the most important aspects of holding a charge card or credit card is to be able to have a reliable means of paying for important and fundamental services such as air fares and hotels.

The precise authorisation procedures for American Express and other charge cards are kept confidential, for the obvious reason that a cardholder who is privy to the procedures might be able to have a transaction authorised when it would not otherwise be. However, the general method of authorisation is for there to be a specific 'floor limit' at each retail outlet (the value of this limit will vary to some degree from one retailer to the next) and for the outlet to permit transactions up to this limit without referring the transaction to the authorisation process unless the retailer has reason to suspect the bona fides of the customer.

Where the value of the transaction exceeds the floor limit the transaction will need to be authorised before it can go ahead. Authorisation above the floor limit usually takes place by means of an electronic link from a terminal in the outlet to a principal computer at Amex's authorisation centre, with the communication taking place via a leased or proprietary telephone line.

The computer authorises the majority of these referred transactions by reference to simple parameters, including whether or not the customer's account has been settled to date and whether the proposed transaction harmonises with the cardholder's usual throughput of charge value. Where the proposed transaction is considered for whatever reason not to be capable of being authorised it is referred to a manual authorisation centre, at least some of which are naturally required to operate in the evenings and at night.

A transaction will be referred to a manual authorisation centre if there is a problem with the cardholder's account (such as that his last payment has not reached his account) or if the transaction significantly exceeds the value of the cardholder's usual transactions.

Time is obviously of the essence in the authorisation process. Typically, a retailer will be waiting for a decision to appear on the terminal, and cannot proceed with the transaction until the authorisation has come through. The cardholder, for his part, will be in the embarrassing position of not knowing whether the transaction will be authorised. American Express aims to complete the manual authorisation decision within about one minute. In this time frame the human authoriser will need to undertake a manual consultation of the cardholder's account details and payment record and decide whether to authorise the transaction by applying to the case in question a body of rules and lore which in essence represents the accumulated expertise of American Express in relation to transaction authorisation. These rules are codified in a training manual which is issued to authorisers, and which is approximately four inches thick.

Obviously no manual process can involve the application of all these rules to a particular case within one minute, and consequently the highly-trained authorisers must rely on their own experience and knowledge of authorisation procedures. Understandably enough, authorisation is a difficult and stressful task. The last thing that an authoriser wants to do is to delay or, worse, offend a creditworthy customer and the authoriser is only too aware that Amex makes no money on unauthorised transactions. But equally the authoriser does not want to approve a transaction that may turn out to be uncollectable or even fraudulent.

In 1984 American Express began to look at ways of automating the larger proportion of the authorisation decisions that were referred to human authorisers. From the beginning, the technology experts who were asked by American Express to look into the feasibility of this automation process were interested in the possibility of whether a rule-based program would be the most effective means on which to base the system, particularly since it seemed to them that the instruction manual was in effect a paper-based set of rules.

The rule-based system which was eventually developed and which had its first installation at Amex's Fort Lauderdale authorisation office in October 1986 was indeed a rule-based system and its success was principally due to the instruction manual being well-suited to automation, particularly since the authorisation rules rely heavily on mathematical criteria rather than judgemental factors.

Overall, the benefits which Amex has derived from 'Authorisers' Assistant' are substantial. They include:

- increased revenue through a *higher volume* of approved transactions. While human authorisers tend to err on the side of caution, the 'Authorisers' Assistant is able to apply more criteria to the authorisation decision than a human authoriser could apply in an equivalent period and so makes fewer decisions not to authorise
- gains in customer goodwill through speedier and more accurate and fair authorisation decisions
- lower authorisation costs due to fewer human authorisers being required.

Case study
THE SANWA BANK'S 'FINANCIAL ADVISOR' SYSTEM

During the mid-1980s the Sanwa Bank, at the time Japan's fifth largest retail bank, was forced to admit that it had a problem. Sharply rising land values, particularly in the Tokyo area, had meant that many of its customers suddenly possessed substantial amounts of spare cash.

There are, needless to say, enormous opportunities to spend such spare money in Tokyo; a city where consumerism is as natural as breathing. However, there is a strong Japanese tradition in favour of saving: partly the result of vivid memories, at least on the part of middle-aged people, of the grinding poverty of the past; partly because financial caution appears to be a Japanese national characteristic, despite the keen interest which the Japanese have in enjoying their money.

In February 1989, I visited Tokyo and met Shoji Sakamoto, the then assistant general manager of the Sanwa Bank in Tokyo, who explained that one result of the Japanese fondness for saving was that the Sanwa bank had found itself in a situation where about 100,000 of its approximately one million customers had more than Y50m (about £250,000) on deposit, and had an average of about Y10m (about £50,000) readily available for investment.

Japanese investors have always been relatively demanding of their investment vehicles. The job of the Sanwa Bank's investment advisers was to advise the bank's customers on asset allocation: that is, allocating their investment funds between different investments. They had a wide variety of investment vehicles available, but not equities (ie ordinary shares), since under Japanese law banks are not allowed to sell equities. So, for example, an asset allocation might consist of 50 per cent Japanese fixed-interest Government securities, 25 per cent Japanese corporate fixed-interest bonds and and 25 per cent overseas bonds.

Obviously the particular mix of assets favoured by one investor will vary from that which is most appropriate to another investor. This principle, that the task of the investment adviser is to make as close a match as possible between the investor's circumstances and requirements was enshrined during the 1980s in the national legislations of several countries, including Japan and the UK.

The point is that there is scope for schematising the different circumstances and requirements of investors according to their own needs and creating a computer system which embodies the parameters which apply to each particular investor. The Sanwa Bank, which like all Japanese banks has an extremely resourceful and ingenious technology department, decided to try to tackle the problem of very many of its investors requiring in-depth help with their investments, and at the same time try to establish a competitive edge over its rivals.

The result was that the Sanwa Bank set its large in-house systems team (comprising about two hundred systems engineers and four hundred programmmers) to work on designing a rule-based system which would, as far as possible, provide a consistent duplication of the investment skills of the bank's most experienced asset allocation experts. Furthermore, since Japanese tax law is a critical factor as far as an individual's asset allocation is concerned, the bank decided to build taxation expertise into the system as well.

The resulting system, branded 'Financial Adviser', which runs on Hitachi PCs networking with a principal computer in Tokyo, is not intended as a substitute for the human investment adviser. Instead, the system gives branch-based investment advisers support with advising customers on asset allocation. In practice, this means that the system does most of the work, with the human adviser primarily being there to take down information about a particular investor and then feeding this information into the system.

Once the system has received the information, the Financial Adviser will compute the best investment portfolio for the investor in question and print out a list of possible investments. These would cover a wide range of suggested investment vehicles, from corporate and Government bonds to special high-interest deposit accounts. Once the system has printed out its suggested portfolio of investments for the customer, it is for the customer to decide whether or not to follow the Financial Adviser's advice. There is not even anything to stop the customer buying investments listed in the portfolio from another bank, but the Sanwa Bank, having recognised this danger, offers a special rate to investors using the system.

The Financial Adviser was, from the outset, a notable success for Sanwa Bank. Sakamoto told me that on average, it enabled each bank branch to provide, daily, approximately ten detailed personalised investment portfolios for customers. Equally important, he felt, was the role which the Financial Adviser played as a marketing weapon for Sanwa Bank. In an ultra-competitive retail banking environment, the Financial Adviser made a significant contribution to positioning Sanwa bank as an innovative and highly resourceful bank which puts the customer first.

Here, as with the Authorisers' Assistant, we see how the essence of the successful deployment was that the rules on which the simulated skill was based could be assimilated and then embodied in a rule-based program. Furthermore, and perhaps even more importantly, the users in both cases had a realistic expectation of what rule-based systems could achieve for them. They were intent on creating a tool, not some sort of device which purports to think for itself.

In conclusion we can say that rule-based systems have significant, if fairly modest, areas of application within the financial sector, and the fact that nowadays they are used increasingly as part of a decision support system rather than as the entire system should not obscure the fact that they are an extremely interesting way of making a simulation, however crude and simplistic, of the human thought process. All the same, the existence of tacit knowledge means that rule-based systems can never reach anywhere near the real thought processes of the human brain.

It is for this reason that the past few years have seen an entirely different approach to the business of programming a computer to replicate human intelligence: the technique known as the neural net.

Neural nets

Neural nets (also called neural networks or neurone nets) caused considerable excitement and interest during the late 1980s among artificial intelligence programmers, who believed that these nets offered the best possibility which had become available, to date, for replicating intelligent human thinking and judgement-forming processes.

The obvious attraction of the neural net is that its design is based closely on what we know of the design of the human brain. The brain is currently regarded as consisting of specialised nerve cells (neurones) connected by specialised connective links (synapses). The neural net is itself based on a similar configuration, with the design of the computer software (and sometimes the hardware, if a chip is slotted into the actual computer) seeking to imitate the brain's own network by simulating what are in effect simplified neurones and the strengths of connection between them.

In *Mind Over Machine*, Dreyfus and Dreyfus draw an analogy between a simulated neural net in computer software and a soap bubble, with the net, like the bubble, being 'an entity composed of molecules each physically attached only to its immediate neighbours and sensitive only to local forces – which is none the less formed by the interaction of all the local forces so that the whole determines the behaviour of the local elements.'

When a neural net is configured within the software in this manner, what should happen in theory is that a given input will cause activity to spread among the simulated neurones according to an arbitrary rule devised by the programmer, based on strengths of connections, and this given input will eventually produce an ouput. Again theoretically, it seems that such a system could be a useful learning system, since the intriguing possibility arises that the system could be made to take onboard a memory trace of how a particular output was produced for a given input, and to produce new outputs for other inputs. However, if this learning process is actually to happen, the neural net must have the capacity *to retain a memory trace of an association between an input and an output.*

Retaining a memory trace is achieved by modifying the strengths of connection. Although this is, in fact, more difficult than it sounds, since the new, adjusted strengths of connection must not only result in the new input yielding the new output, but also all previously learned inputs for which connection strengths have already been adjusted must still yield their correct outputs. The different strengths of connection allow the association to be *recreated* rather than located somewhere and later retrieved as in conventional computer programming. Because the twin concepts of distribution and association are so fundamental to neural nets, these nets are sometimes referred to as 'distributed associative nets', and seen as having a 'distributed associative memory'.

The neural net concept is undoubtedly more difficult than the rule-based system. The great advantage which the protagonists of neural nets claim for these systems is that a properly constructed neural net should have, to some degree, a capacity for self-learning or, as these protagonists prefer to say, 'training'. Supporters of the neural net idea point out, reasonably enough, that a rule-based system can never be any better than the rules it contains, and that if the knowledge base contains a flaw (ie if one or more rules are incorrect or unreliable) then no amount of processing sophistication will remove the flaw from the system.

What is the value of neural nets in today's financial sector? One important point to make here is that many researchers in cognitive science believe that at least some part of the brain's function might indeed be explainable in terms of neural nets. Other researchers would go further than this. For example, Dr Martin Davies, Reader in Philosophy at Birkbeck College, University of London, told me he felt certain that the future of artificial intelligence lay in neural nets, rather than in rule-based systems.

What seems clear is that the *potential* for neural nets could be very great, even giving the opportunity at some stage for artificial systems to be constructed which carry out subjective, even tacit tasks that no man-made computer has ever been able to achieve. Dreyfus and Dreyfus give a tantalising explanation of how the brain – and, by extension, an artificial neural net – might make use of a neural net to carry out an activity which has, to date, almost completely baffled computer systems designers: the problem of visual recognition of a face. This is clearly a task that the brain does extremely well. We are able to recognise the faces of our loved ones, friends and even mere acquaintances from the merest glance. Although some very crude and clumsy visual recognition systems for face recognition have been developed, they have nothing remotely resembling the speed, accuracy and flexibility of the brain's own face recognition facility.

Face recognition is an important skill in relation to the financial sector, since any artificial system that was able to perform at an even reasonably effective level as a face recogniser would undoubtedly have numerous other applications in judgemental areas of the financial sector – particularly those areas associated with decision support and other subjective areas of judgement-forming activity.

It is equally certain that the tacit skill of face recognition gives few, or no, opportunities for being incorporated within a rule-based system. What rules do you follow when you recognise your wife's or girlfriend's (or husband's or boyfriend's) face among anonymous faces in a crowd? The answer is that you do not follow any rules at all, but rather that you make an instantaneous or near-instantaneous recognition based purely on acquired perceptive skills.

Of course, we do not know for certain exactly (or even approximately) how these skills function. Dreyfus and Dreyfus suggested an explanation as to how this might take place, but this is only a hypothesis, albeit an extremely interesting one:

> The neurones and connecting nerves in a certain area of the brain might store, in distributed form as a memory trace, associations between images of familiar faces and names. Many such associations might be stored for each friend's face – each with a different typical expression or seen from a different angle. When we see the face, the light-intensity pattern would interact with the memory trace, and if it approximated to any of the patterns that created the trace, the associated name would come to mind as the output. All known faces would share the same memory trace, and one interaction of input and output would produce the output. No features would be detected or lists searched.

Some aspects of this sound too clumsy to be true; I do not believe that the brain operates by storing multiple possibilities for associations (as a computer would have to) in order to cover different angles, but rather that the brain employs a much more sophisticated, creative facility which is far more flexible than this but less easy to explain. I also think that this explanation assumes a too straightforward connection between a successful recognition of a face and the person's name; since we can often recognise a face but are unable to put a name to it. However, the explanation remains extremely interesting, since in essence it does suggest how a neural net might operate in order to carry out a tacit skill.

Much of the above will appear to be, and is, very theoretical. However, there are an increasing number of software vendors offering neural nets to the financial community both in the US and the UK, and no examination of programming techniques in the financial sector would be complete without a discussion of neural nets. No case study is included here, because I have not found a sufficiently satisfactory example of a neural net in action to warrant its inclusion. Those neural net-based software packages that are offered to the financial sector appear for the most part to be relatively modest self-learning programs rather than any major advance in artificial intelligence.

Having said that, anyone managing technology at a financial institution ought to remain open-minded about neural nets, since they certainly appear to have the *potential* to simulate intelligent judgement-forming thinking more effectively than rule-based systems can. However, we should not forget that there are two major problems to extensive practical deployments of neural nets in the real world. These obstacles should leave the canny technology manager safely cynical about vendors who make great claims for their neural nets.

The first problem is that the idea that neural nets provide a useful explanation of the brain's functioning might simply be wrong. It is easy to see that rule-based systems – relying as they do on logical rules which are expressed verbally and then embodied in a knowledge base – are a long remove from the way that the brain operates, but neural nets might also be a long way from this, for all that they appear to bear an anatomical relation to the brain's composite elements. If the brain does use neural nets for some parts of its functioning (and I think it might) the nets that it uses are enormously more complex than the simple simulations which are the neural nets of today's technology. For one thing, the brain's neural nets are in three rather than two dimensions, with individual nets linking with vast numbers of others on a scale which is certainly impossible to investigate with any currently available technology.

The second problem is that no methods exist at present to achieve something that the brain achieves with great facility: the storage and processing within synapses and neurones of all the delicate shades of thinking and judgement-forming. The brain is clearly adept at doing this by biochemical means, and certainly our understanding of how the brain does this is on the increase, but we are very far from being able to digitise this information ourselves. Instead, all we can do with a neural net is train it to relate certain inputs to certain outputs, and retain a memory trace of certain useful associations.

METHODS OF CONSTRUCTING A FINANCIAL SYSTEM

To move now from the complex and theoretical world of neural nets to the realities of building systems, this chapter concludes with a discussion of the principal methods of assembling the building blocks that have been examined above.

Chapter Five gives a detailed analysis of managing the implementation process of a financial system from initially drawing up plans to post-deployment activity. It is important at this stage, however, to be acquainted with the basic methods of building a financial system, since the four building blocks of the principal computer, the data communications medium, the terminal and programming techniques are only of interest to us here in so far as they can be assembled into a working implementation of financial technology that carries out a useful function.

A financial institution has three basic choices when deciding how to build a new decision support system. Firstly, it can opt for a fully customised system. Secondly, it can select a system based around a package, but modified according to the organisation's own requirements. Thirdly, it can choose an unmodified package.

Figure 2:2 opposite depicts the advantages and disadvantages associated with each of these options.

The advantages and disadvantages of each option are fairly self-explanatory, although some additional comments should be made. Obviously the fully customised system represents the ideal. It has the potential to offer a very close fit to the institution's precise specifications, and if successful, should furnish a high degree of competitive advantage. Nor should the advantages of a successful system boosting staff morale and enhancing the institution's position from a marketing perspective be discounted.

On the other hand, a customised system is indeed very expensive, and may take years to design and implement; even longer if a post-installation monitoring period is included. But even worse than this is the danger that the system will not be completely successfully. The problem here is that the utility of a customised (and usually highly advanced) decision support system can never be predicted and so the chances of successful completion can never be known for certain.

Unmodified packages, on the other hand, probably swing too far in the other direction. The likelihood that they will be successfully implemented is high. They are relatively inexpensive to implement, but they are not likely to fit the user's requirements very precisely, and in an unmodified form, they are certainly not very likely to offer the user much in the way of competitive

	Advantages	Disadvantages
1 Fully customised system	Very close approach to the ideal.	Very expensive.
	No competitor has anything similar.	Lengthy development time.
	A completed system boosts staff morale.	
	A completed system will offer marketing benefits.	May not get finished.
	Close match to business requirements.	
2 Modified package	Considerably less expensive than customised system.	Unlikely to meet all requirements.
	Offers a competitive edge.	
	Farily rapid deployment time.	
	System based on tested package.	
	Package probably comes with maintenance agreement.	
	Marketing benefits.	
	Staff morale benefits.	
	Good completion rate.	
3 Unmodified package	Relatively inexpensive.	Unlikely to meet all requirements.
	Rapid deployment time.	Unlikely to offer much competitive edge.
	Package has been tested before.	May present security problems (owing to standardisation).
	Package probably comes with maintenance agreement. Low risk.	

Figure 2.2 Advantages and disadvantages of the three methods of building a financial system

edge. A further problem with unmodified packages is that they may present security problems, since any computer virus which has infected the package in the past, or any hacker who has been able to access the package, will present a potential threat to the package. The full implications of computer security in the financial technology management process are discussed in Chapter Six.

Unquestionably, the most attractive option from the point of view of most financial institutions is the modified package, which neatly blends the advantages of the fully customised system with those of the unmodified package, while avoiding many of the disadvantages of either.

In practice, since – as this book maintains throughout – a principal purpose of deploying a financial system is to gain a competitive advantage, unmodified packages are not usually very popular, although they are important as an element of an entire system, such as when a particular type of analysis needs to be undertaken as part of a decision support system. Many financial systems are fully customised, despite the high costs of such systems and the danger that they might not be completed successfully (or may be completed but will only provide a fraction of the utility and edge that was initially anticipated). Even where modified packages are used the degree of customisation usually remains high.

An important and encouraging development within the financial technology arena is that an increasing number of vendors are becoming alive to financial institutions' needs for competitive advantage combined with the requirement to conserve costs. As a result, suppliers are developing extremely complex packages which offer such substantial possibilities for customisation that every user of the system will in effect have an entirely different version of it. Examples of such systems are provided in the following chapter.

3 REAL-LIFE APPLICATIONS OF FINANCIAL TECHNOLOGY

Introduction

What role does information technology play in the financial sector? Which specific tasks does financial technology undertake within different types of financial institutions. Can these tasks usefully be classified schematically?

This chapter aims to survey all the major real-life applications of financial technology today. The survey is conducted according to the type of application involved, not according to the technology used, although details of the technology are given. The rationale for basing the survey upon the application rather than the technology is simply that, in the most successful and competitive financial systems, it is the application which drives the mindset, not vice versa.

In September 1992, while attending a launch in London of new branded financial system packages from ACT Financial Systems, probably the UK's largest financial technology vendor, I had the opportunity to ask Paul Foll – technical director of ACT Financial Systems and known throughout the financial technology industry as an expert on matching technology to the needs of an application – what he regarded as the principal reasons why financial institutions deployed technology. Foll identified two reasons, namely:

- the need which institutions have to find new markets and establish themselves in these profitably
- the particularly pressing requirement which institutions have to operate with lower overheads.

Foll said that product development at ACT Financial Systems was profoundly influenced by these two considerations. In terms of specific outworkings, these considerations had, Foll said, led ACT to place great emphasis on offering products which offered a lower cost of ownership. This did not only mean that ACT would do its utmost to offer products which gave users greater flexibility of function at a lower real cost, but also that ACT would seek to sell products which could be used on open systems, and would therefore allow institutions to:

1 extend their systems' range of function on existing hardware
2 enjoy the confidence of knowing that future updates in a particular system which they own will also be fully compatible with the present system and will, in turn, require no additional hardware expenditure.

Many readers will be familiar with the concept of open systems, but for those who are not, open systems are standardised protocols which happen to have proved popular among users and which are consequently favoured by vendors as platforms (ie fundamental software specifications) for software products and entire systems (see Chapter One).

In our discussions, Foll said that ACT did not seek to dictate to the marketplace which open system ought to be used but rather aimed to respond to the marketplace's needs for products that met the largest range of open systems. He said that ACT vigorously resisted the temptation to decide that *one* particular open system or another was likely to become a dominant one in the future, and orientate product engineering around this.

As is always the case when corporate directors say things about their organisations, the proof of the pudding is not in the saying but in the doing. The following case study gives details of one of the ACT products that was launched at the meeting I attended. This case study is very interesting in that it demonstrates how a major vendor is accommodating its products to a wider range of open systems in order to enable users to secure ownership without needing to change to a specific protocol.

Case study
CITYDESK X / CITYDESK VIDEO SWITCH / CITYDESK KEYBOARD

(*Note*: this product description is an edited version of one supplied by ACT Financial Systems. 'Citydesk' is spelt in upper case by ACT, but has been placed into lower case for the purposes here)

Summary

Citydesk is an information and management system for the front offices of wholesale financial institutions. The Citydesk system handles both video and digital information services and is currently (September 1992) being used in over seventy dealing rooms worldwide, with installations at more than three thousand dealing and fund management positions within these dealing rooms.

The strength of the core Citydesk product is seen by ACT as being located in the following three areas:

- functionality
- ease of use
- efficiency and control.

Until the launch of the new version of Citydesk in September 1992, the system was only available in the DOS/Windows and OS/2 Presentation Manager open systems environments. The launch of Citydesk X, a UNIX version of Citydesk, will expand the available options, meaning that users can choose from one, or a combination of, all the above-mentioned platforms.

Citydesk X – product specifics

Citydesk X comprises four main features.

1 *UNIX data server*. This provides workstation distribution of data.

2 *Gallery presentation*. This is a motif-based presentation tool that enables general and tailored display of market data in the form of pages, graphs, records or chains.

3 *Real-time spreadsheets*. Citydesk X drives workstation spreadsheets with real-time data.

4 *UNIX API toolkits*. These enable users to provide Citydesk data to any user-defined application

Citydesk X – benefits

1 *More supported applications*. Full support is provided for applications in UNIX, DOS/Windows 3 and OS/2 Presentation Manager. Users are not restricted to software from a single environment but can choose the application best suited to their requirements. Additionally, bespoke applications can be developed for the most appropriate environment.

2 *Flexibility*. An organisation can 'mix and match' PCs and workstations throughout the front office according to their requirements and budget.

3 *Investment protection*. The ability to mix environments protects users from both unpredictable and predictable developments in technology.

4 *Cost-effectiveness*. In the current economic climate, saving costs plays a crucial role in a financial institution's profitability. For financial dealers already using PCs and involved in trading activity that does not require the

processing power of UNIX, it may be difficult to cost-justify installing workstations at every position. However, certain types of trading activity will clearly benefit from the increased performance offered by UNIX workstations.

ACT Financial Systems offers software for both types of device in one dealing operation and allows those to be mixed on the same network, utilising the same information feeds. This enables highly cost-effective use to be made of technology while at the same time offering the most efficient provision of services for each dealer position. It also reduces costs associated with the operation of the network, the provision of information services (ie from third-party vendors) and maintenance costs.

Comments on the case study

A striking feature of this case study is that it shows the detailed knowledge which ACT Financial Systems has of users' requirements. This knowledge is undoubtedly a major reason for the success of ACT in the financial sector. Incidentally, the organisation frequently recruits directors, sales staff and systems engineers from the financial sector, as do most of the more successful financial technology vendors.

Once the knowledge of the user's needs has been assimilated, ACT clearly devotes considerable effort and research to market products which seek to meet user's needs as fully as current technology allows.

Finally, to what extent do Foll's comments that financial institutions are currently seeking from technology the opportunity to operate profitably in new markets and to secure lower overheads conflict with my own assertions, explored in Chapter One, ie that the primary reason why institutions deploy technology is to gain a competitive advantage? The answer is that there is no conflict, since Foll's remarks are another way of saying the same thing. Securing a competitive advantage is an aim which can be approached from various perspectives. The following lists the most obvious means of achieving this aim, and proves my point:

- reducing costs without reducing profitability
- where possible, reducing costs and *increasing* profitability
- securing more business by making products and services more popular with customers and clients in *existing* markets
- securing more business by making products and services more popular with customers and clients in *new* markets.

In the following survey of real-life applications of financial technology, it is possible to say categorically that wherever a financial institution is carrying out the application effectively and also achieving all or any of the above four methods of gaining a competitive edge, that institution will indeed be establishing such an edge.

Survey of Real-life Applications of Financial Technology – Part One

RETAIL FINANCIAL INSTITUTIONS

Introduction

Retail financial institutions are in the business of providing a wide range of banking services to the general public *and maximising the profit accruing from providing these services*. This latter part of the 'job specification' of retail institutions needs emphasising, because it has often been the case in the past that retail institutions have regarded themselves, and have certainly been regarded, as semi-official organisations with huge, mysterious reserves of cash. Furthermore, sporting a reputation within the financial community which dates back – as banking textbooks are fond of pointing out – to the eighteenth century with its periwigs and coffee houses where merchants met to trade and arrange finance for each other's enterprises, and to which many of the oldest retail banks in the world can trace their origins.

This sense of retail institutions being large, mysterious and infinitely respectable organisations persisted up until around the 1950s – a time when having access to a bank account was still regarded by banks and the general public alike as a privilege rather than a right. However, by the 1960s, with its emphasis on the freedom and rights of the individual, there emerged a new generation which, for all its often ludicrous attempts to be 'with it' and fancy-free, was undeniably the first generation of young people in history with money to spend and, occasionally, save. Moving on to the 1970s it was clear that the role of the retail financial institution was profoundly different from that which had prevailed almost intact since the very days of the coffee houses.

Suddenly, retail banks were competing for business with other banks, and having a bank account was no longer a privilege but something which even sixth-formers and students, with their notoriously unstable finances, could expect to have. Of course, the banks were not interested in sixth-formers and students *per se*, but rather in the earnings potential which they had for the future. Giving young people a few incentives to join a bank was a smart investment if it was possible to retain their business in later years. For example, in 1975 I won a consolation prize of £50 in an essay competition which Barclays Bank organised for sixth-formers. I have stayed with Barclays ever since, and I think they have gained an excellent return on their outlay with my bank charges and interest payments over the years.

In the 1980s, policies pursued by the Reagan Administration in the US and the Thatcher Government in the UK, as well as similar policies pursued in many of the other developed countries, sought to increase the level of competition within the financial sector and particularly in the retail banking sector. In the UK, building societies – which were originally formed in the nineteenth century to provide loans to artisans for house-buying and which have retained their function as mortgage-lenders while becoming major savings houses in their own right – enjoyed a spectacular increase in the range of banking activities in which they could participate, following the passage into law in January 1987 of The Building Societies Act 1986. This gave building societies the right, among other things, to make personal loans and to offer customers accounts which competed with the bank accounts provided by retail banks.

There were other key factors in the construction of a new competitive retail banking environment beyond regulatory developments, of course. Much of the 1980s was a boom decade for developed countries, with consumers enjoying an unprecedented level of choice and power in determining the future of commercial organisations. Retail financial institutions, which even at the beginning of the 1980s possessed a residual exclusiveness and sense of their own superiority to other money-making enterprises, found that they had to become as competitive, hungry for new business and market-oriented as any newly-formed enterprise if they wanted to succeed. It was as if the long history of many of these institutions counted for very little among customers who were above all seeking a better deal from one institution than from another. In search of this better deal, customers were prepared to do something which they had never done before with any sense of concerted purpose: move from one institution to another, if the new institution was offering them a superior service, higher interest, or a combination of the two.

The result of all this was that retail financial institutions found themselves operating in a highly competitive environment, and an environment which shows no signs of becoming less competitive. Efficiency of operation, commitment to customer service and a genuinely innovative and enterprising approach to marketing are all extremely important for a retail institution which wishes to maximise its profitability in today's climate. As in other areas of the financial sector, technology plays an essential role in providing the means whereby an operation can become more efficient, good customer service can be delivered to the customer and services can be marketed to the public.

The best way to begin an analysis of how technology is used by retail banks today is to consider the needs that customers have from retail institutions. These needs can be seen as fitting into two principal categories.

1 *The customer's need for information relating to his account*

Customers need information about the state of their accounts. The more up to date this information is, the better, which is why retail institutions try to arrange for most, if not all, of their facilities for providing information about customers' accounts to operate in real-time. In a real-time information system, the information is continually updated, with the latest updates being available instantaneously. From the point of view of customer service, a serious hazard of not providing information on a real-time basis is that a customer may try to initiate a transaction with a knowledge of the state of his account that is based on earlier, out-of-date information and then suffer the embarrassment – in a supermarket checkout queue, perhaps – of being unable to proceed with the transaction. The need to take every reasonable measure to avoid a customer who is acting in good faith to be embarrassed in this way should be at the heart of any real-time information system.

Another major reason for deploying real-time account information systems is – as was explained in Chapter Two – that they give the institution a much higher level of security than information systems which only communicate with the principal computer on an occasional basis, such as through batch processing. This is because there are various methods which the dishonest can use to circumvent the 'daily cash withdrawal limit' rules from automatic cash dispensing equipment. These rules have to be imposed by an institution for the sake of security if it is using a batch processing system, although many institutions which use real-time systems also impose a limit on the amount of cash that can be withdrawn. However, where a batch processing system is used, the rules can easily be circumvented by multiple copies of a plastic card being made. The batch processing system – which is by definition unable to communicate with the principal computer (and, by extension, with other automatic cash dispensing machines) in order to ascertain what funds the cardholder has already withdrawn that day – will usually mark the card electronically in some way in order to show that it has already been used that day. A copied card will of course not carry that mark. A batch processing system also suffers from the more fundamental drawback that it is unable to ascertain whether the customer has sufficient funds in his account (taking into account any permitted overdraft facility) to make the transaction in the first place.

2 *The customer's need for access to payment facilities*
Customers need to use the funds which they deposit with retail financial institutions in order to pay their bills. It follows that the provision of some facility (or, in real life, various different types of facility) for making payments is an essential part of the range of services which retail institutions need to provide to their customers. Incidentally, it is useful to regard the customer's need for access to cash withdrawal facilities as a subset of the customer's need for access to payment facilities, since in a cash withdrawal situation what is happening, in essence, is that the customer is making a payment to himself.

The two categories of applications of retail financial technology

Retail financial technology applications can be categorised neatly into those applications which involve the customer's direct participation (almost invariably by the customer using a plastic card with a personalised code number or word to complete the authorisation process) and those applications which are undertaken entirely within the retail institution. In the following survey, those applications which involve the customer's participation are referred to as *electronic payment systems*, while those applications which are undertaken within the institution are referred to as *administrative systems*.

Note, incidentally, that electronic payment systems – while having as their main objective the provision of payment facilities to customers – do in fact usually also incorporate a facility for providing account-related information to customers, thereby fulfilling the other principal requirement which customers have from retail institutions.

In both this survey and the subsequent examination of wholesale financial technology, an analysis of how the different types of application make use of technology follows each major category of applications.

ELECTRONIC PAYMENT SYSTEMS

AUTOMATED TELLER MACHINES (ATMs)

Automated Teller Machines (ATMs) are automatic machines for dispensing banking services to customers. They are the most immediately visible type of retail financial technology and are easily the most important electronic payment system.

As payment system devices, they have two main applications:

1 customers can withdraw cash from them and so in effect can make themselves the recipients of the payment service
2 many retail institutions enable customers to initiate payments to third parties via ATMs.

Worldwide, ATMs play a key role in the efforts of most retail banks to win business from customers. Many customers of retail institutions see ATMs as a more typical interface between themselves and their institution than the institution's branch.

There are two principal types of ATM: *through-the-wall (TTW) ATMs*, which are located in the outside wall of the institution's branch or, sometimes, in the outside wall of a large retail outlet; and *lobby ATMs*, which are either located inside a financial institution's branch or in some other place (eg a supermarket or other large retail outlet) where there is likely to be a substantial demand for cash. Many lobby ATMs situated in branches are dedicated to particular functions, eg cash-dispensing, deposit-taking, statement ordering etc. Generally speaking, different institutions have different policies on what particular dedicated functions their lobby ATMs should provide.

Typical facilities which ATMs offer include one or more of the following.

Most common facilities

● cash withdrawal
● balance available on screen
● balance available on paper slip
● statement ordering facility
● deposit facility
● a facility allowing the customer to change his Personal Identification Number (PIN) or personal code.

Other facilities

- traveller's cheque withdrawal
- payment facilities to third parties (the customer must provide details of the payee in advance to the institution)
- loan arranging
- purchase of investment products
- purchase of insurance.

Figure 3.1. shows the front configuration of a typical ATM, with the different operating parts that the customer sees.

ATM sharing

The high cost of ATMs, the wastefulness of large numbers of ATMs which all belong to different financial institutions being located every few yards in

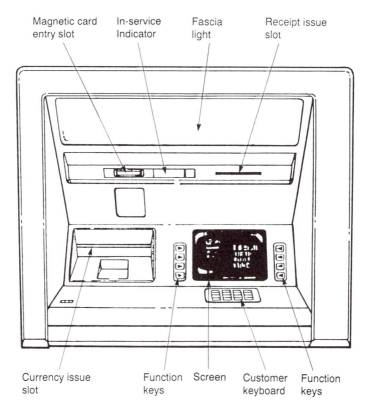

Magnetic card entry slot   In-service Indicator   Fascia light   Receipt issue slot

Currency issue slot   Function keys   Screen   Customer keyboard   Function keys

Figure 3.1 Front configuration of a typical ATM.
Source: NCR Ltd

city centres, and – less obviously but equally importantly – the sophistication of telecommunications switching facilities which allow different transactions to be routed quickly and cheaply through a complex network to the relevant institutional recipient, all make the idea of *ATM sharing* an extremely attractive notion.

The idea behind ATM sharing is very straightforward. Individual institutions share their ATMs with other institutions, who have the option either of deploying their own shared ATMs, or – which in practice only happens if the institution is very small – not deploying any ATMs at all but issuing their customers with cards that operate in the shared ATMs.

ATM sharing arrangements can be simple agreements, backed by the implementation of the appropriate technical procedures, between one or more institutions which provide for the sharing process. However, in most countries it is more usual for those institutions participating in the sharing arrangement to create a wholly or partially separate organisation to manage the sharing technology, ensure that all transactions are satisfactorily reconciled and that institutions receive the fees (paid by the customer in most cases) which they are due for their ATMs having been used, and – most importantly of all from a competitive perspective – act as a focus and energiser for marketing activity based around encouraging customers to use the sharing service, and seeking to recruit new institutions to the service. Obviously, the more institutions that participate in the ATM sharing service, the more cost-effective that service will be.

A logical and important extension of the principle of national ATM sharing is that of international ATM sharing, which involves a financial institution's ATM network being connected to the network or networks of one or more instititions located abroad. Although there is no particular reason why a lone institution should not conclude an international sharing arrangement with a foreign institution, in practice international sharing tends to take place between shared ATM networks rather than between individual institutions.

Whether an institution is involved in national or international ATM sharing, it can reasonably expect to gain the following benefits from its participation in a sharing service.

1 *Marketing appeal of the shared network*. In an increasingly competitive retail financial sector, perhaps the primary benefit to an institution of participating in an ATM sharing arrangement is that customers like using plastic cards and display a high level of recognition of branded shared networks. When a customer wants a new type of account, the knowledge that with the account will go a card that gives the customer access to all the

ATMs operated by a particular branded shared network will be an important, and possibly decisive, factor in the customer's decision to opt for the account.

This marketing benefit of participation in a shared network is sometimes overlooked by institutions, concerned as they are with the more tangible financial issues. However, in time to come, as the financial costs and benefits of shared network participation become routine, the *intangible* appeal of the branding to the customer will become the dominant factor in the benefits which an institution accrues from such participation.

In a nutshell, customers like to be part of exciting trends and fashions, and it is indicative of the vast changes that have swept the financial sector during the past twenty years that branded ATM networks have become as much a perceived (and actual) trend and fashion as a fashion in clothing and music.

Proof of the importance of the intangible charisma of a shared network is surely found in the US, where ATM sharing is at least five years ahead of that in any other developed country and where it is common for shared networks to have deliberately 'exciting' and 'dynamic' names, such as, for example: 'Magic Line,' 'New York Cash Exchange' (NYCE) and 'PLUS'. The last mentioned is an interstate shared ATM network and competes vigorously with the Cirrus network for the title of largest shared network in the US.

2 *Quality of customer service*. Financial constraints, a limit on the number of branches which an institution operates or a combination of these factors, will restrict the number of ATMs which an institution could provide if operating the ATM network independently. ATM sharing will give the institution's customers access to a much greater number of ATMs, thereby making the institution's services more attractive to the customer.

Clearly, there is a close relation between the importance of this benefit and the increase in personal and business travel both within, and across, national borders. Since there seems no indication that personal and business travel is doing anything other than continually increasing, this benefit must correspondingly become an increasingly important one.

3 *Cost savings*. The institution will be able to make substantial cost savings compared with the cost of continually extending its ATM network on a purely independent basis. There is always a fee to pay for joining a shared network, but this is invariably less than the cost of deploying even a small number of additional ATMs, let alone a large ATM network.

4 *Higher transaction revenue*. Because institutions usually manage their relationship with customers so that customers pay for ATM withdrawals just as they pay for cheques used, institutions gain more revenue from customers

the higher the number of ATM transactions which customers put through the system. This will also apply where the ATMs used by the customer are part of the shared system.

5 *Network branding*. Where the shared network has its own branding, the institution will gain substantial benefits in terms of market awareness as a result of the branding of the shared network.

6 *Better resources*. A shared network, whether branded or not, will almost certainly have more financial resources and know-how available specifically for ATM deployment and associated research than even the largest lone institution could.

7 *Additional benefits*. Shared networks offer institutions a variety of other benefits, the precise nature of which depends on the precise terms on which the institution has joined the network. Examples of such benefits are: access to opportunities to participate in international ATM sharing; potential involvement in national and international conferences on ATMs and the chance to share expertise with other experts; and the chance to participate in leading-edge research projects such as 'smart' cards (ie plastic cards with a microchip onboard which offer a much higher level of functionality and security than do magnetic strip cards) and projects which examine new types of applications of ATMs.

In this latter context, there seem many interesting opportunities, as yet unexplored, for a shared network to use its ATMs as communications devices for both financial and nonfinancial purposes, and at the very least as methods for cardholders to summon emergency assistance for any reason.

The effectiveness of ATM networks as communications devices has been seen in rudimentary form when financial institutions and police have liaised together to catch card fraudsters, with the institution being able to give information instantly to the police about which ATM the fraudster is using (assuming that the ATM operates in real-time) and the police springing into action. Several fraudsters have been caught red-handed in this way.

ELECTRONIC FUNDS TRANSFER AT POINT OF SALE (EFTPOS)

EFTPOS is an electronic payment method which involves goods or services being paid for at the point of sale (frequently abbreviated to POS). EFTPOS transactions are sometimes authorised automatically by the card being swiped through the magnetic cardreader or manually by the customer inputting a PIN into a hand-held pad, but where the transaction value is within the house limit there is often no remote authorisation and the transaction is completed by the customer signing a paper voucher.

Although the fundamental principle behind EFTPOS is the same however the transaction is initiated, there are four different ways in which the actual debit can be made against the customer's account. These are:

1 real-time (instant) debit against a current or savings account
2 real-time debit against a credit account
3 debit after the usual clearing period (three days in the UK) against a current or savings (thrift) account
4 debit after the usual clearing period against a credit account.

The method of debit

The choice as to whether the debit takes place against a credit or current account is, assuming that the facilities for both are available, very much up to the customer. There are arguments in favour both of the debit taking place in real-time or after three days; the principal ones being that real-time debit allows customers to keep careful track of their expenditure but forces them to forego the 'float' during the clearing period, whereas debit after the clearing period gives them the float but is less efficient in terms of allowing them to keep track of the state of their accounts.

Many financial institutions have proved to be unwilling to commit themselves to one form of debit rather than to another; presumably because, although real-time debit appears to be the most 'perfect' form of EFTPOS, it involves the requirement that EFTPOS should operate in real-time at any time. Most institutions have to date preferred to retain the option that even a system that is essentially a real-time system should be able to operate in float mode on occasion. However, as EFTPOS technology improves, we can expect to see most systems becoming real-time, mainly because of the immense advantages, from the point of view of security, that accrue to a real-time system.

Benefits of EFTPOS

Any discussion of the benefits of EFTPOS ought to focus on the benefits – and detractions – of EFTPOS from the point of view of financial institutions, retailers (who have to deploy the system in their own outlets) and customers. Figure 3.2 opposite shows the advantages and disadvantages of EFTPOS to each of these three categories. Since, however, the most important group which needs to be convinced of the benefits of EFTPOS is obviously the

Financial Institution	Retailer	Customer
Advantages		
1. Enormous opportunities for generating commission revenue exist. 2. Widely implemented, EFTPOS would greatly reduce the mass of cheques which institutions must process every day.	1. Cash handling costs reduced. 2. Fewer dishonoured cheques. 3. Better central management control of payments in. 4. Lower bank transaction charges. 5. More productivity in the back office.	1. No need to carry cash, fewer security problems. 2. Transaction can be made quickly and conveniently. 3. Customer can monitor state of account on a transaction-by-transaction basis in some cases. 4. Possible increased status. 5. No need to write a cheque. 6. No need to carry a cheque book.
Disadvantages		
1. Initial investment required is high. 2. No clear evidence is available that most customers want EFTPOS. 3. Many retailers are opposed to EFTPOS. 4. Single national EFTPOS do not often exist.	1. No clear evidence exists that allowing a customer to debit a current account is an incentive for customers to spend money that would not otherwise be spent. (With credit cards there *is* this incentive.) 2. Unauthorised transactions could cause loss of customer goodwill.	1. PIN or other authorisation code must be memorised. 2. Card may be lost. 3. If system debits instantly customer loses three-day grace period provided by cheques. 4. If cashier cannot get authorisation customer may suffer embarrassment. 5. The customer may simply be indifferent to EFTPOS.

Figure 3.2 Advantages and disadvantages of electric funds transfer at point of sale

customers, the benefits of EFTPOS to users requires some further elaboration.

It should be said at the outset that the benefits of EFTPOS to customers are not as self-evident as the benefits of ATMs. It is likely, none the less, that EFTPOS will eventually become a dominant payment method in all the countries where it is implemented – indeed in the UK it has become this already – but any financial institution which wishes to participate in an

EFTPOS scheme has to accept that it cannot assume – as it perhaps can with ATMs – that the system will automatically be popular with customers. One important problem here is that people have been used for about twenty years to paying for things by credit card, but the whole idea of EFTPOS focuses more on current or savings accounts than credit cards (even though a credit card transaction initiated electronically is a form of EFTPOS).

Another problem is that whereas an ATM, being a machine, allows a customer to beat a retreat from it with the minimum of embarrassment if a transaction is not authorised – such as if there are insufficient funds in the customer's account – an unsuccessful EFTPOS transaction will expose the customer to having to deal with a human cashier and (possibly) the curious stares of those others in the queue behind.

Although there is an undeniable need for a process of education to explain to customers what EFTPOS is and how it works, financial institutions can be confident that EFTPOS will eventually find its public. Much of the success of ATMs is surely due to the simplicity of the selling proposition or concept: you stick a card into a slot in the wall and money comes out of another slot. There may be buttons to press and other functions available, but the basic proposition remains.

EFTPOS has an equally straightforward basic propostion: you give a card to someone in order to pay for your purchases. Add to this the observation that customers generally enjoy using plastic cards, which are probably seen by many customers as conferring status, and one has ample reason to believe that the eventual future of EFTPOS must be a bright one.

Shared EFTPOS networks

An area of uncertainty for larger financial institutions seeking either to become involved in EFTPOS or to extend their current involvement is the question regarding the extent to which they ought to become involved in shared EFTPOS schemes, as opposed to developing their own initiatives.

Experience has shown that, as with ATMs, institutions tend to seek to obtain the best of both worlds by developing their own proprietary initiatives at first, and then participating in a shared EFTPOS system when they feel either that there are no further competitive advantages to be gained from remaining independent, or that participation in a shared network is essential for continued financial viability, or both. The difference is that the option of running a proprietary EFTPOS scheme is limited to the very largest institutions, since whereas a proprietary scheme involving ten ATMs is better than one involving no ATMs, an EFTPOS scheme will be of little use unless its covers many thousands of retailers – albeit perhaps in a specific region rather than necessarily on a national basis – soon after its inauguration.

The advantages to an institution of joining a shared EFTPOS scheme are as follows:

- *quality of customer service*: a shared scheme will almost inevitably have more retail outlets in it than a proprietary scheme, thereby giving customers access to a better level of service
- *cost advantages*: terminal sharing should bring institutions significant cost benefits, both in terms of the opportunity to spread terminal installation costs among a number of institutions and also in terms of reduced marketing costs, since the shared network will probably promote itself from a central source, and these promotional costs can be shared among participating institutions
- *higher knowledge and expertise*: the sharing of knowledge and expertise is likely to lead to higher levels of these throughout the network
- *higher levels of security*: a shared network is more likely to have access to substantial funds for computer security than a proprietary network and, given that the transaction switching system works properly, a shared network ought to have the resources and know-how to incorporate an extremely high level of security.

TELEPHONE BANKING

Telephone banking is a means for a financial institution to provide an at least partially automated banking service to customers via the customer's own telephone. Since all telephone banking systems make use to some extent of electronics in the communications equipment, it can be called a form of electronic payment system, with customers able to give banks a range of instructions, including payment instructions, over the telephone.

As the professional and leisure lives of banks' customers have ranged over wider geographical areas, the central role of the local banking branch in the delivery of banking systems has changed into only being one location at which a customer may wish to initiate a transaction, with customers also being interested in initiating transactions at other branches. The most typical scenario for most customers nowadays is that they initiate some transactions at a branch near their home, but a greater number of transactions at a branch near their place of work.

We have already seen how customers have turned to ATMs – and more recently to EFTPOS – to conduct transactions and make payments by remote means. Many customers have also come to rely heavily on manual telephone and postal liaison with their banks in order to arrange payment facilities and obtain account information. Market research, an example of which is seen in Figure 3.3 below, demonstrates the appeal of branchless banking to customers.

- One in five people had not visited their branch in the last month.

- One in ten people had not visited their branch in the last six months.

- Over half (51%) said they would rather visit their bank as little as possible.

- Over a third (37%) used cash dispensers rather than withdrawing money over the counter inside their bank.

- On the last visit to their branch, one in three people had left without speaking to any bank staff.

- Nearly half (48%) had never met their bank manager. Of those who had, over a third (36%) said the meeting was over a year ago.

- Almost 40% (39%) complain that there are too many queues at banks.

- Almost 40% (38%) find it inconvenient to visit the bank because of short opening hours.

- Over a quarter (27%) wished they could do more business with banks by telephone.

Figure 3.3   The appeal of branchless banking to customers
Source: First Direct (Battelle, August 1990)

In the light of market research such as this and simple observation of the public's changing habits regarding how they use their bank it should come as no surprise that an important feature of the retail financial sector in the 1990s and beyond has been and will be a greatly increased demand among customers for direct bank-to-customer banking *which does not involve a visit to the branch*. Financial institutions, for their part, are responding vigorously to this demand and are competing with each other to provide effective facilities for the remote delivery of banking services. The surge in competition over the provision of these services shows every sign of rivalling the initially US-wide and then Europe-wide competition over ATMs which took place in the 1970s and the 1980s.

Options for delivery of remote banking services

There are two principal options for the delivery of remote banking services. These are:

1 services based around a personal computer (PC) located in the customer's home
2 services based around the customer's home telephone.

Experience to date has shown that the telephone-based option is a much more useful one than the PC-based option. The immense advantage of the telephone-based system is that it makes use of a tool which most customers will already have – the telephone. Similarly, most people are familiar with the telephone, whereas only a small minority of people are already adept at communicating via a computer. Furthermore, it is usually less expensive for institutions to set up an automated, 24-hour service involving some kind of automated response system than to install a computer system and communications device that will provide the PC user with the 24-hour service which he is entitled to expect.

Telephone banking services offer great potential both to institutions and their customers. A very full range of banking services can be offered by the telephone, thereby reducing the customer's need to visit the branch during opening hours. Details of balances can easily be obtained over the telephone from an automated voice system, statements can be ordered, and payments to prearranged third parties can be organised. The only transactions that cannot be handled satisfactorily by telephone are cash withdrawals and account deposits, as these involve the handling of money and cheques.

Note that there are three major technological options for telephone banking. What all these systems have in common is that they feature the customer making contact with his bank by telephone and communicating with an automated prerecorded voice which offers various options that are either activated by a voice response system (ie the automated voice recognises certain words or phrases that the customer uses) or else by a tone telephone (which the customer may already have). Tone telephones are proliferating in most developed countries, but where a customer does not have access to one he can obtain a tone pad which makes the requisite tones and which can be held against the voicepiece of the receiver.

The different technological options for telephone banking are discussed in detail in the section below on electronic payment systems' technology.

Lessons drawn from the US experience of telephone banking

Telephone banking is well established in the US and plays an increasingly important role in its retail financial sector. There are two principal reasons why telephone banking has established itself relatively quickly in the US.

These are:

1 the great size of the US, and the important role which travel plays in the lives of most people, offer an obvious incentive to financial institutions to provide an efficient remote banking service

2 US banking legislation generally prohibits banks from operating outside their own state, which means that customers can usually only use their bank when travelling outside their own state if they make use of remote banking facilities. Note, incidentally, that this regulatory factor is also an important reason why ATM sharing established itself in the US rapidly during the 1970s and 1980s.

Some US financial institutions began their telephone banking service by offering what was simply a manual service where the customer would talk to real cashiers. This sounds fine, but since telephone banking is designed to undertake many routine transactions rather than only the more complex matters, human cashiers are wasted on most transactions, with automation being a far more attractive alternative. Most US banks have now switched to automated telephone banking services, and reserve person-to-person contact for the more complex and difficult transactions.

Telephone banking is advancing on all fronts in most developed countries. It offers straightforward and important benefits to customers – who can carry out many routine banking functions from their own home – and to institutions, which do not need to build and staff as many branches as they would otherwise be obliged to, and which can relieve congestion in branches. There is also the opportunity for institutions to gain some revenue from their telephone banking service by charging customers for using the service, although most institutions prefer to keep these costs down or even do away with them completely. Institutions tend to believe that the savings in bricks-and-mortar and staff costs which telephone banking offers is quite enough of a justification for it.

The benefits of telephone banking to institutions and customers alike is such that it is difficult to believe that telephone banking will do anything other than continue to expand in the future.

THE TECHNOLOGY BEHIND ELECTRONIC PAYMENT SYSTEMS

AUTOMATED TELLER MACHINES (ATMs)

From a technological perspective, ATMs can be regarded as consisting of three elements:

1 a safe
2 a facility for an electronic link to a principal computer via a data communications network
3 an electromechanical unit for interfacing with the customer.

An ATM system provides a typical example of a financial system which makes use of all the four building blocks that were examined in Chapter Two. Specifically, an ATM system makes use of these in the following manner.

Principal computer – this will be the central computer which handles all the remote data storage and retrieval functions of the system and with which the ATMs communicate. An important role of the principal computer in an ATM system is to handle the authorisation process if the system is operating in real-time.

Most, if not all, ATM systems used in today's financial sector make use of principal computers that feature fault-tolerance, either in the hardware or the software. Note, too, that while mainframe computers are still used for the ATM systems deployed by large retail financial institutions covering an entire country or large regional area, minicomputers are increasingly used for all but the very largest ATM systems, with PCs being employed in some cases as the principal computers of small ATM networks.

Finally, it should be mentioned that the security problems associated with ATM systems that are not operating in real-time has meant that batch-processed ATM networks are becoming increasingly unfashionable. For example, in the UK, since October 1992, there are no longer any ATM networks operating in any other mode than real-time.

Data communications medium – this will consist of a leased or proprietary telephone network that constitutes a WAN. Where ATM sharing is involved, one or more additional remote switching devices are required to communicate with the other participating financial institutions and ensure that all shared transactions are switched across the network in an efficient and timely manner.

Terminal – an ATM can be regarded as a specialised computer terminal dedicated to carrying out certain banking functions. Clearly, it differs significantly from the more familiar 'workstation' type of computer terminal in that the user is restricted to a limited range of functions and that the standard keyboard or mouse interface is replaced by an alphanumeric board for keying in a PIN, and various buttons for initiating transactions.

Programming techniques – there is no universal programming software for ATM and EFTPOS systems. The type of software used will depend on the hardware chosen. However, two important observations can be made:

1 there is an increasing tendency for financial institutions to use packaged software for ATM and EFTPOS applications rather than designing their own software
2 the programming language COBOL is rapidly establishing itself as the leading programming language for ATM and EFTPOS applications, the principal exception to this is that where a PC is being used as the principal computer for a small ATM or EFTPOS network, the most common programming language used is probably the language known as C.

Sequence of functions

The overall sequence of functions of an ATM system are typically as follows.

1 Plastic card inserted into slot.
2 ATM registers account number (contained in magnetic strip on card) and requests cardholder to enter PIN.
3 PIN entered. ATM requests functions required while PIN is checked against account number. If real-time authorisation is used, PIN is checked against data contained in principal computer. If batch processing is used, PIN is checked against PIN held in magnetic strip on card.
4 Transaction unauthorised – cardholder asked to enter PIN again (usually only one further attempt is permitted before card is retained by the ATM).
5 Transaction authorised – transaction proceeds.
6 Transaction completed – card is returned to cardholder. In a real-time system, the ATM immediately relays details of the completed transaction to the principal computer. In a batch processing system, the details of the transaction will only be relayed to the principal computer when the messages are transmitted.
7 The cardholder's account is updated by the principal computer to accommodate the transaction.

ELECTRONIC FUNDS TRANSFER AT POINT OF SALE (EFTPOS)

An EFTPOS system is approximately analagous to an ATM system, with the building blocks being made use of in the following manner.

Principal computer – as with an ATM system, this is the central computer which handles all the remote data storage and retrieval functions of the system and with which the EFTPOS terminals communicate. An important role of the principal computer in an EFTPOS system is to handle the authorisation process if the system is operating in real-time.

Data communications medium – as with an ATM system, this consists of a leased or proprietary telephone network that constitutes a WAN. Where EFTPOS sharing is involved, one or more additional remote switching devices are required to communicate with the other participating financial institutions and ensure that all shared transactions are switched across the network in an efficient and timely manner.

An EFTPOS communications system can also operate in real-time, on a batch-processed basis, or on either mode at different times.

Terminal – an EFTPOS terminal can also be regarded as a specialised computer terminal dedicated to carrying out certain banking functions. It is even more specialised than an ATM since its functions are usually restricted to providing an electronic means (typically via a cardreading mechanism) through which details of the card and the transaction can either be relayed immediately to the principal computer or else stored within the terminal and relayed when the other batched messages are relayed.

Programming techniques – these are very similar to those associated with ATM systems, and for this reason are discussed above in the section on programming techniques for ATM systems.

Sequence of functions

The overall sequence of functions of an EFTPOS system are typically as follows.

1 Cashier takes plastic card from customer and inserts it into cardreading section of EFTPOS terminal. Authorisation may be made by means of a separate hand-held pad into which the cardholder can key in his PIN. Otherwise the only authorisation method will be the cardholder's signature on a paper voucher. However, if the cardholder's account is out of order and the cardreader is operating in real-time, the transaction may be disallowed.

2 Transaction disallowed – card is returned to cardholder (or, in exceptional cases, retained by cashier).

3 Transaction allowed – details of transaction may be keyed into the EFTPOS terminal by cashier and relayed instantly (real time system) or subsequently (batch-processed system) to the principal computer. In other systems the financial institution will only know of the transaction when the paper voucher reaches it – usually after a period that is approximately analagous to the cheque clearing period.

TELEPHONE BANKING

Telephone banking also makes use of the building blocks, although in a very different manner to an ATM system or EFTPOS system.

Principal computer – in a telephone banking system, this is usually the central computer of the financial institution. Although sometimes a separate computer (typically a minicomputer or even a powerful PC) will be used to power the telephone banking system, with an interface being used between the separate computer and the principal computer in order to ensure that information relating to accounts and transactions can be relayed between the two computers, and if necessary also to the customer.

Data communications medium – the data communications system for a telephone banking system differs from that of an ATM or EFTPOS system, since – by definition – the link between the customer and the institution is through a voice line. Data communications will be used by the institution in its own offices, via a LAN. Otherwise, where the PC-type of telephone banking system is used, this system will of course function with a WAN.

Where a homebased PC is used as the interface for the telephone banking system, a large real-time data communication system will be required. Such a system would be similar in application to that for an ATM system, with the homebased terminals being operated by customers in much the same way as ATMs, with the obvious exceptions being that the homebased terminals cannot dispense cash or accept deposits.

Programming techniques – in true telephone banking systems where voice communications is used, the data processing element is usually contained almost entirely within the institution's premises rather than being required to communicate with a terminal. Packaged telephone banking systems are available, and many will run on powerful PCs or on small minicomputers. Again, COBOL and C are the most common programming languages here.

Sequence of functions (voice telephone banking system)

1 Customer lifts handset and dials number of telephone banking service.
2 Automated voice welcomes customer to service and provides auditory cues for either customer's vocal commands, tone inputs from tone telephone board or tone inputs from tone pad.
3 Customer undertakes transactions, receiving vocal confirmation from the automated system that the transaction has been completed, and also receiving any requested information about the condition of the account(s); ie account balance information.
4 Customer replaces handset.
5 Completed transactions are reconciled to customer's account, which is updated accordingly.

Technological options for telephone banking

There are three major technological options in voice telephone banking. Each option has made significant progress over the last few years towards becoming cost-effective and practicable solutions. In all instances, the telephone banking systems respond to the caller in a clear speaking voice, which is created not by crude simulation but by digitising a real voice speaking the range of expressions that are required to communicate the various functions of the system. The technological options are as follows.

1 *Tone telephones/voice response.* An increasing number of modern push button telephones send an audible multifrequency tone down a telephone line. This tone can be interpreted electronically by a receiving computer, which can be made aware of which buttons the customer has pressed. In this technological option, the customer input is therefore made by buttons being pressed on the telephone handset.

As we have seen, customers who do not have access to tone telephones can still make use of this type of telephone banking system if they are supplied with a tone generating device by the institution that operates the system.

This option is by far the most widespread technological option for telephone banking, and has very much reglegated the other two options below to the status of 'also-rans'.

2 *Preprogrammed telephones.* It is possible to provide customers with special telephones featuring different keys which, when pressed, will select the banking service that is required. These telephone are very easy to operate since the interface can be made extremely simple. On the other

hand, this option has the serious disadvantage that it does away with the principal benefit of the telephone banking system: the fact that the customer can use a device which he will almost certainly have in the house already, and with which he will be very familiar, so that telephone banking becomes a 'user-friendly' type of electronic payment service.

3 *Voice recognition*. Some telephone banking systems, particularly in the US, are able to recognise the *spoken* instructions of customers within a range of words and expressions that has been programmed into the system beforehand.

In theory, these systems have the great advantage that they allow the customer to 'talk' to the computer – albeit in a stilted and formal manner – rather than be obliged to use the less natural process of pressing buttons. On the other hand, in a society where mechanisation and automation is a part of almost everyone's life, pressing buttons to execute commands is only slightly

be more natural than talking in the kind of artifical way that voice recognition systems demand from their customers.

However, the big problem here is that voice recognition systems often do not work properly, and until the technology of the recognition system reaches a level where failures are as infrequent as failures in the tone communications process, voice recognition technology will remain an interesting gimmick rather than the basis of a reliable and workable large-scale telephone banking system.

MANAGING ELECTRONIC PAYMENT SYSTEMS

There are two principal management aims in relation to deploying electronic payment systems.

1 *Cost-effectiveness*: the deployment should have as low as possible a cost in relation to the additional revenue that is likely to be generated from it. In other words, the deployment should be as profitable as the institution can reasonably expect.

2 *Acceptability to customers*: the deployment should be such that is likely to have the maximum chance of proving popular with customers.

Both these objectives are easy to formulate but rather less easy to achieve. In practice, it is difficult for an institution to predict what the take-up of an electronic payment system is likely to be or what revenue it is likely to generate. There are, however, certain guidelines which can be followed in order to maximise the likely profitability of an electronic payment system. Some of these guidelines relate to gaining an essential understanding of the different stages of evolution of electronic payment systems, and the need to become involved with a particular system at the stage that is appropriate for the institution in question.

There are also extensive guidelines relating to the entire deployment process of electronic payment systems and other types of financial technology (see Chapter Five).

At this stage, we can usefully introduce a theory which is not my own invention but which I have named *The Theory of the Evolution of Electronic Payment Systems*. This provides a convenient yardstick for assessing the stage of evolution, and indeed the likely ultimate prospects for the success of, any electronic payment system under consideration.

It states that there are three phases of evolution of an electronic payment system, with the corollary that it is essential for any financial institution seeking to deploy a particular payment system to be aware exactly of which evolutionary phase the system occupies at any one time. According to this theory, the three evolutionary phases are:

- the inception phase
- the growth phase
- the maturity phase.

Note that the particular phase which applies to a payment system will depend within which country the payment system is being deployed since payment systems evolve at different rates in different countries. For example, ATM and EFTPOS systems involving smart cards are in a growth phase in France – which has proved itself a pioneer in smart card applications – but are very much at an inception stage in the UK, as indeed they are in most other developed countries.

Broadly speaking, the three phases of inception, growth and maturity relate, respectively, to:

- *inception*: the initial development of the technology and the ironing out of problems
- *growth*: the period during which the effectiveness of the technology is proven in the marketplace
- *maturity*: the period of acceptance of the technology and its widespread use by financial institutions and their customers. In the maturity phase, it can usually be said that if an institution is not deploying the technology, it will probably be at a serious competitive disadvantage to rival institutions.

The specific characteristics of each evolutionary phase are described below.

The inception phase

- the technology is still being developed and some technical problems remain to be ironed out
- the technology is not widely available commercially
- substantial investment will be required by any institution which seeks to deploy the technology. This would generally preclude the development of technology in the inception phase by any but the largest financial institution or computer systems house
- an element of risk will inevitably be inherent in the development. This can hardly be avoided, since ultimately the institution has no way of being certain that the technology in question will prove acceptable to the bank's retail customers (in the case of retail banking) or will be found to be useful and profitable by the bank's staff

The growth phase

- the technology is widely available commercially
- the technology is increasingly accepted by the people for whom it is intended
- since much of the major expenditure on development will have been made by the organisations which pioneered the deployment, financial institutions wishing to deploy this technology will probably not need to face high development costs
- institutions which do not deploy this technology will be under increasing competitive pressure to do so
- there is a distinct tendency in the retail financial marketplace in favour of increased deployment of this technololgy
- the technology has not yet attained a point where the majority of institutions provide it

Note: although the last two characteristics may appear contradictory, this is not in fact the case, since the overriding characteristic of the growth phase is that implementation of the technology is in a state of dynamic change, with more and more institutions becoming interested in deploying the technology, although saturation point is still several years away.

The maturity phase

- the technology is being used by most, if not all, institutions

- there is widespread acceptance of the technology among the customers for whom it is intended
- customers expect institutions to have the technology and those institutions which do not have it available are likely to be at a severe competitive disadvantage
- further gains in competitive advantage can only be made by providing refinements of the technology

The implications of the theory

The progression of many types of electronic payment system through the three stages is usually a reasonably steady one, but this observation should not be allowed to obscure the fact that financial technology managers can never afford to be complacent about how the market will react to a new form of payment system.

Experience shows that those types of electronic payment system which are likely to be successful are those which demonstrate actual, or potential, benefits to financial institutions as *marketing tools*: that is, methods by which customers can not only receive the institution's services but are also likely to be impressed by the system sufficiently to want to use the service more often or even to encourage their friends and relatives to use it. This, in essence, the point at which an electronic payment system becomes a highly effective marketing system, is the point at which an electronic payment system starts to help an institution to win new customers.

However, what financial technology managers must always bear in mind is that *technology creates opportunities for, but does not guarantee, successful deployment of an electronic payment system.* Given the choice, a technology manager would probably do best to err on the side of caution when considering whether or not to deploy such a system, because if the system is rejected by the public the costs of rejection would probably far outweigh any competitive advantage that would have accrued from a successful deployment. The point is that an experienced manager will know when the time is right for a deployment to be made – that is, when the system is in the growth phase unless his institution wants to take the gamble of becoming involved with a pioneering technology.

Having examined electronic payment systems from various perspectives, it is now appropriate to apply a similar treatment to those systems used by retail financial institutions which handle administrative matters. As with the section on electronic payment systems, the survey first looks at the nature of these systems and then goes on to consider the technological aspects of deploying these systems and general management issues.

INTERNAL SYSTEMS

These can be divided into two categories, as follows:

1 internal systems used to assist staff to deal with customers
2 internal systems used for purely administrative purposes.

INTERNAL SYSTEMS USED TO ASSIST STAFF TO DEAL WITH CUSTOMERS

1 Counselling and sales systems

These are systems, used typically in the financial institution's branch, which assist staff in providing a variety of advice to customers, with the ultimate objective that the customer will be offered a particular solution by the institution. This solution will usually relate to an investment product, insurance product or other type of sales product.

Counselling and sales systems of this nature provide a very wide range of functionality, with the following being the most common applications of them:

- gaining a picture of the customer's entire finances
- making a loan application
- understanding the customer's investment requirements
- purchasing investment instruments
- providing the customer with a choice of current (checking) or savings accounts, and allowing the customer to see the features of each of these
- handling a mortgage application.

One way of looking at counselling and sales systems is to see them as a 'humanised' form of ATM, which sounds a tortuous idea until one reflects that ATMs came *before* this type of system. The development of counselling and sales systems was principally due to the following factors.

1 Due to the success of ATMs, financial institutions were finding that a high proportion of customers were not using the branch at all, or only rarely. At one level institutions were pleased with this, as it meant that the workload of routine transactions on their branch-based staff was lower and ATMs could process such transactions more efficiently than staff as well as less expensively. On the other hand, institutions knew that they had to bring customers back into the branch if they wanted to sell a range of financial services to the customers

2 Changes – discussed earlier – in the regulatory climate of most developed countries introduced a greater degree of competitiveness within the retail financial sector, thereby requiring institutions to fight harder for competitive advantage if they wanted to maximise profitability. The old style of doing business, whereby the institution operated on the assumption that customers would come into the branch to enquire about such additional services as loans, mortgages and other financial services no longer applied. Institutions saw only too well that if they did not adopt a more proactive approach to selling these services then customers were likely to buy the services from other institutions. This was particularly the case in the light of the unprecedented development, during the 1980s, of a willingness on the part of customers to switch to another institution if they felt that the other institution would offer a better level of service.

Note that in terms of developing counselling and sales services, the issue of *useability*: that is, good design of the user interface (with the user being either a customer, or a member of staff, or both) becomes of great importance (see Chapter Four).

2 Countertop teller systems

These are the systems which are used by cashiers when the customer visits a branch and makes a routine banking transaction with a cashier. These systems can typically handle the following transactions:

- cash deposits
- cash withdrawals
- cheque deposits
- cheque withdrawals
- ordering statements
- providing details of a balance
- passbook updating.

In the 1970s and early 1980s, the 'usual' way in which retail financial institutions' customers made a transaction was to visit the branch and deal with a cashier. The automation of countertop cashier systems began in the early 1970s in most institutions, and was already fairly advanced by the time ATMs began to establish themselves (early 1970s in the US, mid to late 1970s in other developed countries).

Such was the proliferation of ATMs that by the mid-1980s at the latest, by far the *majority* of routine transactions were handled by ATMs, with institutions having achieved great success in persuading customers to use ATM facilities.

Why, then, do we still see queues of people inside institution branches, waiting to be served by a cashier? Surely ATMs could do away with such queues completely?

Some institutions believe that they could. In the UK, for example, the Midland Bank (now owned by the Hongkong and Shanghai Bank) has followed a remarkably ambitious policy of branch automation, with customers not only having access to TTW ATMs outside the bank's branches but also having access to a range of dedicated ATMs within branches, with these ATMs carrying out specialised functions such as, deposit facilities, cash withdrawal facilities, statement ordering and balance provision. The Midland Bank still operates some cashiers with access to countertop terminals, but the bank clearly hopes that these cashiers will not be required very often.

The Midland Bank has enjoyed considerable success from its branch automation activities; the financial difficulties from which it suffered in the early 1990s and which led to its takeover appear to have been caused by other factors, principally the bank's small size relative to its competitors. However, anybody who visits a Midland Bank branch, or indeed any branch of an institution which has pursued an ambitious branch automation policy, will none the less notice many people using the manual cashier terminals. It would seem that there will always be people who use these terminals, with the following being the most likely reasons for this.

1 *ATMs and other automated machines do not always work.* Unfortunately the downtime (ie the time when they are not operating) of these automated machines is usually high, with few institutions being able to offer what is truly the '24-hour, 7 days a week' service that they like to refer to in their self-promotion.

2 *Some customers have business which is not capable of being automated.* Many customers, particularly corporate customers, have business to transact which cannot easily be automated, or which it is not practicable for institutions to automate due to the small level of demand for it. Examples of such business are:

- large cash withdrawals
- large cash deposits
- open credits (ie regular withdrawals to a weekly prespecified level)
- many routine corporate transactions (although some institutions, such as

Barclays Bank in the UK, have now introduced an ATM card for businesses)

● general queries.

3 *Some customers do not yet have the facilities for gaining access to automated systems.* For security reasons, most institutions require that some time should elapse between a new customer joining the institution and being allowed a card and PIN which give access to automated facilities.

Generally speaking, this need for a quasi-probationary period is receding, with institutions increasingly promoting immediate access to automated payment facilities as a benefit of a particular account. However, even here a customer may prefer to use in-branch facilities until he feels familiar with using the automated systems.

4 *Some customers do not like using automated facilities at all.* We are supposed to live in an age where everyone delights in using technology and has great facility with it. In fact, many people – and not just the elderly, either – do not like using automated facilities and prefer to do their business with a human cashier. This appears particularly to be the case with customers of financial institutions that trade on their status (eg American Express in the US and elsewhere, and Coutts in the UK) but all institutions have customers who are afraid of, or simply do not like, technology.

Institutions have hardly been helped, in this respect, by the recent spate of negative publicity in several countries relating to so-called 'phantom' withdrawals, whereby customers have complained that an amount has been debited on their account from an ATM withdrawal which they are absolutely certain they did not make. Although the majority of phantom withdrawal complaints are probably due to the customer being absent-minded, or forgetting, that he had given the card to someone else and told them his PIN number; other complaints are due to attempted fraud on the part of the customer or due to theft of the card.

All the same, institutions have not done themselves any good at all by insisting that their computer system can *never* make a mistake, either by spontaneously generating a transaction or (which seems more likely) by filing a transaction to the wrong account. The public have every reason to distrust an institution which claims that its system is infallible, since although computers do not in fact often make mistakes, the human beings who operate them do, and ultimately all 'automated' systems have points at which errors can occur due to human error.

INTERNAL SYSTEMS USED FOR PURELY ADMINISTRATIVE PURPOSES

In addition to the retail financial systems discussed so far, retail financial institutions also make extensive use of administrative systems. The principal functions which these systems undertake are as follows:

- creating, updating and maintaining customer accounts
- calculation of interest charged or paid out
- inputing and reconciling transactions sourced through ATMs, EFTPOS, telephone banking and branch-based systems
- handling all the institution's own accounting requirements
- handling all regulatory compliance
- generating letters and/or cheques for despatch to customers on a wide variety of matters
- compilation of statistics to assist in the institution's overall operational and marketing activity.

As can be seen from the above list of functions, and as common sense tells us, the administrative requirements of a retail institution require the rapid and efficient handling of a very large amount of data. A detailed understanding of the data storage hierarchy (explored in depth in Chapter Two) is essential for any financial technology manager working with administrative systems.

THE TECHNOLOGY BEHIND INTERNAL SYSTEMS

INTERNAL SYSTEMS USED TO ASSIST STAFF TO DEAL WITH CUSTOMERS

1 Counselling and sales systems

Principal computer – these systems often operate on a stand-alone basis: that is, they would be self-contained and not necessarily have any communications element at all. They can also be used in such a way as to communicate in real-time with a mainframe or Midrange computer, or microcomputer.

Where the system is fully self-contained, the principal computer will most likely consist of a PC with customer information stored on a hard disk. In some cases a powerful PC workstation – often regarded as amounting to a Midrange computer – would be used, but for most applications a PC would suffice.

Data communications medium – there may not be any data communications involved, but if there is, this would simply be a LAN, allowing the system to obtain customer information from the branch's own computer system.

Terminal – where a PC is used on a stand-alone basis the terminal and the principal computer are in effect the same.

Programming techniques – most institutions develop their own counselling and sales system software on an in-house basis. The usual programming languages are COBOL or C (for PCs).

2 Countertop cashier systems

Principal computer – this will usually be the branch's own principal computer, which is typically a Midrange machine or powerful PC Super-Server.

Data communications medium – there are two kinds of data communications involved here. Firstly, the countertop terminal will communicate (almost invariably in real-time) with the branch's principal computer. Secondly, the branch's principal computer will offload details of transactions completed by the cashier system to the institution's own principal computer, with the offloading sometimes taking place on a batch-processed basis, but more often happening in real-time, for security reasons.

Terminal – a countertop cashier terminal is a dedicated device designed to accommodate all the relevant range of transactions and also to communicate with the branch's own system.

Programming techniques – again, COBOL is most typically used as the programming language for such systems.

INTERNAL SYSTEMS USED FOR PURELY ADMINISTRATIVE PURPOSES AND BRANCH AUTOMATION

Principal computer – this would be sited at the head office of the institution and would be a mainframe or very powerful Midrange computer.

Data communications medium – in an administrative system, the principal computer will need to communicate in real-time with a wide range of local and remote terminals, with communications also existing between any local or remote computers which operate subsystems, such as systems for ATM networks, EFTPOS, telephone banking and branch automation.

Terminal – many different kinds of terminals would be involved in the system, ranging from workstations at which administrative information is inputed to the system, and including all kinds of terminals which communicate with subsystems that in turn communicate with the institution's principal computer.

Programming techniques – although COBOL is the main language used to program these administrative systems, it is inadvisable to be dogmatic about this as institutions, and their vendors, are constantly developing new types of programming techniques for administrative systems. The same is true, to a slightly lesser extent, of the other internal systems.

One of the most important new programming techniques is known as 'object-orientated' (OO) programming, which aims to deal with a problem facing all retail institutions: the need to deploy software which can easily and inexpensively be updated to accommodate changing products, changing account features and other factors which yield to change.

OO programming involves tackling the programming problem by breaking it down – at a conceptual level – into a series of intermediate steps or individual 'objects'. In OO programming, a team of programmers will often work on a complex task by having each individual programmer undertaking to program one particular object, with these various sections of the program later being developed into a single, integrated program.

A major advantage of this OO technique is that individual programmers, who may well be experts in one specific programming function but may know far less about other functions, can work on their own module or modules without necessarily needing the expertise to understand the nature of other modules being programmed within the same overall program. Although, the overall, final program will encapsulate every one of the individual modules.

Chris Elliott, a sales manager in the finance division at leading branch automation system vendor Siemens Nixdorf Information Systems, told me he believed that by using OO programming methods, institutions 'should be able to cut development time and costs without compromising existing investment in traditional applications'. Elliott added, 'Traditional development methods involve devoting about 40 per cent of time available to maintenance or in reworking the application. I am confident that OO can cut this to about 10 per cent, thereby making the total amount of time spent on analysis and design far more productive.'

He concedes, however, that institutions can be put off by the 'initial high costs of implementing an OO design methodology', but insists that, 'these costs are soon recovered by the increased productivity of the development over a shorter period of time. It is generally true that the longer a project continues, the higher the costs. By cutting development times costs can be cut, often by as much as 25 per cent for some large organisations. As a result, financial institutions can be much more reactive to changing market conditions.'

MANAGING INTERNAL SYSTEMS

Earlier in this chapter I suggested that the key to successful management of electronic payment systems is gaining an understanding of The Theory of the Evolution of Electronic Payment Systems, with its three phases of development. I believe that the key to successful management of internal systems is more of a practical problem, involving the selection of the correct vendor of the system.

The reason for this is that institutions are increasingly looking to select packaged systems which handle all aspects of internal function, from basic administration to counselling and sales as well as the countertop cashier function. Some institutions do still prefer to develop a fully customised system, but it is nowadays more usual to buy in a package and customise it with specific features.

The different advantages and disadvantages relating to choosing a packaged system, a partly customised and a fully customised system have already been explored (see Chapter Five for the entire development process of a financial system).

What should be emphasised now is that technology managers should – given that they have ensured a very high level of performance and reliability from their internal systems – seek to have the widest possible range of functions for the lowest cost. Since the functions which internal systems must carry out are constantly changing, this does suggest that a form of OO programming may be the best method of constructing such a system.

Similarly, the ideal package to buy in is one which provides a 'core' level of functionality and additional, optional modules which can be added to the core system (after modification, if necessary) as and when required. Systems which are architectured in this fashion are known as 'toolkit' systems and they have a particularly important role to play in financial institutions' internal systems, which need to meet all the following objectives:

- speed
- accuracy

- wide range of functionality
- cost-effectiveness
- adaptability to changing conditions
- operation on an open protocol. This allows new types of externally developed software to be used on the system.

Survey of Real-life Applications of Financial Technology – Part Two

WHOLESALE FINANCIAL INSTITUTIONS

Introduction

Wholesale financial institutions are in the business of providing a wide range of banking services to corporate clients, many of which may themselves be financial institutions. Wholesale financial institutions do not operate retail banking accounts – although they may have associated organisations which do – and undertake many activities on their own behalf as well as on behalf of customers.

As with retail banks, wholesale banks have found themselves operating in an increasingly competitive environment during the past twenty years. Regulatory factors have played an important role here and, in particular investor protection legislation which has been passed in most developed countries since around 1980. Nowhere is this better typified than in the UK's Financial Services Act 1986, which introduced a major new self-regulatory framework for wholesale banks.

The wholesale banking world is poorly understood by people who do not work within it, and is often not well understood by those who do. For many laymen, it is a remote, mysterious, even slightly shady world where people stare at computer screens for much of the day and make telephone calls to other people who sit in similar circumstances in other institutions. Occasionally, as in the UK during September 1992, the public is forcibly made aware that the activities of wholesale bankers (in this case foreign exchange traders) can affect something as fundamental as mortgage interest rates and the value of the pound. However, after the television news has screened the usual shots of people sitting at computer screens and making telephone calls the wholesale banking scene fades, for most people, into the obscurity from which it came. This, one must immediately add, would not greatly bother wholesale bankers, as most are not particularly interested in what the public think of them.

In the following analysis my definition of a wholesale financial institution is deliberately wide, and in fact includes any organisation whose business involves, in any sense, the trading or managing of money or any kind of financial instrument. This would include banks; securities houses; stockbrokers; investment managers and related organisations. Some of these firms would, of course, have customers among the general public but remain as wholesale banks because they will be trading or managing instruments on behalf of those members of the public rather than running accounts which are clearly retail banking accounts.

At first sight the objective of surveying every possible application of technology by wholesale banks looks impossible, and it would indeed be unrealistic to list every single individual application, but it is certainly possible to consider the major generic types: that is, the principal classes of technological application into which different individual applications can be categorised.

As with retail financial technology, it is useful to draw a distinction between those technological applications which are essentially money-making and profit-generating and those which are concerned with administration. In the wholesale banking environment, it is conventional to use the term *front office*, or front-office system, to describe that part of an institution, and the staff functions, which are primarily involved in making money for the institution, and the term *back office*, or back-office system, for that part of an institution, and the staff functions, which are mainly designed to handle the institution's administrative tasks. This is, however, a somewhat oversimplified distinction. There are two reasons why this is so.

1 *Front office/back office linkages*. As we shall see, one of the primary benefits of technology to wholesale institutions has been to create opportunities for the front and back office to be linked in real-time or on a batch-processed basis. Some commentators have begun to use the term 'middle office' to describe this linking process, and to imply that the front and back office distinctions are no longer appropriate. However, there clearly *is* a distinction between the direct money-making functions of an institution and the support functions, which is why the front and back office terminology is pursued here. Even though back offices can themselves sometimes become a direct source of revenue, as when a back office acts as a clearing firm, the distinction remains fundamentally sound.

2 *Profitability can be maximised in both parts of the institution*. It is pedantic to deny that people such as traders and investment managers are involved in making money for a wholesale institution in a way that support and administrative staff are obviously not. However, both the front and the back office offer institutions the opportunity for significant financial efficiences and cost savings. This was particularly true in the difficult operating climate which most wholesale institutions experienced in the early 1990s, when the relatively narrow profit margins of most trading activity in relation to the amounts of capital which had to be tied up with that activity made it more true than ever that, in business, you make money by not spending it. Any wholesale institution seeking to maximise profitability had to pay as much attention – and arguably even more attention – to keeping costs down as to earning money in the marketplace.

Many wholesale banks found it very difficult to adjust to this new scheme of things after a 1980s of boom conditions, when making money was easy and spending money was even easier. Spending money on technology, in particular, was much less of an option than had been the case in the 1980s, and information technology departments of wholesale banks grew as lean as the systems houses which they had swamped with orders a few years earlier.

The recessionary climate of the early 1990s will not last, but it seems unlikely that wholesale institutions will ever again be as free-spending on technology as they were in the 1980s. In either event, for wholesale bankers a knowledge of the most efficient and effective way to deploy technology within the range of typical front- and back-office applications has never been more important.

FRONT-OFFICE APPLICATIONS

Introduction

This analysis of the front-office applications of technology in wholesale banks is in two parts.

The first part looks at the hierarchy of information which front-office institutional bankers need in order to carry out their work. The second part lists all the principal generic applications of technology in wholesale banks.

The rationale for this approach is that all front-office applications in wholesale banks have certain important aspects in common relating to the basic categories of information that are used. Broadly speaking, there are two categories: *raw information* – that is, basic price and market information; and *decision support* (or value-added) information – that is, more heavily analysed information which plays an essential role in helping the trader or investment manager to arrive at a decision: a decision, that is, which should ideally be a better one than a decision arrived at by a rival trader or investment manager in a different institution (or even in the same institution).

Obviously the *precise nature* of the raw information and the decision support information used by different types of traders and investment managers will vary. To take a simple example, a foreign exchange trader will want raw information about the prices of different foreign exchanges in different markets, whereas an equities trader will want information about the prices of different equities in different markets. However, from the point of view of analysing these applications of technology, the differences between the precise nature of the information used by different types of traders and investment managers can usefully be regarded as superficial. What matters is gaining an understanding of to what use the information is put in relation to the user's entire decision-forming process.

Note that, due to the complexity of front-office applications, it is more convenient to discuss the technological and management issues alongside the discussion of applications. However, there is a summary of these issues at the end of the section.

I THE INFORMATION HIERARCHY

The financial information industry might be a very high-tech, modern industry, but its roots go back a long way. The man who was almost certainly the world's first financial information vendor was born in 1816 in the German town of Kassel. Of Jewish parentage, his name was Israel Beer Josaphat. In 1844 he became a Christian, and did what most Hollywood movie stars do early on in their careers: he changed his name. The name he chose was Paul Julius Reuter.

As a clerk in his uncle's bank in Gottingen, Germany in the 1840s, Reuter made the acquaintance of the eminent mathematician and physicist, Carl Friedrich Gauss, who was at that time experimenting with the electric telegraph, one of the first useful practical applications of the nascent science of electricity and magnetism, and an application that was to become important in news dissemination.

In the early 1840s, Reuter joined a small publishing firm in Berlin. After publishing a number of political pamphlets that aroused the hostility of the authorities he moved to Paris in 1848, a year of revolution throughout Europe. Reuter began translating extracts from articles and commercial news and sending them to papers in Germany. In 1850 he set up a carrier pigeon service between Aachen and Brussels, the terminal points, respectively, of the German and the French-Belgian telegraph lines. Since, by using his services, his customers could obtain faster access to financial information from the countries involved than could their rivals, Reuter's business prospered.

Moving to England in 1851, Reuter opened a telegraphic office near the London Stock Exchange. At first his business was confined mostly to commercial telegrams, but with daily newspapers flourishing, he persuaded several publishers to subscribe to his service. One of his major successes came in 1859 when he transmitted to London the text of a speech by Napoleon III foreshadowing the Austro-French Piedmontese war in Italy.

Throughout the growth of the news agency side of Reuter's activities, the dissemination of financial information went hand in hand with the development of the news agency activities. When, in the 1860s, underseas cables (including cables that crossed the Atlantic) began to be laid, Reuter was able to develop his service to other continents.

Now a UK-registered public company, Reuters is the world's largest financial information vendor in terms of number of customers and staff. Hot on its heels, however, came an astonishing array of organisations: some big, some small; but all competing energetically and aggressively for market share.

Screen-based information

In today's wholesale banking sector, by far the highest proportion of information reaching users comes via computer screens. Typically, these screens will be networked within a local area network (LAN) into a configuration of other screens (with the number of screens thus networked varying from five to about five hundred, depending on the size of the user organisation) and fed and controlled by a central computer: typically a mainframe or a mini, although some PCs are nowadays sufficiently powerful to power a PC network themselves.

As we have seen, it is useful to distinguish two major categories of screen-based information reaching users.

1 *Raw information*. Much of this will consist of real-time market information, broker information and online news.

2 *Value-added information.* This is screen-based information which has
been configured or otherwise processed in such a way as to offer the user an
additional degree of utility. The term 'value-added information' is most
commonly applied to this type of information. However, I prefer the term
'decision support information' which best expresses the function of such
information as being to support decisions. Raw research information will
not provide the same degree of decision support power as value-added
information.

There is a clear hierarchy of financial information, ranging from information where the value-added element is quite small – such as graphical
displays of historical information – and onwards to systems where the
value-added element is substantial, such as in a system programmed to
match an index or generate investment decisions based around quantitative
principles. The *decision support hierarchy* (my term) is also examined
below.

Raw information

The following are the principal categories of raw information which are of
importance to a user.

1 Market information
This information relates to the prevailing market price and volume of shares
and other investment instruments.

2 News information
This means news relating to the countries where the relevant financial
market is located. The news may be specific to a particular financial market
(eg the announcement of the results of a particular company); economic (eg
the announcement of a change in the interest rate or rate of inflation); or
general but with specific financial repercussions (eg an important political
development).

3 Broker information
Some brokers supply screen-based information as an extension to, or
replacement for, their written research information service. These proprietary brokerage screen-based services tend to be operated on a confidential basis and are usually only available to a broker's clients. As such,
they are not commercially available to all-comers and so are not listed
here. Sometimes a small charge is made for the service, often a rental cost
for the computer screen (if supplied by the broker). Screen-based broker

information either has the advantage of carrying a strong opinion, or the disadvantage of being too one-sided, depending how one looks at it.

Implementing raw information

There are basic requirements which institutions have from raw information.

1 *Cost-effectiveness*. In today's highly competitive financial sector, the need for screen-based research information to be cost-effective is of extreme importance. Although at first sight many of the pricing policies laid down by the major financial information vendors (who are, in all fairness, themselves constrained in this respect by the need to make a profit on top of the fees that they must pay to exchanges) are relatively rigid, in practice there is often ample room for negotiation, particularly – as we have seen – if the user organisation is purchasing a complex mix of types of information.

2 *Accuracy and reliability*. No amount of sophistication in terms of screen-based information will be of any avail if that information is not reliable and accurate at all times. Investment decisions made on the basis of inaccurate information are likely to be expensive errors at best, and potentially disastrous at worst. Unfortunately for users of screen-based services, it is almost impossible to check the reliability and accuracy of screen-based information while this information is being relayed. Information originating from a domestic exchange may possibly be capable of being checked reasonably rapidly through a third-party source, but this is hardly likely to be the case with information originating from abroad.

Since the recipient will probably be unable to check the accuracy of the information as it is relayed, there is very little that can be done beyond ensuring that the vendor chosen to supply the information is reliable in the first place. In practice the reputation and experience of the world's major financial information vendors means that the information they supply is in almost all cases an accurate reflection of that which they receive, but since in most cases (with the exception of self-generated news services) they are only relaying information which they themselves have received from an exchange, there is little that can be done if the exchange has made an error. The speed and accuracy of today's real-time datalinks means that an error due to technology is infrequent, although not impossible.

Clearly, where a user is executing a deal based on a particular price displayed on a screen, a built-in checking process in effect exists, since the broker with whom the deal is being made will – if the brokerage is conducting its business ethically with its clients – be quick to notify the user if the manager is bidding too high or too low for a particular stock. The real danger in receiving inaccurate information lies in constructing a strategic or tactical (ie a long-term or short-term) investment plan based on this information. The only practical advice that can really be given here, apart from a reminder of the need to ensure that one is buying screen-based information from a reliable source, is to point out that, as when relying on computers in other fields, care should be taken not to assume that information is infallible merely because a computer is relaying it.

3 *Comprehensiveness.* There is an obvious tension between cost of raw information and the comprehensiveness of this information, since the cost of raw information is always linked to the breadth of this information: which means in effect the range of instruments covered on a particular market (if the market trades more than one type of instrument) and the number of markets surveyed. Special requirements, such as information about the world's more obscure markets, will add proportionately more to the bill than information coming from the better known markets, which is why the cost of screen-based information will be a factor in portfolio diversification among different countries.

Vendors normally charge for their services on a basis whereby users enjoy a reduced marginal cost per terminal the more terminals receive the service. However, since even a reduced marginal cost may be quite high, users should be absolutely certain that every single terminal which receives the service actually needs it. It is by no means rare for a user company to wind up buying in a service for far more terminals than really is necessary. The cause of this is sometimes a desire not to offend certain senior managers by not giving them a particular service even when they have no obvious need for it, although a more common cause of such 'over-buying' is the sales patter of an enthusiastic vendor representative convincing the user that the more terminals that have the service, the better.

In fact, precise matching of information needs to the information purchased is the key to cost-effective use of all types of screen-based information. Economies can often be made. If, for example, a team decides to make an investment in various stocks issued by a country in which the company does not already invest, there may well be no need for more than one terminal within the user organisation to receive information on the price of those stocks. After all, the worst that can happen in this scenario is that one user may on occasion have to peer over a colleague's shoulder or borrow the terminal for a while.

Within this essential constraint to minimise the subscription to screen-based information within the information needs of the user organisation in question, it remains the case that the information which the organisation buys in must be sufficiently comprehensive for the users to have the information they need at their fingertips. There are obvious dangers in attempting to skimp on the cost of screen-based information by relying on published information that may take several days to arrive in the user's office. Where screen-based information is concerned, good handling of the tension between comprehensiveness and cost requirements is essential.

Digital and video feeds

The difference between digital and video feeds is important to note at this juncture.

Digital feeds are streams of data relayed in computer-readable format. They may be relayed so as to appear on a proprietary screen operated by the vendor that supplies the information. *Equally, however, they may be relayed to any screen that employs a communications protocol with which they are compatible.* The great advantage of digital feeds is that they can be configured by the user into an unlimited range of formats customised to a particular user's own requirements.

A further important benefit of digital feeds is that a number of feeds can be incorporated on a single screen, presenting a user with only one screen to survey. However, since users do not tend to trade on a minute-by-minute basis, they are unlikely to benefit from the single-screen information source as would a trader, for whom this would mean important additional efficiency. All the same, many users would welcome the space saving on or above their desks which a single screen would represent.

Video feeds, on the other hand, are data feeds which can only be relayed to dedicated video terminals. These are almost invariably sold or leased to the user by the vendor. They permit little flexibility and very little opportunity to customise the screen; the user is basically restricted to the vendor's own specification of the screen. There is thus very little opportunity beyond any built-in selection of options for a user to use video feeds to gain a competitive edge. Another major drawback of video feeds is that they tie a user in with a particular vendor. Reuters and Quick (for whom video feeds and video terminals are extremely important) are two examples of leading information vendors which have come under fire in the past for continuing to sell video technology because (as critics claim) this obliges the user to buy the whole service from datafeed to screen, even if the user would prefer to buy only the datafeed, and configure the feed on a customised screen display.

Furthermore, a user using video services is obliged to have a separate screen for every video service, which can often lead to an unwelcome accumulation of screens on or above the user's desk.

Since video technology is less advanced than digital technology, its death-knell was being sounded in the mid-1980s by commentators on the financial technology who predicted that digital would shortly overrun video. However, this has not happened, and the reasons are easy to identify.

The first, and undoubtedly most pressing reason, is that digital feeds cost more than video feeds, both in terms of the actual feed and the screen configuration. The added cost is based upon a variety of factors, including the communications technology required and the cost of designing customised screen configurations. Although there is some truth in the principle that the cost of digital feeds will inevitably come down as more vendors move into the market, the technological complexity of digital compared with video means that digital will probably remain more expensive for the foreseeable future.

In the heady atmosphere of technology spending and apparently ever-increasing profits on the back of the world's bullish equity markets, it was understandable that digital's eventual triumph over video would be assured. However, in October 1987 the lengthy bull market came to an abrupt end, and in the singularly depressed and exhausted securities industry which followed it, the essential need was to reduce costs in order to deal with reduced fees and reduced profits. The last thing any user organisation or trading company wanted was additional costs caused by deploying more expensive new technology. Digital feeds, like all financial technology in this period, were not extended within many securities industry participants. Although since then the situation has improved, users have found themselves operating within highly competitive scenarios where the need to minimise technology costs seems to have become a permanent feature of the industry.

The second reason was that the major information vendors did not switch their services to digital to the extent that they were expected to do. Although there is probably some truth in the cynical allegation that vendors had become perfectly aware that by continuing to supply video-based services they could continue to secure high profits from in effect 'capturing' their customers – who were obliged to buy or rent dedicated video terminals from the vendor in question – it is equally true that the depressed market for financial technology which followed the 1987 Crash led vendors to be extremely cautious in terms of deploying speculative new technology which depended on a very positive commitment from customers in order to be profitable.

The result of these two related factors has been that video has not only retained its importance within the screen-based research world, but actually increased its share of the market in many areas. Although even leading vendors of video technology have launched digital systems alongside their video services, these digital services have often been adjuncts to video services rather than replacements for them. For example, the London Stock Exchange's TOPIC service is a video-based service which is primarily designed to be used in conjunction with the dedicated TOPIC video screen. However, the TOPIC service is also available from the LSE in digital format for configuration on a customised basis within the user's own computer system and on the user's own terminals. Despite this, by far the majority of TOPIC users continue to gain access to TOPIC via video-based rather than digital-based technology.

Video continues to retain a particular supremacy in Japan. This should perhaps not surprise us: the technologically dextrous Japanese have after all always been more keen on technology which has a high practical utility than on technology which is deployed simply because it is on the wavefront of progress. The leading Japanese financial information vendor Quick – which in Japan has a virtual monopoly of the market for Japanese price information – is essentially a video supplier despite also having a digital product. A major, significant, vote of confidence in video-based technology was given in 1989 when Sanyo Securities opened in Tokyo the largest dealing-room in the world. This room, which is approximately the size of a football field, was designed around video technology.

Choosing a vendor of raw information

The main criteria which ought to be considered when selecting a vendor of raw information are as follows:

- *cost of the information*: what will the vendor's service cost? Note that you must factor in the charges for terminal rental/lease/purchase as well as the charges for the information itself.
- *flexibility*: the vendor should be able to promise flexibility when the user wants to add or delete new services. There should be reasonable contract terms for doing this, without penalties such as payment for a lengthy minimum term.
- *reliability, accuracy and speed*: the user should be confident that the vendor has all these attributes. Often the best way to check this is to take up client references.
- *invoicing practice*: what will the vendor's invoices look like and to what extent will they be itemised? Who will deal with your enquiries relating to invoices?

- *coverage*: what breadth of coverage (ie countries covered and markets covered within those countries) can the vendor offer? What level of news coverage does the vendor offer in addition to market price information?
- *terminals required*: what terminals will be required? On what terms are they supplied?
- *digital or video*: is the service available in digital or video format? Note that even if you have opted for a video service, you may well want to convert this to digital in time to come. You need to assess the level of resistance which the vendor has to the future prospect of losing a video customer, tied down to using a particular terminal, and gaining a digital customer (if the service is available in digital format) who will not be tied down to using the screen supplied. You may well find that the level of resistance here is higher than you expected;
- *compatibility for integration*: to what extent will the vendor's services be capable of being integrated within other information services that you are buying in?
- *customer service*: who will look after you? How will problems be resolved?
- *existing clients*: does the vendor have existing investment management client organisations of a comparable size to your own organisation? Can you talk to these clients?
- *financial stability*: is the vendor financially stable? Remember that if there is a relatively high capital cost of beginning to work with a new vendor in terms of screen installation and (probably) the deployment of switching systems, there will be a danger that this capital expenditure will be wasted if the vendor suddenly goes out of business, or has to sharply curtail its activities.

II DECISION SUPPORT INFORMATION

Decision support systems provide screen-based information which is used within wholesale institutions – particularly institutions involved in securities trading and investment management – to aid the decision making process.

When examining different kinds of decision support system it is extremely useful to distinguish between different systems according to their level of analytical power.

Making such a distinction based on analytical power is especially useful because it allows a clear analysis of the resources to which users can have access when making investment decisions. Since the process of making investment decisions is at the heart of the user process, an analysis of the technology which supports decision-making must be of great importance to the user industry as a whole.

What precisely constitutes a decision support system? With no widely accepted definition of the term, any meaning attached to it must be to some extent arbitrary, but a good definition would be something like *any screen-based service which offers information that assists in the decision-making process beyond simple market and news data and administrative information.*

Note that this definition assumes a certain level of sophistication in the nature of the information. In particular, the definition excludes:

a) raw research information such as market prices and news
b) back-office administrative information such as details of portfolio compositions and information regarding funds available for investment. However, some of the more important back-office systems are included in this directory.

Even a cursory consideration of those services which can be described as 'decision support' clearly reveals the existence of a hierarchy of decision support information. Put simply, some decision support services provide a greater level of decision support than others do.

A useful term to use here is *decision support power*. This can be regarded as the extent to which a decision support service assists with a decision. It does not necessarily define whether a system will make the user money or not, because that will depend on the quality of the decision, not on the level of decision support provided. Decision support power, therefore, is not a measure of the *quality* of the support provided (ie whether the service helps a user make a higher proportion of correct decisions, but rather a measure of the *thoroughness* of the service, that is, the extent to which the service assists with decisions.

Figure 3.4 shows typical generic examples of decision support services in an ascending level of decision support power.

The following explains the nature of the listed applications in detail.

a) *Historical price displays in tabular form.* These are displays of previous prices in simple tabular or column form. No attempt is made to present the information graphically.

b) *Historical price displays in graphical form.* Here, the program within the system is able to present the display of previous prices in a graphical forms. Most systems that are able to do this feature a remarkable level of graphical facility; enabling the user to focus on a particular historical period and examine price changes minutely throughout this period or to 'pull back'

LOW DECISION SUPPORT POWER

INCREASING DECISION SUPPORT POWER

- Historical price displays in tabular form
- Historical price displays in graphical form
- Multiwindow configurations providing customised information displays simultaneously
- Risk management systems (algorithmic or formulaic operation)
- Technical analysis systems
- Quantitative analysis systems
- 'Artificial intelligence' systems (rule-based, neural nets)
- Indexation systems involving weightings or tilting
- Indexation systems involving full index replication

HIGH DECISION SUPPORT POWER

Figure 3.4 Examples of decision support services listed according to level of decision support power

from the display and look at changes over a lengthy historical period, such as several months. Probably the most common historical period surveyed by users is ninety days, although the exact historical period which interests one user or another will vary from manager to manager.

c) *Multiwindow configurations providing customised information displays simultaneously*. One of the most satisfying results, from the user's perspective, of the greatly increased data processing power and windowing capability which personal computers and minicomputers have developed over the past ten years or so is the opportunity for managers to buy in at a reasonable cost packages which offer a very high level of flexibility regarding displaying real-time and historical information from whatever markets interest the user. Not only do such systems often have up to ten different windows, each with their own tabular or graphical displays, but the systems are often able to provide price information from whatever brokers are offering the best price for a particular investment instrument.

Such on-screen sophistication of data presentation not only requires that the incoming data feed is in digital format, but also that the computer on which the system is running has enough processing power to process and re-present the data in the desired configuration. However, such is the power of today's PCs and minicomputers that the requisite processing power is almost always available.

d) *Risk management systems*. These are systems which provide information about the level of risk in a particular portfolio or individual instrument under management. Typical examples of risk management systems used within the financial industry are systems to assess the risk of holding a particular stock or group of stocks, or to assess the risk involved in holding an option, or general assessments of risk deriving from a market's volatility (volatility risk).

e) *Technical analysis systems*. These are graphical displays of historical price information, but with additional, essentially predictive analysis added to the displays in order to boost the level of decision support power.

Technical analysis is a form of analysis of investment instruments and financial markets which is based upon the premise that a study of historical (ie past) movements in the prices and corresponding volume of the instruments or markets under scrutiny reveals important information about future price movements.

f) *Quantitative analysis systems*. These embody various theories of risk management and portfolio diversification.

g) *Artificial intelligence systems*. As was discussed in detail in Chapter Two, artificial intelligence (AI) systems are not really intelligent, but rather constitute a form of simulated intelligence, with the two principal methods by which such simulation occurs currently being rule-based systems and neural nets.

h) *Indexation systems involving weighting or tilting*. This kind of indexation involves creating a portfolio of investments which are an approximation (based on various different approaches to investing) of a particular market index, the idea being that experience has shown that most investment portfolios do not in fact outperform the hypothetical market index. This kind of indexation seeks to obtain the benefits of index-matching portfolios but to modify the portfolios slightly so that they seek to gain a performance which is better than the index – although in real-life the performance level might also be worse.

i) *Indexation systems involving full index replication*. These seek fully to replicate the index.

Decision support and technology

In theory many tasks performed within the applications listed in the decision support hierarchy could be performed manually. It is certainly true, for example, that technical analysis was practised successfully several years before computers were developed. Similarly, many of the calculations involved in quantitative analysis can be carried out manually, although these calculations are admittedly very laborious. However, in practice the computer offers such huge potential for running decision support applications with enormous speed, accuracy and reliability – not to mention the very considerable interface advantages which computer screens have over paper-based information – that it is inconceivable that the applications contained within the decision support hierarchy would be possible at all without computerisation.

With the processing power of today's PCs and minicomputers already exceeding that of the mainframes of the early 1980s, processing power is rarely a problem for user organizations which wish to deploy the latest decision support systems. However, there are some very important practical issues which a user organization must address prior to deploying a decision support system at whatever level of the hierarchy. Paying due attention to these practical issues will save the organization time and money in the short, medium and long term.

Planning a decision support system

Whereas the choice of a vendor of raw information – or a vendor of value-added systems with a fairly low level of decision support power – is usually simply a question of choosing between different vendors, developing a decision support system is more complex, particularly since most decision support systems are to some extent customised. The remainder of this introduction looks in broad terms at how such a system should be specified and developed.

Naturally enough, the institution must first decide what function the system will need to carry out. Here, the decision support hierarchy is useful for enabling an institution to specify with great precision the level of decision support power that it will want the system to provide.

Arriving at an estimate of the level of decision support power required is a matter that will depend on a wide range of factors, in particular the following:

1 *What level of competitive advantage should our system provide?* It must above all be borne in mind that the purpose of installing a decision support system is to gain a competitive advantage. There should be no question of ever installing a system simply because the technology is available, or, even worse, in order to make some sort of internal political point (many

ultimately failed systems are started for precisely this reason).

Competitive advantage deriving from higher front-office performance is only one area of an institution's activities where competitive advantage can be obtained. However, it is an extremely important area, and there is every reason to build a decision support system if there are good grounds for believing that its installation will help overall trading or fund management performance.

2 *How well will the system harmonise with our overall investment objectives and strategies*? Such harmonisation is vital from the beginning. An important cause of half-hearted development cycles, which lead inevitably on to lacklustre and very likely failed systems is an inadequate recognition, in the planning stage, that a system must be matched to the overall investment objectives of the organisation that is installing it, rather than these investment objectives being forced to comply with what the system can do. A small, traditional investment management organisation or private bank catering for a few corporate clients may well not require a decision support system at all, but may be able to manage with raw screen-based research information only.

Similarly, an institution whose pension fund clients are firmly opposed to any kind of passive investment is hardly likely to be interested in a system designed to undertake indexation. On the other hand, a go-getting US investment house which is eager to maximise returns across a wide variety of derivative-based and underlying market-based portfolios will very likely need a sophisticated decision support system capable of configuring data on-screen in a wide variety of customised displays, as well as offering a facility for quantitative analysis and even rule-based or neural net operations.

3 *How much can we afford to pay*? No user should ever undertake the development of a decision support system unless the organisation is sure that it has an ample budget for the system's development. There is almost no such thing as a decision support system which comes in under budget; a good rule of thumb is to assume that the system will ultimately cost twice the original budget estimate and then allow yourself to be surprised if you have anything less than this sum. Fortunately, the great increases in processor speed and the proliferation of open systems have meant that many of even the most powerful decision support systems can run on hardware that may well already be installed in the office or which can at least be enhanced to give the requisite level of processing power. However, the cost of software development can still be very high.

Unlike a back-office system, which tends to pay for itself through the somewhat unglamorous – but none the less effective – means of reducing staff costs and administrative costs and generally by streamlining the organisation deploying it, a front decision support system has to earn its keep in the arduous, demanding area of real-life day to day use. Users will want results from it in terms of improved decision-making; the accountants who authorised the budget for it will want to see it in action, making money for the organisation.

There are, however, less obvious and immediate cost benefits of installing a decision support system. For example, installing such a system may allow the organisation to pitch for an account realistically that would not have been accessible without the system in place. Similarly, the system might extend the range of services which the organisation can offer its clients, and thereby generate greater productivity based on the system. But perhaps the most important cost benefit which has in practice been observed by user organisations which install new technology is the clear benefit in the front office which installing a more efficient back-office system almost invariably seems to bring.

This benefit usually stems from users being to a large extent freed from the more mundane administrative aspects of their job and being able to devote more attention to the actual task, such as, for example, the management of the assets for which they are responsible. Since for any institution, higher performance of funds under management not only increases the likelihood that new business will be won, but actually leads to a direct cost increase in revenue – management fees being linked to the value of the funds under management – the cost benefits in the front office of installing a more efficient back-office system are often almost immediate.

4 *How willing will our staff be to use the system?* On the face of it this may seem a trivial problem, but it is not. Information technology managers working within user organisations (or external suppliers selling to them) are only too aware of the resistance which many users have towards the 'black box' which they feel will at best prove a waste of money and may at worst lead to their own redundancy. Experience shows that this fear of technology is often worse among senior staff – those who began their careers in the 1950s and early 1960s, say – who were brought up in a society without computers and who will very often not only be ignorant of technology but also fearful of it. Of course, this is by no means true of all senior users, many of whom have made admirable efforts to become acquainted in detail with a technology in which their own education gave them no grounding whatsoever. However, there is no doubt that the problem of making technology acceptable to users tends to become more grave the further up the ladder of seniority one goes.

There is no simple solution to the problem of making technology acceptable to users. In any case, some scepticism as to the real benefits of a system that is being proposed is not only natural but actually healthy. Even in today's user industry, where so much emphasis is placed on cutting costs and exercising caution over technological spending, ill-conceived technology projects are often put forward and these must be weeded out at the earliest stage. Even with the experience of the over-ambitious, unsuccessful systems of the 1980s to guide us, some systems are still being designed that have little or no chance of fulfilling the hopes of those who commissioned them.

Given that the system's aims are realistic and that there is general agreement that the system should go ahead, it will still be necessary for the completed system to win the trust and co-operation of the staff who are using it. There is no substitute here for the confidence that arises from satisfactory use. Once users can see that a decision support system is helping them to improve their performance, they will tend to warm to it. But one problem, deriving from human nature, will always remain: where users who are using a decision support system score a success, they will almost invariably attribute this to their own skill. Where an investment decision goes wrong, blame will almost always fall on the system.

5 *How quickly do we expect the system to be obsolete*? In today's fast-moving financial technology world, no system can represent the best available current technology for more than a year or so. However, a system will still be useful, even if it no longer represents state-of-the-art technology. What is required is a balance between the need to keep technology up to date and the need to be economical in technological spending. The precise balance which a user organisation takes will depend on the organisation, but a reliable and useful system should never be discarded merely because it is no longer state-of-the-art. The governing criterion here is utility and practical effectiveness rather than adopting a more advanced technology for its own sake.

6 *Can we solve the technical problems?* No new technological project should be allowed to start unless the user organisation is certain that any technical problems which the system will cause can be solved. This may seem like an obvious guideline, but it is remarkable how many would-be deployers of new systems become so carried away by their own enthusiasm for the system that they forget that the more ambitious and complex the system the more technical problems it is likely to bring.

In essence, the key to ensuring that technical problems do not disrupt, delay or even curtail a new project is the need to ensure that the new system will either be compatible with existing technology deployed or else can be made compatible by being interfaced or networked into existing systems. In some cases a user organisation will be prepared to create an entirely new in-house technology protocol in order to accommodate the system, but this is the exception rather than the rule.

With the fairly rapid proliferation of open systems around the user community, technical compatibility is starting to cease being the problem that it once was. For example, a user organisation which has chosen UNIX as its in-house protocol, should not only be able to install (and modify, if required) any UNIX-based packaged system, but should be able to adopt without difficulty any customised system built on the UNIX protocol.

Of course, where a decision support system requires powerful Midrange computers such as AS/400 or Sun or HP workstations, it will be necessary to ensure that the hardware is in place. But all new hardware requirements should have become clear at the planning stage.

7 *How likely is it that we will be able to bring this project to a successful conclusion?* This is perhaps the most important consideration of all, since unless the project is completed successfully – which means that the technology must not only work at a prototype stage but also must be capable of successful real-life implementation – none of the practical or cost benefits of the system will apply.

Regrettably, it is impossible ever to be absolutely certain that a new technological project will be brought to a successful conclusion. Certainly, a packaged system that is bought in from an external supplier will bring with it a very high likelihood that it can be installed successfully – and the user organisation will have the possibility of redress to the supplier if it does not – but such a system may by its standardised nature offer little in the way of competitive advantage.

None the less, the days when (as in the 1980s) many projects were enthusiastically started when they had a realistic likelihood of success that was no more than about 70 per cent, are over. No user organisation would be advised to commission a project unless they were sure that there was a 90 per cent or more likelihood that it would succeed. There is of course no way of being certain what the likely percentage for a particular system will be. The percentage can only be estimated based on successful deployments elsewhere and on the likelihood that the skill of the implementation team, the budget, managerial enthusiasm and eventual staff acceptance will all be adequate to make the system work.

The next stage – the actual development and deployment of a decision support system – is comparable with the deployment of other types of financial system (see Chapter Five).

LISTING OF FRONT-OFFICE APPLICATIONS

The listing in this part of the chapter covers every principal generic application of technology in wholesale financial institutions' front offices. Each particular application is listed under a subheading, as follows.

Information reception

- reception of current and historical information on prices of financial instruments
- reception of current and historical information on values of market indices
- reception of information on financial news
- reception of information on general news
- reception of current and historical information on foreign exchange fluctuations
- reception of information on economic indicators (eg interest rates)
- reception of information on counterparties' requirements
- reception of information on counterparties' credit position
- reception of information on potentially profitable arbitrage opportunities

Note: 'Historical' means any information relating to a previous time period. Among the most common historical parameters are ninety days and seven days (ie closing prices for each of the previous ninety and seven days, respectively.

Decision support facilities

(in ascending order of 'decision support power')

- presentation of historical price displays in tabular form
- presentation of historical price displays in graphical form
- multiwindow configurations providing customised information displays simultaneously
- risk management systems (algorithmic or formulaic operation)
- technical analysis systems
- quantitative analysis systems
- 'artificial intelligence' systems (rule-based, neural nets)
- indexation systems involving weightings or tilting
- indexation systems involving full index replication

Trading systems

(these applications cover all financial instruments, and foreign exchange)

- systems for negotiating with counterparties via a screen
- systems for concluding screen or telephone-negotiated deals via a computer (note: many systems which wholesale institutions deploy to this purpose are intended for 'retail' transactions: that is, relatively small transactions carried out on behalf of individuals rather than corporate or institutional clients)
- systems for concluding profitable arbitrage deals

Investment management systems

- multicurrency systems for the storage and retrieval of details of portfolio composition
- multicurrency systems for the storage and retrieval of details of portfolio valuation

Communications systems

- systems for networking workstations carrying out any of the functions in the subheadings above
- systems for communicating with counterparties via Local Area Network (LAN)
- systems for communicating with counterparties via Wide Area Networks (WANs)

Additional notes on front-office technology

Analysing front-office technology in terms of the financial technology 'building blocks' (ie the principal computer, the data communications medium, the terminal and programming techniques) is very useful. The following general points should be made.

Principal computer – for most front-office applications this will be the institution's main computer, which will probably be a mainframe if the institution is large (ie with numerous branches nationally and internationally) or a Midrange computer or PC/LAN arrangement for smaller institutions. Fault-tolerance is recognised by wholesale institutions as being of great importance, and essential where online transaction processing (OLTP) is involved. OLTP features in many front-office applications, with the most important types of OLTP being:

- reception of real-time information from third-party vendors
- negotiating with counterparties in real-time via the system
- concluding transactions with counterparties in real-time.

Note that in these cases both the third party (ie the information vendor or counterparty) must also operate a fault-tolerant system if the likelihood that the system goes down is to be reduced to a minimum.

Data communications medium – as with all data communications used by financial institutions, this will either be via leased or proprietary telephone lines, configured in a LAN or WAN. The most important point to make here is that the impetus in front-office deployments in favour of integration of function means that most institutions prefer to deploy systems which feature such integration. Integration is usually seen in a single workstation, with one operator gaining access via a single screen to a wide range of information reception, decision support, trading and investment management functions. However, the data comunications medium also plays an essential role in integrating different workstations which have different functions, and thereby ensuring that each workstation user has access (albeit often only a controlled access) to the functions of other workstations.

Terminals – in wholesale institutions, 'dumb' terminals (ie those with no onboard processing power) have lost a great deal of ground in favour of terminals with substantial onboard processing power. Such terminals are, as we have seen, often known as workstations.

IBM PCs or IBM clones or compatible PCs remain the most popular within the financial industry, with DEC PCs and Hewlett-Packard PCs probably being the next most popular.

Programming techniques – institutions have considerable choice and flexibility in selecting or designing software to operate most front-office applications. The only exception here lies in the area of information reception, when users must either be compatible with the information vendor's system or become compatible. Many institutions regard this pressure to conform to a vendor's format as annoying and even oppressive, but as there has been a polarisation in the financial information industry around a few powerful and influential vendors, institutions usually have little choice but to make themselves compatible with the vendor's system. However, the pressure is not all one-way, since vendors have had to yield to institutions' growing unwillingness to buy in proprietary video reception equipment – which can only be used to receive that particular vendor's services. As a result, even those vendors (eg Reuters and Quick) whose financial information business was originally founded on proprietary video systems, have launched alternative digital facilities.

There are numerous packages for different front-office functions. Some packages are extremely powerful and bring with them many years of practical experience in meeting the real-life front-office problems and challenges of wholesale institutions. However, unfortunately, many packages are not good and do not come close to doing what they are supposed to do. How, then, should an institution decide which packages – if any – are right for it? There is no easy way of doing this, but the case study at the end of this chapter suggests one methodical and effective way of sorting out the good from the bad.

Front-office systems can also be fully customised, but the great expense of this option means that even where an institution wants a high degree of customisation, it will probably prefer to buy in a package and enhance it rather than start from scratch.

Front-office systems for wholesale banks feature many different programming languages. The only hard and fast rule governing whether a particular language is suitable for a front-office application is whether the application program can be designed economically and whether the system does what it is supposed to do. There is no other rule. COBOL is, as with all areas of financial technology, widely used as a legacy of the mainframe systems used in the past, but is is not usually very popular with programmers. LISP is often used for rule-based applications and C is growing ever more popular for PCs.

BACK-OFFICE APPLICATIONS

Introduction

Back-office systems are perhaps not the most exciting area of a financial technologist's activities, but they are extremely important and play an essential role in a financial institution's bid for competitive advantage.

Without efficiency, speed, reliability and accuracy in the back office, any competitive advantage gained in the front office through the skill of staff or the sophistication of the front-office system will be reduced or – even worse – lost entirely. Back-office functions are admirably suited to being carried out by technology; indeed, it is inconceivable that any institution would nowadays wish to operate a back office that was not highly automated.

In their eagerness to deploy the most advanced information reception and decision support systems in the front office, financial technologists often neglect the back office. They do so at their peril, since not only must a back office operate effectively if competitive advantage is to be maximised over-all, but official regulatory and clearance organisations are increasingly demanding of the quality of the administrative information supplied by institutions. These demands are such that only the most advanced back-office systems will be likely to provide them in an efficient and timely manner.

Back-office functions

The following are the principal back-office functions of a financial institution.

Accounting

- storing and retrieving information relating to the institution's own internal accounting
- storing and retrieving information relating to an account held with a particular client or counterparty
- operating a bought and sold ledger
- storing and retrieving details of costs and ongoing profit and loss.

Administrative

- storing and retrieving data on a wide range of administrative issues, particularly relating to:
  a) costings
  b) personnel
  c) premises
  d) technological resources.

Compliance

- meeting compliance requirements specified by regulatory bodies and/or clearance houses and supplying compliance-related information

Risk management

- storing and retrieving information relating to credit limits of particular client accounts, and notifying traders of these limits as and when appropriate
- storing and retrieving information on credit limits relating to particular

instruments, and notifying front-office staff of these limits as and when appropriate.

Transaction settlement

- initiating transaction settlement procedures with external counterparties
- reconciling details of completed trades with internal accounts and client accounts
- notifying front-office staff of details of completed transactions.

Notes on back-office technology

Back-office technology can also be analysed in terms of the financial technology 'building blocks'. The following general points can be made.

Principal computer – for most back-office applications this will be the institution's main computer, that is, a mainframe or a minicomputer. Fault-tolerance is less important for back-office applications than for the sensitive front-office applications, but in practice it is none the less often used in order to ensure that administrative, accounting and other support functions are not interrupted.

Data communications medium – this will typically be within a back-office LAN. The most important development in back-office data communciations is for institutions to be increasingly interested in the possibilities for competitive advantage that arise from them connecting their back-office networks to the front office, and thereby giving front-office staff access to useful information relating to such factors as:

- status of transactions
- state of client accounts
- compliance information (such as relating to capital requirements)
- risk management information, particularly regarding the total exposure to a particular instrument within the firm (so that an additional trade or investment does not take the firm's total position beyond a level that is regarded as advisable).

Terminals – the terminals used here would be similar to those used in the front office: that is, IBM or compatible workstations and other types of proprietary workstations. The fact that back-office terminals are nowadays usually the same as front-office terminals facilitates the process of linking back-office terminals to those in the front office.

Programming techniques – most institutions nowadays use one of the many available back-office packages, enhancing these as required. The relative sameness of most back-office functions means that there is ample scope for package vendors to provide powerful, multifunction and multi-currency products.

Similar kind of challenges face institutions in selecting back-office packages as in choosing those for the front office. The following case study shows how an in-house integrated system was constructed around both front- and back-office functions.

Case study
DUBIN & SWIECA CAPITAL MANAGEMENT'S 'HIGHBRIDGE CAPITAL CORPORATION' SYSTEM

How does a successful derivatives fund management organisation with strict budgetary and time constraints create a highly complex new in-house trading and administration system if no readily available package comes remotely close to doing the job?

In the autumn of 1991 this was the challenge facing Joseph Rosen, chief information officer (technology director in UK parlance) of New York-based Dubin & Swieca Capital Management. Founded in 1984 as a managed futures house, Dubin & Swieca had, by 1992, more than $700 million under management and a client list that included some of America's largest pension funds. According to cofounder Henry Swieca, much of the firm's success was due to managed futures being a particularly potent investment instrument when markets are showing great volatility.

In October 1991 Swieca and fellow cofounder Glenn Dubin had decided to form a new firm under the Dubin & Swieca umbrella. This new firm, to be known as the Highbridge Capital Corporation, would manage funds based on a variety of complex equity derivatives, including equity futures and options, equity indices futures and options and the increasingly popular derivative instruments Preferred Equity Redemption Cumulative Stock (PERCS) and Long-term Equity Anticipation Participating Security (LEAPS). Highbridge Capital Corporation would be using a 'market neutral' strategy: that is, the firm would be seeking to exploit opportunities resulting from changes in the underlying volatility of stocks, with the principal relationship under scrutiny being that between a particular corporation's common stock and some of the derivative instruments tied to that stock.

The computer system, when completed, would not only need to provide a rapid and accurate facility for trading and fund management according to this complex process with a relatively wide range of stocks, but would also have to be an effective tool for all administrative activity associated with the new firm, including – in due course – all relevant compliance functions. Finally, the system would need to be networked into Dubin & Swieca's own in-house network, which has about forty workstations.

As a former information technology consultant and an author of three books on financial technology, Rosen knew that the task which Dubin & Swieca had set themselves could be done, but that it would not be easy. Between the formulation of the plans and the creation of the system lay an immense minefield of dealing with and selecting vendors in no less than seven specific areas of functionality, namely: executing and clearing; front-end portfolio analytics; order-routing networks; portfolio/client management and accounting; market data; risk analysis and management; and trading and inventory control. Figure 3.5 (overleaf) shows how Rosen envisaged the different areas of functionality being networked within the completed system. 'I do not know of any comparable system in the derivatives world which sought to unite so many different levels of functionality,' said Rosen. 'In particular, I do not know of a system which was planned to be developed and deployed within less than a year.'

With the cofounders setting the target date of 1 September 1992 for the deployment of the system and the first day of trading for Highbridge Capital Management, the option of choosing a packaged system was obviously an attractive one; or rather would have been attractive if the right package had been available at the right price. 'We did of course spend some time at first considering going down the package path,' Rosen said. 'However, we realised quite soon that no single off-the-shelf package would be able to provide the full range of functionality that we wanted, and those few that came remotely close to fulfilling our objectives were far too expensive, with figures well in excess of $1,000,000 being regularly quoted. We decided that the only option was to build the system ourselves.'

And so, in November 1991, Rosen and his team began a laborious and painstaking process of seeking out vendors who could supply a system or product to carry out at least one of the seven areas of functionality, and whose system or product would run on Dubin 9 Swieca's in-house platform. This is a Novell Netware Local Area Network (LAN), powered by three file servers and using IBM-compatible 486 PCs running Windows 3.1.

The first contact with vendors was always made by Rosen in person. He is a great believer in the need for an information officer to spend a large part of his time engaged on continually evaluating vendors by immersing himself or

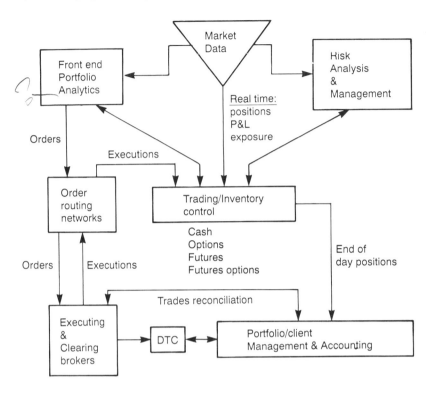

Figure 3.5 Highbridge Capital Corporation: equity and derivatives money management support structure

herself in any sources which provide vendor-related information. In Rosen's case the sources he prefers are write-ups in journals and books and discussions with colleagues in other organisations both in the US and internationally. Rosen is very optimistic about the type of vendors with whom he prefers doing business. 'I don't like dealing with one-man bands,' he says, 'Because no matter how enthusiastic and talented the proprietor is, the fact remains that there are no guarantees that the vendor will still be in business in the future. On the other hand, as a medium-sized company ourselves rather than multinational, we find that very large vendors aren't always interested in giving us either the level of service that we require or the realistic quotations that we expect. As a result, we generally prefer to choose vendors who are medium-sized organisations, like us, and who – again as we can claim to be – have established an excellent track record, are sound financially and have a secure future.'

Not that Rosen was burdened with preconceived ideas about vendors when he made his initial contacts with them. From the very first phone call, he was evaluating and assessing the vendor, even taking into account such factors as speed of answering the telephone ('more than ten rings is bad news') and the courtesy and helpfulness of the person who answers the phone. Equally important, Rosen feels, is the promptness with which telephone calls are returned. 'If they don't get back to you promptly when you are a potential client,' he said, 'It's a fair bet that they'll be just as slow, or even worse, once you've installed one of their systems.'

Once Rosen had made contact with all the vendors in each area who he thought were potential suppliers, and had product and corporate information from all of them, he set to work evaluating the information which he had obtained from them in the light of what he already knew about the vendor. The next stage was to invite several vendors from each area of functionality to visit Dubin & Swieca's offices in the General Motors building on Fifth Avenue. 'The benefits of this are reciprocal,' Rosen said. 'We want to see them, and they want to see us. Although it's unlikely that any financial technology vendor in New York would not have heard of us, we accept that vendors will want to see us in our own location and realise that we are a successful and ambitious organisation which means business. Once we have had this meeting with vendors in our own offices, we expect an opportunity to see them in *their* premises. It's astonishing how much you can learn about a vendor from a visit to their offices. If the reception area and offices generally are dirty and untidy, and if staff are impolite and look harassed, it's probable that some aspects of the vendor's business are run in an equally slovenly manner. Of course, the main thrust of the visit to a vendor's premises is to attend a discussion with the principals and see a demonstration of the system, but you can often learn as much about a vendor when you are arriving for and leaving a meeting as you can when you are actually in the meeting.'

The next stage, for those vendors which passed muster on the round of initial meetings, was for Rosen and his team to see the product or system up and running at a client site. 'Obviously you don't really know whether a system will do what it's supposed to do until you see it in action in a live site,' said Rosen. 'But seeing the system or product in action was only part of this further vetting procedure. In every case we asked vendors for client references and made sure to take these up. It's astonishing how many clients tell a very different story of an installation and their general relationship with the vendor compared to the vendor's side of the story.'

Rosen added: 'In taking up these client references, what we aimed to find out was, above all, the vendor's responsiveness to problems and – equally important – to changes in the client's requirements; how smooth (or rough) the installation process was and how well the vendor met agreed cost and time constraints. We tried to uncover any particularly favourable or unfavourable stories. One problem which often recurred – and which from my experience in technology consultancy I know is also a frequent problem in the consultancy business – was that clients complained that they met the vendor's senior personnel, and even the principal, when the sale was being made, but that these senior people were no longer involved in the installation process. It seems to me that vendors who treat clients in this way are orientated around making the sale rather than providing the service, and I think this should be regarded as a serious negative factor.'

By now the selection process had reached the shortlist stage, with between two and three vendors being shortlisted for most areas of functionality. *Most areas* because one problem which Rosen and his team encountered on their search was the difficulty that in a few areas of function (Rosen prefers not to say which ones) he found only one good vendor, with the somewhat embarrassing consequence that Dubin & Swieca had Hobson's Choice over this vendor. Needless to say, vendors with something resembling a monopoly are well aware of this. However, Rosen was able to negotiate terms that fitted in with the project's overall budget.

The shortlist stage consisted primarily of the product or system being tested by Dubin & Swieca in a pilot scheme. In some cases Dubin & Swieca paid for using the pilot, in other cases it did not, depending on what the vendor's terms of business were. However, Rosen generally expected that vendors would bear at least some of the cost of installing and running the pilots themselves. 'The biggest problem facing a potential user such as ourselves is that so many third party products and services don't do what they are supposed to do. It is obviously in every vendors' interest to prove that they are an exception to this.'

The final stage of the process involved extremely detailed scrutiny of the vendors' contracts by Rosen and Dubin & Swieca's lawyers. As Rosen put it, 'Vendors try to get away with whatever they can. Detailed contract examination and hard negotiation of points that seem unreasonable, are an essential part of my job.'

With a determined and businesslike approach towards the vendor selection process, Rosen and his team found that the process went relatively smoothly and that assembling the selected vendors (the precise names of whom Rosen insists on keeping confidential) and building the system could be completed by the summer, which made 1 September 1992 a feasible date for the launch of the Highbridge Capital Corporation.

The system, while up and running, is in a continual process of evolution and among the next developments planned are a full tie-in of the system to the general ledger and accounting of *all* the funds which Dubin & Swieca operates. Ultimately, additional customisation of the system will – with vendors' permission – result in a system that is close to being a fully customised, in-house originated resource. In the meantime, Dubin & Swieca has an innovative and powerful derivatives trading, management and accounting system which has cost – given that some vendors charge every month and so an accurate statement of what the system costs is not easy to produce – less than half the amount which a vendor of an unsatisfactory package would have demanded. In this case at least, the do-it-yourself approach has worked.

4 UNDERSTANDING TECHNOLOGY

COMPUTERS – THE ULTIMATE TOOL?

Introduction

This chapter sets out the belief that anyone who is interested in deploying financial technology (and, indeed, any other type of technology) to maximum efficiency, ought to develop an attitude towards computers which emphasises the essential nature of computers as *tools to assist us*, not sophisticated gadgetry to hinder and annoy us.

This may be seen as a straightforward and even obvious point. However, I firmly believe that a failure to understand what technology is, and what it is not, is behind many of the problems that plague financial technologists; in particular:

- a system being abandoned in the development stage because it becomes clear that its original objectives were unrealistic
- the failure of a system to carry out its original objectives
- the failure of a financial technologist to understand what these objectives were
- where the technologist does know what the objectives were, the failure to communicate them satisfactorily to the institution's staff
- the failure of individual members of staff to like using a system (or, more correctly stated, the failure of a system to prove likeable)
- the failure of individual members of staff to use a system to its maximum potential

- the failure of the institution to get maximum value for money out of a system
- the failure of the institution to extract maximum competitive advantage out of a system.

Later in this chapter, all these problems are addressed and solutions suggested.

Of course, we should not overlook the point that these problems are sometimes due to technical, rather than conceptual, difficulties. However, in today's financial technology environment, where, by and large, the right level of processing power and technical expertise can be obtained *given that the original objectives of the system are realistic*, it seems to me almost axiomatic that in most cases the majority of the above problems stem not from technical deficiences but from a misunderstanding on the part of financial technologists, or other staff, or both, to understand what computer technology really is, and where it fits into the overall scheme of tools that human beings use.

COMPUTERS AS TOOLS

Man is a tool-maker. Anthropologists are increasingly coming to regard tool-making as the attribute which decisively sets man apart from other animals, and in particular from the other primates. In the past, the possession of a highly evolved brain or a subtle vocal language have been seen by many anthropologists as the unique attributes of mankind, but it is becoming clear that our understanding of cetacean intelligence may be grossly underestimated. Research has shown that many animals have evolved complex systems of sonic, ultrasonic and even magnetic communication, and that we might have placed an undue emphasis on terrestrial vocalisation simply because this happens to be how we ourselves communicate.

Fossil evidence provides ample evidence for the hypothesis that what distinguished early hominids (ie man-like apes) from their ape cousins was an ability to fashion tools for specific purposes. This being the case, we can very reasonably assume that man started to be man when he began to make tools. The argument, while to some extent tautological, is none the less useful.

Let us, for example, imagine that a technological miracle lets you view life on the plains of what is now southern Africa, 2,600,000 years ago. Among the animals of the primeval savannah you would probably see small monkey-like creatures which usually walk on their hind legs and whose bodies are covered in hair. Gazing at them, you might think that they were an extinct species of ape. Yet, if you observed their dexterity as they fashion sharpened sticks to hunt their prey and crudely shaped stones to serve as primitive knives, you might find yourself wondering whether these creatures did in fact become extinct, or rather, in the fullness of time, evolved into something else: a race of beings who could satisfy their hunger by a visit to a restaurant and consequently have the time to read a book such as this.

The so-called apes are nowadays referred to as *Australopithecus*, and they lived between about 2,000,000 and 3,000,000 years ago. The famous fossil, christened 'Lucy', is the remains of part of a skull of a sixteen-year-old Australopithecus female. The physical appearance of our ancestors who lived so long ago was not indeed so much different from monkeys. Although it is possible that the preferred means of locomotion of these creatures was on their hind legs, it is impossible to be sure of this, and they may have only stood on their hind legs when picking berries off bushes, and fruit from trees. What is certain, however, is that even by the end of the Pliocene Epoch, 2,600,000 years ago, Australopithecus had staked their claim to be the forerunner of modern *homo sapiens*. They used tools.

In a rather pedestrian fashion, the *Encyclopaedia Britannica*'s Macropaedia article on Tools defines a tool as an 'implement or device used directly upon a piece of material to shape it into a desired form.' This definition is certainly appropriate for many types of tools – including some highly sophisticated machine tools of our own time – but a better definition, and one which gets to the essence of what a tool actually is, would be something such as 'an implement or device which facilitates the extension of man's natural capacities.' Using this definition as a yardstick, we might regard a stick as a means for stirring up a fire without burning the hand. A telephone is a means for people to talk to people who are located in places out of earshot, and since the telephone is so convenient and removes the need to shout, it is also useful when we wish to talk with people who are within earshot but not very close by.

Defining a tool as an extension of our natural capacities is interesting, for it emphasises the fact that tools are centred around humans: a human-centricity that is so obvious, it is not usually noticed. But what is undeniable is that the design of the tools we use is entirely dependent on our physical characteristics as human beings. An alien species, with very different physical characteristics from our own, might have a set of tools that would look completely unfamiliar to us yet carry out precisely the same functions as our own tools carry out.

Our own physical characteristics also place an absolute constraint on the design of many tools. The design of telephones has changed greatly since they were first used about a hundred years ago, and will doubtless change considerably in the next hundred years, but no future telephone designer, no matter how innovative, would want to design a gap between the mouthpiece of less than about six inches, which is approximately the distance between our right or left ear and mouth.

Sometimes it is only a particular human physiological characteristic that enables a tool to work at all. For example, without the benefit of one fundamental fact of human physiology – that the retina of the human eye retains an image for about 1/10 of a second after the image has faded – television and computer screens would all seem blank to us. An alien species whose eyes were more efficient than ours and displayed no retinal image retention would not see an image on a television or computer screen.

These two ideas of computers as tools and tools being objects – built to extend our own natural capacities – which are designed around fundamental human physical attributes, are central to the discussion in this chapter. It is reasonable to consider computers as a particularly important tool – perhaps indeed the *ultimate* tool – because computers are used, in essence, *to extend our own natural ability to control information*. Moreover, as reasoning creatures, our control of information is more than merely a step beyond our control of the physical world; it actually *increases* and *enhances* our control of the physical world. This being the case, one would expect a tool that extended our ability to control information to have numerous applications in both the world of information and the physical world. A glance at real-life computer applications, which literally cover almost every single aspect of human life, tells us that this is indeed so.

Furthermore, it is difficult to deny that the developed world is moving into a scenario where the manipulation of information is becoming more important for the advancement of civilisation, the smooth running of society and the comfort and convenience of the individual than any other specific manipulation of the physical world. This being so, the computer has a serious claim to be known as the ultimate tool.

Viewing computers in this way is both exciting and somewhat bewildering. With only about fifty years of intensive computer development behind us, we have to accept that we are only at the very beginning of the computer age. This is a disconcerting, even terrifying observation, for computers have made such a massive impact on our world in forty years that it is difficult for anyone to dare to predict what kind of impact they will have made on the world in another fifty years, let alone in a further one hundred years. Furthermore, the pace of development is so fast that what different people understand by the term 'computer' is to some extent a reflection of the person's age and knowledge of computers.

Generally speaking, the younger a person is, the smaller are the computers in their definition of the term; simply because the pace of change in the computer industry is in favour of increasingly small machines. Unlike telephones, which must always have a mouthpiece and earpiece that are about six inches apart, the only design constraints of computers are imposed by limitations in computer technology. For example, the fact that our technological generation has currently chosen to build computers so that they look like televisions sitting on top of typewriters does not mean in any sense that computers will always look like this, any more than the fact that the first computers which looked like long rows of bookcases meant that computers continued to look like that.

Indeed, the rapidly evolving physical appearance of computers indicates the rapid development of computer technology, overall. It is very likely that Alexander Graham Bell – who invented the telephone about one hundred years ago – would quickly recognise a modern telephone – even a cordless telephone – as a descendant of his invention. However, a computer pioneer of the 1940s, if he had not been apprised of intermediate developments, would by no means necessarily recognise a modern personal computer with its screen and keyboard as a computer, and it is not difficult to imagine that in the future computers could take forms which we ourselves could hardly recognise as constituting computers. Imagine, say, a computer which is made out of a special plastic that can be as flimsy as cloth or as hard as iron depending on whether it is rolled up in one's pocket or spread out on a desk. It is not easy to conceive of such a device, but a computer pioneer of the 1940s would probably have found the idea of a portable desktop computer equally difficult to imagine.

The point is that computers are only as useful as we can design them to be useful. Since the technology which they incorporate is constantly evolving, computer design is in a very real sense constantly evolving, too. But no matter how much computer design evolves, the computer will not be a beneficial tool unless it is easy to use. With all developed countries having access to computer technology, computer usefulness – or, to use the more commonly accepted term, computer *useability* – has indeed become the principal problem of computer design. The rest of this chapter addresses this problem.

Why computer useability is a problem

Computers are, as we have seen, a tool. Unfortunately, however, they do not look much like the more familiar mechanical tools – tools like a hammer, axe and knife – which have been around in some form since prehistoric times. Computers look unusual, even unnatural.

Not only that, but we know that they are extremely complex 'inside'; so complex that only experts can build them, and in most cases even experts need to use other computers in order to build them. Furthermore, we also know that computers do extremely important things. They help to send people into space; they assist in keeping jet airlines airborne; they store an entire nation's telephone numbers; they operate a bank's national ATM network. Computers are expensive, too, with even the ones that sit on our desks costing about a month's salary and with some of the largest computers costing more than most of us earn in a lifetime.

Everything, it seems, conspires to make people feel one, or all, of the following feelings about computers:

- awe
- bewilderement
- fear
- hesitation in learning how to use them
- enormous respect
- trepidation.

Few people, on the other hand, would experience any of these feelings in connection with mechanical tools. No grown person would fail to understand, for example, what the purpose of a hammer was and if they feel respect for the tool it is only because they know that if they miss the tack which they are trying to hammer into the wall they may hit their thumb, or worse. The immense ease with which simple mechanical tools have slotted into our lives can be shown by the fact that the names of most simple tools have become verbs as well as nouns: *fork*, *hammer*, *knife*, *nail*, *screw*, *spoon* and so on.

However, you can't '*computer*' anything, and although certainly the word *compute* does exist, this is a fairly technical term which few people would use unless they were professionally involved with computers. The English language does not have a word which means 'to use a computer' and this fact is a good indication of the very different way in which computers are seen compared with how simple mechanical tools are regarded.

By now you might be thinking this is all very well but I (ie you, the reader) *am* a professional and I am perfectly at home with computers. True, this is probably the case and I daresay that you use a computer more often than you hammer a tack into a wall, too, but if you refer back to the title of this book – *Managing Technology in Financial Institutions* – the reason why the discussion in this chapter should be of great interest to you will be clear, or ought to be.

Question: why are financial institutions in business?

Answer: to make profit.

Question: how do they make profit?

Answer: from handling the finances and financial dealings of private individuals, corporations and other financial institutions.

Question: what role do computers play in this activity?

Answer: an extremely important, all-pervasive role. They are used by private individuals and staff alike.

Used by private individuals and staff alike. Exactly. You may be an expert in computers and fully familiar with them, but your institution's customers and possibly your colleagues are not – and just as it is your institution's customers who generate your institution's profit, it is your colleagues who meet the customers' needs and enable profit to be maximised. Both types of user must be able to use the computers which your institution deploys – and for which you will be at least partly responsible – with maximum ease, efficiency and – no need to be afraid of using the word – *enjoyment*.

Useability is rather more than mere usefulness, although that is a good starting-point. With regard to computers, we can employ the term *useability* as a convenient shorthand for everything connected with understanding a computer and using it easily, efficiently and enjoyably. A computer with a high level of useability facilitates people's understanding and use of it; a computer with a low level of useability does not.

 Useability is a major issue with computer deployment and an issue that has all too often been neglected in the financial technology arena.Some financial institutions have begun to look at it in detail and a few institutions have in fact deployed systems which feature a high degree of useability, but generally useability is something which financial technology managers tend to regard as something of an afterthought, once the system has been developed and they realise that some sort of attention needs to be given to the 'user interface'.

This attitude is neither helpful to staff nor – more importantly – to customers. It is they who will have to use the computers and it is they who will soon tire of using computers that are difficult to use. There is, of course a difference here in that staff will be motivated to persevere with a computer system even if it is difficult to use, whereas customers will have far less patience and will very likely walk away from the computer if they cannot use it easily and effectively. Note that in today's financial world, where computers are often the primary point of contact between an institution and a customer, walking away from a computer is often the same as walking away from the institution. The computer useability fraternity likes to distinguish between those who are obliged to use a computer (eg staff) and those who can choose whether or not to use the computer (eg customers) by referring to the 'obliged' set of users as *nondiscretionary users* and by giving the term *discretionary users* to those who can choose whether to use the computer or not.

Although, as I have suggested, the best way to regard computers is to see them as a tool, there is not much point denying that they are obviously a very complicated type of tool. The danger is to make a mental leap beyond that observation and to conclude that *because* the computer is such a complicated tool, we should therefore accept a situation where we are its servants, rather than its masters. Such a conclusion, while it may seem absurd to anyone who is professionally involved with designing and deploying computers, is in fact regularly in the minds of many discretionary and nondiscretionary users. It is often dangerously easy for computer professionals to forget how bewildering and daunting computers often seem to people who are not expert in their use. What we need to do, therefore, is to think through the problem of useability and to provide a set of practical and useful guidelines for good useability.

Designing for good useability

One of the most interesting books on useability – and essential reading for anyone wishing to explore further some of the ideas in this chapter – is *The Psychology of Everyday Things* by Donald Norman (see bibliography for reference). A professor and director of the Institute for Cognitive Science at the University of California, San Diego, Norman sets himself the task in his remarkable book of looking at the problem of computer useability in terms of the design problems of everyday objects, including many simple tools. In his preface Norman supplies the basic rationale for equating the design philosophy of everyday objects with the design philosophy of computers and information systems. He writes:

My previous research project, was on the difficulties of using computers and the methods that might be used to make things easier. But the more I looked at computers (and other demons of our society, such as aircraft systems and nuclear power), the more I realised that there was nothing special about them; they had the same problems as did the simple, everyday things. And the everyday things were more pervasive, more of a problem. Especially as people feel guilt when they are unable to use simple things, *guilt that should not be theirs but rather the designers and manufacturers of the objects.* (my italics)

Earlier in the preface Norman, reflecting on his own experience, had said:

Over the years I have fumbled my way through life, walking into doors, failing to figure out water faucets, incompetent at working the simple things of everyday life.

"Just me," I would mumble. "Just my mechanical ineptitude." But as I studied psychology and watched the behaviour of other people, I began to realise that I was not alone. My difficulties were mirrored by the problems of others. And we all seemed to blame ourselves. Could the whole world be mechanically incompetent?

There are few of us who would disagree with Norman's basic hypothesis here that simple, everyday things are, indeed, difficult to use. The following list is compiled merely from my own experience. No doubt you will have your own everyday useability bugbears. Here are a few:

● oven controls that make it impossible to understand at a glance which switch governs which of the (usually four) hotplates

How often have you turned the wrong switch when operating one of the hotplates on your stove? Never? Hardly ever? I do it frequently.

● department store doors where it is difficult to know how to open the door.

Apparently most department stores are more keen that customers see through the glass doors and into the shop than knowing how to open the doors, and in particular whether to push or pull.

● washing machine controls which provide no self-contained clue as to which number program does what

Washing machines are good examples of machines which, while undoubtedly extremely useful, often contain more features than is absolutely necessary. If you lose the manual you are usually completely stuck.

Very well, this is fairly light-hearted. You might even wonder what it has to do with computers. The answer is that it has everything to do with them; since if simple, everyday items have useability design problems, complex items such as computers will inevitably have potentially far more serious useability design problems.

The one factor mitigating this to some degree – although it really should not mitigate it at all – is that one of the strange things that happens when people use complex tools is that at the beginning of the using process, they are inclined to consider that their inability to use the tool successfully is entirely their own fault.

I regard this as a strange phenomenon, since when a purely *mechanical* tool is obviously badly designed, no one will think that it is they, and not the tool, which is at fault. If someone handed you a hammer with a glass head and a flexible rubber handle you would not blame yourself for being unable to use the hammer; you would think that it was a badly designed hammer – and you would be right. With complex tools, however, people rapidly develop a strange guilt about their inability to use the tool properly and blame themselves and this is generally true of both discretionary and non-discretionary users.

In either case, no financial technologist should for one moment be prepared to accept the conclusion that such guilt on the part of either a discretionary or nondiscretionary user is anything but disastrous. *For the discretionary user, the next step after feeling this guilt will probably be to walk out of the branch and go elsewhere. For the nondiscretionary user, who is obliged to stay in the office during working hours (although he might not feel obliged to remain with the institution indefinitely if problems with using technology are a constant problem) inability to use technology properly will inevitably reduce his efficiency and morale.*

David Blunkett, the UK Labour Member of Parliament – who happens to be blind – summarised this whole issue in a letter to the UK newspaper the *Independent* in June 1990.

To all manufacturers, not merely of tape recorders but of all office equipment, please keep the best of the old whilst making the changes which help you market your new products. If the consumer is dissatisfied with the product it is the producer and not the user who is at fault! Too often these days you are made to feel that there is something slightly strange and old-fashioned about you, if you don't like the over-organisation of products which make the job take longer and make the learning process more complicated.

At this point the objection might be raised: *yes, but what about the learning curve?* Surely anyone who uses a complex tool has to accept that there must be some sort of learning period before the tool can be mastered?

The most effective reply to this objection is not an answer but a question: what is the point of deploying the tool in the first place? When the deployment relates to financial technology, which is after all the ultimate focus of the discussion here, we have seen in earlier chapters how this technology is deployed for several reasons, with the main one being to win competitive advantage for the institution. This being the case, it should be obvious to anyone that *no institution can afford to deploy financial technology which has anything but the very shortest of learning curves, and ideally no learning curve at all.*

Discretionary users, we may be assured, will walk away from a system at the first sign of difficulty or discomfort (physical or psychological) in using it. Nondiscretionary users may not be so keen to walk away, but they may be equally intolerant of a system that is not easy to use. Anyone who cares about the useability of any technology must remember that *new technology is innately threatening, no matter what degree of expertise the user has, or believes himself to have.*

Human beings are most comfortable with objects that they know, trust and like, just as they are most comfortable with other people who they know, trust and like. New objects, like new people, are at first seen as threatening because the person using the new object has not yet learnt to limit the psychological discomfort that the contact with the new object brings. Now, if the object concerned were a jet aircraft or a car, then the user has very little choice but to master the use of the device before he can expect to feel pyschologically comfortable with it. The technical requirements of an object which flies very fast through the air or which drives fast along a road mean that some process of learning how to use them is inevitable. Financial institutions' customers, however, are not usually prepared to accept that any learning curve at all is necessary and why should they be? Besides, even if customers were prepared to tolerate a more lengthy learning curve, the need for good useabiity would remain. After all, someone who is training to be a pilot or a motorist, while alive to the need to master the use of a complex piece of technology, will be as impatient of any obvious useability problem in the technology as any discretionary user of a financial system.

Before moving onto the particular useability problems of computers, the discussion so far in this chapter can usefully be summarised as follows:

1 reaching the understanding that computers should first and foremost be tools to help us rather than sophisticated gadgetry to hinder us helps to protect against many serious, and expensive, failures of financial systems
2 as tools, computers are in a direct line of evolution from the tools used by our ancestors

3 the purpose of computers, as with any other tool, is primarily to facilitate an extension of our natural capacities
4 people have different ideas about what computers actually are because computer technology has evolved rapidly and is still evolving rapidly
5 the useability design problems of computers are closely related to the useability design problems of many simple everyday objects
6 both discretionary and nondiscretionary users of financial technology will quickly grow impatient with computers that are not easy to use and the use of which fails to provide psychological comfort.

With these points in mind, we can move on to look more closely at the particular useability problems of computers.

As we have seen, it is reasonable to regard computers as a complex tool, in the same way that a jet aircraft and a car are complex tools, although we should remember that merely because a computer *is* a complex tool does not give its designers the right to demand a lengthy learning curve from users. However, if one thinks the matter through a little further, it is clear that not only are computers complex tools, but they are a *special kind of tool* because all the important things that they do take place at a microscopic level, and are in any event invisible. This has always been the case ever since computers were made out of electromechanical components, and it is particularly true in this era of the microprocessor.

In *The Psychology of Everyday Things* Donald Norman succinctly summarises why computers present special problems for the useability designer.

The abstract nature of the computer poses a particular challenge to the designer. The computer works electronically, invisibly, with no sign of the actions it is performing.

This is the very heart of the matter. What makes the computer unique as a tool is that the relationship between the physical actions of the user and the results of these actions within the computer's internal mechanism is completely invisible to the user, since these actions are dependent on the movement inside the computer's microcircuitry. The only way that the user can influence these operations is via the *user interface*, that is, the electromechanical framework available for making the computer do what the user wants it to do. *However, unlike most tools – even most complex ones – no physical action on the part of the user will produce an automatic and direct effect upon the computer.* Every single aspect of the user's control over the computer must be built into the user interface.

Furthermore, it is essential to understand that the physical controls – such as a keyboard, joystick or mouse – which form the hardware of a typical computer's user interface system – can only ever be symbolic aids to help the user manipulate an action to which he has no real access.

This is a difficult concept, and can best be clarified by means of an analogy, such as this one from the legal world. Criminal trials are held because there is no way of reliving the events of a crime other than in a symbolic, imaginary sense (although there is nothing symbolic or imaginary about the punishments which guilty criminals must suffer). Similarly, there is no way of seeing exactly what is going on inside a computer (for example, we cannot instruct individual electrons to move along a conductive surface in a particular direction), so we are obliged to create entirely artificial controls which are useful because they give us a symbolic and imaginary understanding of what is going on inside the computer. For example, when we press a button on top of a joystick in order to 'fire' at a 'enemy' on the computer screen, all we are doing is instructing the computer to alter the visual configuration of the screen so that certain images move in a particular direction. There is no concept of 'firing' within the computer, but this concept is useful from the point of view of how we instruct the computer to do what we want it to do.

What all this adds up to, for the computer useability designer, is that he must shoulder the entire burden of enabling a human to use the computer. Not only this, but the designer has no easy answers – no 'givens' – to how the user interface ought to be configured other than knowing that he wants the user to be able to do a certain thing with the computer. In other words, the user interface design must be designed from scratch (which is not, of course, to say that other experience in user interface design will not prove useful to the designer). However, the very fact that there are no 'givens' allows the designer to enjoy considerable scope for creativity in how he solves the design problems; with the necessary caution that since the designer can enjoy considerable creative freedom, the opportunities for getting things wrong must also be regarded as very high.

There are, of course, certain popular devices which have been found to be very useful and acceptable in creating user interfaces. Examples of such devices are the familiar keyboard, joystick and mouse which are found in such abundance in so many user interfaces. Note, incidentally, that even the terms 'joystick' and 'mouse' are attempts to familiarise essentially unfamiliar types of physical hardware by relating them to more familiar worlds. However, there is absolutely no need for the designer to be hide-bound by these familiar devices, and even if he decides to use some or all of them, there are an infinite number of ways in which they can be configured.

Similarly, many users have found that 'icons' (ie small symbols denoting certain 'operations' which the computer can be instructed to carry out) are extremely useful as a means of giving a succession of instructions to the computer, with the icons being especially useful when deployed in conjunction with a mouse. Even so, one important criticism of many icon-based user interfaces is that they restrict the user more than is necessary in terms of what the user can do with the computer. User interface designers are frequently guilty of a failure of imagination, and icon design is one area where this failure is frequently apparent.

To use an expression for which I am indebted to Ian Clowes, a consultant in human-computer interaction with Logica in Cambridge, England, what the user really wants in the human-computer interaction process is to be a 'magician', who is able to achieve whatever he needs (within reason) from the user interface. Most icon-based systems do not recognise this need and instead tend to restrict the user to mere reality. As Clowes pointed out to me, the user does not want metaphors that restrict him solely to reality; he wants metaphors that let him do as much as he can comfortably recognise and with which he can feel most at ease.

To use an example supplied by Clowes, a wastepaper basket icon on a screen is a useful metaphor because it is easy for the user to understand that if he uses his mouse to send a document to the wastepaper basket, the document will be thrown away, but that the icon allows retrieval later on if necessary (sometimes only for a certain time-period), just as in real life there is a period when a document has been thrown into a wastepaper basket but can still be retrieved because the basket has not yet been emptied. In this case, 'putting' a document into the wastepaper basket icon gives the user some leeway in changing his mind. However, there may well be numerous other instanecs – such as where a user wants to get rid of all earlier versions of a document so as to avoid confusion with a later, improved, version of the document or where the user wants to avoid the danger of an unauthorised person reading a secret document – where the user wants to 'destroy' the document completely without a period during which it could be retrieved.

In this instance what the user would really like to do is to have (say) a firebreathing dragon (or an icon representing one) which sits quietly in the office until needed to incinerate a document that is required to vanish without trace (even shredders leave some trace). Although firebreathing dragons are not normally found in offices, it would be simple to create a dragon icon for a system, and to use this icon as a way of erasing documents completely. This is – literally – an example of how, if the user interface can imagine his users as being magicians, this can give the user more useable features than would be the case if the metaphors involved were restricted purely to being representative of the world of reality. Incidentally, this example is useful in suggesting the potential – much of which is still relatively unexplored – that computer games have for providing useful hints for designers of user interfaces for more formal systems.

The wastepaper basket and firebreathing dragons are both metaphors, and the concept of the metaphor is central to good computer useability design. Metaphors facilitate communications between humans and computers by creating an illusion to which the human can easily relate. In the human-computer interface sense, metaphors are mental structures used to create understanding. Metaphors are usually expressed visually or linguistically, although there is, on the whole, a tendency among user interface designers for metaphors to be expressed visually wherever possible.

A popular high-level metaphor to allow a user to interact with a computer is where the software provides the user with a metaphorical 'toolbox'. Indeed, the very term 'information technology' could even be seen as a general metaphor for all computer systems.

If there is one general trend that can be pinpointed in the use of metaphors within user interfaces, it is that the user interface appears to be all the more effective the more the metaphor relates to the everyday, rather than seeks to glorify the technology for its own sake. Any metaphor that does seek to glorify, or even emphasise, the technology must be regarded as highly suspect, since what the user interface designer really wants to achieve is a state where the user is as far as possible unaware that he is communicating with a computer at all.

To take an important example from the financial world, the world's first automated teller machines (ATMs) appeared in the 1970s. They were designed so as to emphasise in their appearances the computerised aspect of the technology. These first machines often had names like 'Compubank' or 'Computer Teller' and featured screen-based dialogues in which the ATM was personified as a robot. This metaphor was presumably based on the notion that people using an ATM would find the prospect of interacting with a computer particularly interesting or exciting, and that this metaphor would somehow let them accept the idea of doing business with a computer more readily than they would otherwise have done. This is, to put it mildly, a very debateable notion. People use an ATM because they want it to do certain things for them: provide them with cash from their bank account, give them information about the state of their account, allow them to order statements and similar normal banking functions. These are all normal banking functions; why should the user want to become involved in a dialogue with a robot? The answer is that he doesn't, any more than someone buying a coffee from a hot drink vending machine wants to become involved in a dialogue with the vending machine.

In the development of ATMs, and as ATMs moved from being a technology at the inception stage to being a technology at the growth stage, the 'robot bank' metaphor was discarded by user interface designers because, far from making the ATMs more acceptable to users, it made them less acceptable. In fact, many new technologies go through a phase where the technology is first emphasised in the user interface and then de-emphasised. In the case of ATMs, the robot bank metaphor was replaced with different, more humanistic metaphors which aimed to create the highest likelihood that the user would forget the existence of the computer completely.

Instead, ATMs were given names such as (to quote real-life US and UK examples) 'Speedbank', 'Magic Line', 'Cash Exchange' and 'Cardcash', which emphasised the principal benefit of the ATM: speedy access to banking services, and in particular fast access to cash.

VIRTUAL REALITY AND METAPHORS

Virtual reality is a form of computer technology which has as its ultimate aim the simulation of real-life sense data so that a user can interact with a computer and yet be obtaining a powerful simulation of reality. A type of virtual reality has been used commercially for more than twenty years in aircraft simulators, which have now reached an extremely high level of sophistication, with computer graphics providing a replication of the view through an aircraft's window which looks very similar to that which the pilot would see in real life, and hydraulic mountings for the simulator which enable the pilot to experience the twisting and turning of the aircraft as it responds to the pilot's controls.

True virtual reality, however, aims to take the simulation one step further by providing the user with equipment and software which as far as possible seek to remove from his mind the fact that he is interacting with an artificial device at all.

To date, virtual reality technology is relatively crude, with the leading edge of development taking place in the US. The entire essence of virtual reality is a system which provides the user with the kind of complex feedback to his actions that he would obtain in real life. Achieving this is not only extremely complex technically, but also requires an immense amount of computer memory. Even arranging for a virtual reality graphic to change its configuration in response to a movement in the user's head (assuming that the user is employing a virtual reality visor) requires a complex program and a great deal of computer memory to effect.

At present, virtual reality technology can only provide the kind of simple approximations to reality which, using a visor and – in some cases – a glove, can very roughly simulate certain visual and tactile sensations to a degree which gives this technology the potential to be an amusing entertainment in a games arcade. However, with a certain leap of imagination we can conceive of a virtual reality system which – using technology that probably lies at least ten or twenty years in the future – makes use of a virtual reality 'suit'. This, when used in conjunction with a visor, could offer users a range of tactile sensations which would provide as accurate a replication of reality as the sophistication of the software allowed. Such a system would offer thrilling – and daunting – possibilities to mankind and could be as potentially beneficial or dangerous as the most powerful pharmaceutical drugs. Furthermore, it is likely that the solving of the type of problems which would be encountered on the way to developing such a fullbody virtual reality system would open up important technological avenues and provide spin-off products much as the US space programme produced important spin-offs. How, for example, does one replicate the sensation of a gentle breeze blowing on the user's face as he takes a walk through a forest? Furthermore, such a system would raise daunting technical, even ethical, problems.

A technical problem might be the extent to which the system – which could clearly provide the user with a degree of pleasure – should also be permitted to furnish the user with a level of pain. An ethical problem might be the extent to which a virtual reality system – which could, presumably, be designed to incorporate a level of sexual gratification – might encourage emotionally immature people into types of behaviour which might be socially dangerous; although, by the same token, such a system might provide a totally harmless way for people with deviant – or even psychopathic – tendencies to indulge in their urges without injuring anyone.

Nevertheless, these are issues which will need to be confronted in the next century rather than now. In the meantime, focusing on practical applications, as we are here, it need only be said that virtual reality is a technology which has certainly not yet reached the inception phase within the financial industry of any country but the US, and which is still highly experimental there.

However, virtual reality looks like offering great potential to the financial industry once the technology reaches the inception phase, which it may possibly do during the late 1990s. The reason why virtual reality has a great potential within the financial sector – and perhaps particularly in the wholesale banking sector – is that it could offer computer useability designers immense opportunities to create user interfaces which allow users to manipulate complex financial data in a higly efficient manner, perhaps by using metaphors which allow users almost literally to 'get a handle' on the data. There may be particularly exciting possibilities here within the wholesale financial world, where traders and investment managers need to deal with a complex range of incoming market data, analytic resources and back-office information most of the time and where none of the keyboard, mouse and even touch-screen user interfaces currently available seem to facilitate the handling of this information.

Guidelines for good useability design

Finally, what guidelines should a useability designer follow if he is to maximise the useability of a particular computer system? I have extrapolated the following list of suggested guidelines from my own research into and observation of the computer useability industry over the past few years, but readers should see this list as the starting point for their own thinking on this subject rather than as representing by any means the last word.

1 *Give the user access to powerful metaphors*
As we have seen, users do not merely need metaphors which confine them to the world of reality, but need metaphors which give them the opportunity to exercise as much control over the user interface system (and, by extension, the computer system) as they feel comfortable to exercise. If this means giving the user access to 'magical' metaphors, then so be it.

2 *Make the relationship between the controls for a particular action and the action itself as clear and logical as possible*
The relationship between the controls of a particular action and the action itself is often referred to by computer useability designers as the 'mapping'. Where possible, mappings should be 'natural' and relate to a familiar world to which the user can easily relate. An example of a natural mapping is where the user touches a wastepaper basket icon on a screen if he wants whatever is on the screen to be discarded with a possibility of retrieving the screen's contents at a later stage if necessary. Note that a good mapping might also refer to a technology which, while not as advanced as the computer technology world, is also sufficiently familiar to the user for the reference to be a natural one. Computer keyboards are a good example of such mappings. You touch a button with a letter on it and that letter appears on the screen. Our distant ancestors, who were unfamiliar with typewriters, would not easily have understood this mapping, but our familiarity with typewriters means that we do understand it. Sometimes mappings refer to worlds of which we do not ourselves have any direct experience, but which we find glamorous and exciting. The obvious example here is the computer joystick. Few of us have flown an aircraft, but the joystick mapping is sufficiently attractive for us to find it interesting in its own right.

3 *Make the required operations very clear and easy to understand*
This is an extremely obvious point, but it needs stating, and all too often it requires restating, too. Whatever metaphor and mapping is chosen for the

user interface, the user should be able to tell almost at once – and ideally at a glance – how the user interface operates. One great advantage of natural or familiar mappings such as icons, touch-screens, keyboard and joysticks is that it should be immediately obvious to the user how the user interface operates. However, some use of language and/or symbols will probably be inevitable, and the following subguidelines must be borne in mind:

- avoid abbreviations where possible. Research shows that reading is a matter of visual recognition and abbreviations tend to slow the visual recognition process
- if your language uses the Roman alphabet, spell long words (say, longer than six letters) or entire phrases using upper and lower case, just as the words would be spelt in a text. IT TAKES DISTINCTLY LONGER TO READ A LENGTHY ACCUMULATION OF CAPITAL LETTERS than it does to read a sentence composed primarily of lower-case letters
- use familiar, everyday, language. Wherever a long word can be replaced by a shorter, everyday, word, use it
- make sure that symbols are immediately recognisable. If they are not, use language instead.

4 Be polite to users

Think everything through from the user's perspective and ensure that the user interface treats users courteously, helpfully and positively. The user interface should not be designed so that mistakes by the user are greeted with insulting or off-putting 'error messages' or by penalties (even unintentional ones) such as that the user loses work which he has completed or is completely unable to progress the application. Bear in mind that a good user interface should implicitly recognise that a user is going to make mistakes and should not only allow for this but allow user deviations from the expected norm of interaction to provide useful and positive feedback to the user about how to make the best use of the system.

5 Make the range of alternative actions within the user interface visible to the user

Too many user interfaces require the user to remember different alternative actions or sequences of actions. Placing such a memory burden on the user not only reduces the speed and facility with which they can handle the system but is also likely to disenchant them with using the system at all. Useability designers must make the most of the computer screen's potential for giving users verbal guidance on how to use the system.

6 *Don't require the user to refer to the accompanying manual more than is absolutely necessary and consider doing away with it completely*

When a user has to refer to a manual, this is in effect a failure of the user interface. Sometimes, with a complex piece of technology, occasional references to the manual may be inevitable, but this is not at all the case with financial technology applications, where the user should in almost all cases be able to understand how to use the computer and the application by referring to the financial system itself. Any complex instructions are invariably better presented on the computer screen than in a manual. Once you send your user to a manual, you run the risk that he might not come back.

Finally, bear this in mind:

not even the most brilliantly conceived and ingenious computer system can do all that it was designed to do – or even a small part of what it was designed to do – unless the brilliance and simplicity of its operation and purpose is matched by the cunning simplicity of its user interface.

If computers are indeed the ultimate tool, and man the ultimate tool-maker, then we need to extract the maximum benefit from computers if we are to inherit the best of our evolutionary heritage. If, on the other hand, we do not extract the maximum benefit from computers then we are squandering our evolutionary heritage and perhaps even destroying it.

To show good useability design in action, here is an illustrated case study involving a system deployed by the stockbroking arm of a UK clearing bank the National Westminster Bank. The useability design and system design was undertaken by Henley-on-Thames useability designer AIT Limited.

Case study
NATWEST STOCKBROKERS TOUCHSCREEN DEALING SERVICE

Background

The Touchscreen instant payment dealing service, Suffolk, was launched to provide private individuals with a simple and visible method of buying and selling British Gas shares following its privatisation in 1986.

Selected NatWest branches were issued with PCs with a touch sensitive screen, linked to a mainframe computer. Certain parts of the buying and selling process, for example obtaining the latest price, are carried out by touching designated areas of the screen.

The service provides sellers with a cheque for the proceeds at the time of dealing. It is available to individuals whether customers or noncustomers of NatWest.

The service has been used for all subsequent privatisation issues and for the water privatisation issue in 1989 it was extended to cope with up to fifteen companies at the same time. The Suffolk system has proved very successful and high volumes have been achieved. In the Regional Electricity Companies privatisation over 28,000 trades were carried out in one day and the total over 6 weeks was over 270,000.

In 1988 a new Touchscreen service, SHADE (SHAre DEaling), was developed enabling customers of NatWest to buy and sell shares in the top 100 companies for conventional Stock Exchange account settlement. SHADE has since been extended to over 500 stocks and has also been opened up to investors who do not bank with NatWest. This service is not aimed at the very high volume achieved at the time of a privatisation issue

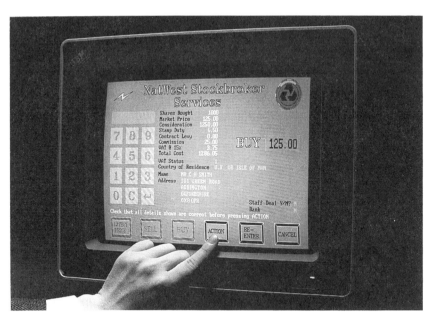

Figure 4.1   The transaction screen user interface for the NatWest Stockbrokers share dealing service.
Source: NatWest Stockbrokers

but over 5,000 trades have been carried out in one day through the system and its capacity is higher.

With Touchscreen, NatWest have succeeded in bringing the stock market to the high street.

How 'Suffolk' works

An investor, whether they bank with NatWest or not, may go into any of the 278 NatWest branches which have a Touchscreen and request the price of the latest privatisation issue. Where there is more than one stock the required stock is selected from the list shown on the screen, and the current buying and selling prices are displayed. These prices are the best buying and the best selling prices published by all market makers at that time. If the client wishes to proceed with the purchase or sale the quantity to buy or sell is entered and the breakdown of figures which will appear on the contract note are displayed on the screen showing what funds, if the deal is completed, the customer will receive or will have to pay.

The customer's name and address and other details are entered into the system and the deal is then completed. The price first shown is guaranteed provided the deal is completed within five minutes, even if the price changes in the market. For sales, the contract note and a settlement cheque are printed and for purchases only the contract note is printed.

Examples of the volumes transacted through Suffolk are:

	Total transactions	Peak day
British Gas	168,000	23,400
British Airways	69,000	16,800
Rolls Royce	89,000	20,800
BAA	86,000	26,100
Abbey National	174,000	23,000
Water	134,000	27,500
Regional Electricity Co's	272,000	28,000

How 'SHADE' works

The screen prompts for either the mnemonic code for the required security or there is a search facility on the first letters of the company's name. Once the stock has been selected the current buying and selling prices are displayed. Like Suffolk, these prices are the best buying and the best selling prices in the market among all market makers at that time.

If the customer wishes to proceed, the amount to be sold or bought is entered. If the customer wants to raise or invest a set amount this is entered and the system calculates how many have to be sold or how many shares can be bought. Details of the transaction are then displayed on the screen illustrating all the figures that will show on the contract note.

The customer's full name and address and, where available, bank details are then entered. The deal may still be aborted up to this point. Once the customer confirms that all the details are correct the deal is completed. The contract note is then produced on the spot and for sales a Talisman Sold Transfer form is printed.

NatWest customers buying shares have their bank account debited on the Stock Exchange settlement day. Noncustomers, however, pay by cheque or cash at the time of dealing. For sales, NatWest customers have their accounts credited on settlement day and nonNatWest customers either have their bank account credited or, if no bank details are entered, they are sent a cheque.

Equipment used

The model of PCs installed in branches are based on the IBM PS2 range. The communication links are through an internal network although certain branches do use British Telecom lines. These are linked to the IBM network and mainframe computer.

Typical real-life problems and their solutions

Finally, let us return to the problems outlined at the beginning of this chapter, and consider how an understanding of the issues discussed in this chapter could help solve them.

Problem:

- a system being abandoned in the development stage because it becomes clear that its original objectives were unrealistic

Solution:
Bear in mind that computers are tools designed to solve problems, not bewildering white elephants. The unrealistic objectives should not have been formulated in the first place, any more than you would think of using a hammer to make a telephone call.

When designing a system, you should have ready access to knowledge regarding which objectives are unrealistic and which are realistic and if you do not have ready access to this information then find out what you need to know.

Above all, do not be bamboozled by slick-talking systems salesmen that computers can work miracles. They can't. Remember that when it comes to thinking for oneself, earthworms have one over on computers any day.

Problem:

● the failure of a system to carry out its original objectives

Solution:
There is nothing magical about putting a system together. You should plan the entire implementation process from the outset and you should know in advance what is going to happen at every stage. If you aren't confident (and do not have reasons for being confident) that the system will finally do what it is supposed to do, you shouldn't be planning it. No one builds a bridge and then finds out whether it will support the weight of the traffic that will pass over it. One expects civil engineers to find out this sort of thing beforehand.

Problem:

● the failure of a financial technologist to understand what these objectives are

Solution:
It sounds as if someone is launching into the development process simply because their rivals are building something similar. Any financial institution which starts a programme for systems deployment without being crystal-clear about the objectives of the system is either corporately insane or irresponsible.

Problem:

● where the technologist does know what the objectives are but fails to communicate them satisfactorily to the institution's staff

Solution:
The staff are probably afraid of computers and regard them as semi-mystical instruments of redundancy and early retirement. The staff must be educated in a more positive (and more realistic) manner.

Problem:

- the failure of individual members of staff to like using a system (or, more correctly stated, the failure of a system to prove likeable)

Solution:
Unless a member of staff is being deliberately obstructive (which *does* happen), it is difficult to see what motive a staff member would have to find a computer a problem. The problem is probably in the useability design. Call in a good useability designer.

Problem:

- the failure of individual members of staff to use a system to its maximum potential

Solution:
Is someone afraid of the computer? Do they think it will explode if they press the wrong button? They need education, and the computer might need some refinements in its user interface.

Problem:

- the failure of the institution to get maximum value for money out of a system

Solution:
The institution needs to explore all the possible benefits which the system can provide. It is more than likely that the system is being underutilised. Even if this is not demonstrably the case, a small modification of the program may bring considerable benefits in terms of increased functionality or – which may be even more relevant – increased flexibility of existing functionality.

Problem:

- the failure of the institution to extract maximum competitive advantage out of a system.

Solution:
Obviously, not enough thought has been given to deciding how exactly the computer should be used as a tool to gain a competitive edge. Ideally this

thinking should take place when the system is being planned, but even now it may not be too late. Take a long look at what the competition is doing and see how exactly your system can either do what they are doing, but do it better, or else do something that they are not doing. Unfortunately, adopting this approach may reveal to you that you ought to have a new system to achieve these competitive advantages. In this case there would be no alternative but to start again, and plan things better this time.

Which brings us neatly to the next chapter.

5 MANAGING THE IMPLEMENTATION PROCESS

Introduction

There is nothing magical about putting a system together. This statement, which appeared towards the end of the previous chapter, can be used as a convenient starting point for this chapter, which looks at the specifics of deploying a computer system within a financial institution.

It is surprising that many financial technologists, even those with extensive experience in implementing a financial system, often regard the implementation process as a voyage into the unknown.

Such a voyage sounds vaguely romantic, but there really is nothing romantic about bringing a project in well over budget or abandoning a system half way through because it has become clear that it will not be able to carry out the objectives agreed at the outset or completing a system but finding that rival institutions have already deployed systems that make your new resource obsolete before it has even been fully deployed.

There is only one way to minimise the likelihood of these problems occurring and that is to front-load the project in terms of planning. It was the great Dr Johnson who said, 'Marry in haste; repent at leisure' and much the same might be said of implementing a financial system. 'Implement in haste; repent at leisure.' The difference is that, whereas the fellow in Dr Johnson's aphorism was stuck with his bride, anybody who is responsible for a major failure in financial systems implementation is likely to find that they do their repenting at home, while they wait for a reply to job applications.

No one wants that to happen, so let us get things right at the outset.

When I was planning this book I was keen to find a case study which would illustrate all the points that I propose in the following discussion. I cast my mind through all the financial system implementations that had come to my notice during the past few years and I wondered whether any of these could usefully be written up as an instructive guide.

The problem was, every real-life implementation that I studied seemed to me to contain some element, some part, that had been fudged or which had turned out well by accident rather than by design. Now, I am well aware that things sometimes work out well in the financial technology industry, contrary to all expectations, and that fudging (by which I mean putting some degree of trust in fate to make things go properly) also sometimes works, but such examples hardly seemed instructive here.

Of course, I encountered – and still encounter – numerous examples of how *not* to do it, and it is true that they might have considerable instructive value in much the same way that people can sometimes be dissuaded from smoking by being shown a cancerous lung in a jar. Indeed, I know of one case which involved a leading Wall Street investment bank losing more than one million dollars in a project that involved building a complex system for arbitrage between derivatives and underlying stocks. However, discussing this case in detail, and giving the name of the bank, would be a sure way to land in a libel court.

In any event, in a chapter such as this, which aims to focus on general issues which the reader can then apply to his individual case, it may be that case studies – inevitably focusing on the particular as they do – are superfluous anyway and would only serve to dilute the text and detract from the main arguments. I have therefore resolved to omit them.

The challenge of implementation

For any financial technologist, the task of deploying a new type of financial system will be one of the most interesting and important challenges that faces him. Even if you yourself are not likely to have anything to do with the actual implementation process; even if you will delegate much of this task to an external consultancy or a financial systems house, you will probably find what follows to be of interest, particularly because – as will become clear – I believe that no external organisation deserves to be given a completely free hand in managing the implementation of a financial system.

Throughout what follows I have tried to focus on the key issues at every stage. Some of the material is discursive, but I have attempted to boil down the advice to particular principles where possible. The intention has been to focus on the specific tasks that must be completed at each stage of the implementation process.

STAGE ONE: PREPARATORY PLANNING

As the tail end of the last chapter has already suggested, it really is impossible to spend too much time on the planning of a new financial system. Most systems that either fail or go wildly over budget or which are abandoned at some point during the implementation period, suffer from inadequate preparatory planning.

As soon as an idea for implementing a new financial system has gone beyond the casual stage, a group of people should be formed which will be responsible for the planning process. This group of people will typically include a member of each of the following:

● senior management
● practitioners (eg traders and back-office staff)
● information technology department.

In addition, there will usually be outsiders involved from the outset. These people will typically include some or all of the following:

● management consultants
● software engineers
● financial systems specialists (eg with experience in a specific package or programming language).

Once this group has gathered together, it is as well to choose a *project manager* at the beginning. Some institutions use external consultants for project management and get on very well with this. There are in fact some consultancies which offer specialised project management consultant. However, it is difficult to see why an institution does not take the obvious step of using an in-house member of staff as the project manager. Using an in-house person will maximise the likelihood that the institution will be in control of its own project.

As regards the precise choice of project manager, the person chosen should be senior enough to have authority over all the other people who will work on the project, yet not so senior that he is engaged on other demands and is remote from the project at hand.

The following directives are the minimum undertakings necessary for all planning committees.

1 Analyse the motives for the implementation

Why are you considering the implementation?

Is the implementation simply a 'knee-jerk' reaction to a rival institution's implementation?

If so, are you sure that it will give you the opportunity to gain competitive advantage and serve your customers better? If not, why do it?

Decide whether you are following an 'attacking' or 'defensive' strategy. An attacking strategy is one where you are seeking to out-compete your rivals; a defensive strategy is one where you are seeking to minimise damage caused by a competitor seeking to out-compete you. Ideally, your implementation should be based around an attacking strategy. If you conclude that you are following a defensive strategy, could you convert it into an attacking strategy (eg by adding new features and functions to the system)?

How do you want to profile your institution? Are you go-ahead, dynamic, hungry for new business or are you more traditional, cautious, keen to maintain long-lasting relationships with customers who may be shy of technology? Ask yourself other searching questions, in particular:

- what are our main areas of business now?
- what are likely to be our main areas of business in five and ten years' time?
- what kind of computer facilities are we offering our customers now and how could these facilities be improved?
- what kind of computer facilities are we offering our staff now and how could these facilities be improved?
- what area(s) of our operations do we feel could be made more efficient and cost-effective by the deployment of technology?
- are we all right as we are? If not, why not?
- are we big enough to make the implementation?
- could we handle the additional business that the new system might bring?
- is it technologically feasible to achieve what we want to achieve?
- can we afford to change? The answer to this particular question will depend on what meaning your accountants attach to the word 'afford'.

If the answers to too many of the questions above are negative, do not be afraid of abandoning the idea of initiating the implementation: at least for the time being. It is much better to admit the unfeasibility of a projected implementation at an early stage than to proceed with it to save face and then be obliged to scrap the idea at a more expensive later stage.

2 Formulate a feasibility study

This study should focus on the following factors:

- a realistic expectation of what the system could be expected to achieve for your institution
- a statement of why the institution ought to initiate the implementation

- a statement of why the proposed system is technologically possible
- cost justification
- an estimate of how long the system will be viable and useful as a generator of competitive advantage before entering technological obsolescence and confirmation that the period of useful service is likely to justify the cost and effort of deploying the system
- the feasibility study should also usefully focus on the particular stage which the system occupies within the evolution of financial systems (ie inception, growth or maturity phase – see pages 95–7 for a discussion of these terms); in most cases an institution should only contemplate an implementation of a system that is in the growth phase, where the essential feasibility of the technology has already been proven in the marketplace, and where the institution not only has the real prospect of gaining a competitive advantage from implementing the system, but may in time to come run into problems competing with its rivals if it does *not* deploy the system.

The feasibility report's purpose is to *investigate* (rather than simply to seek to confirm or deny an uninformed supposition) whether, in broad terms, the system is a realistic possibility for the organisation and to give the reasons for its conclusion. There should be no attempt to present the feasibility study as a foregone conclusion. It is much better to abort a suggested system that looks likely to be of doubtful value or to present major technical problems rather than to persist with it.

STAGE TWO: DEFINING THE SYSTEM'S REQUIREMENTS

Once a basic decision has been made to proceed with deploying a new system, the project can enter the second planning phase. Here, definite decisions are made about what precise functions the system will need to carry out and how acceptable a system which carries out those functions is likely to prove to its intended users.

The precise functions of the system can generally be arrived at by refining the findings of the feasibility study until they make as close a match as possible to the needs of the institution. Care must be taken to ensure that the needs of the institution do not exceed those functions which are feasible. A system's failure to do that which it was originally designed to do is perhaps the most common of all system failures and this danger can be guarded against by erring on the side of modest rather than extreme ambitions. Remember that a financial system is a tool which must do the same thing, or similar things, over and over again if it is to be successful; the task must be feasible and practical all the way along the line.

The following are the principal questions that must be answered on the way to a comprehensive definition of the functions of the system:

- why are we deploying this system?
- within what areas of our activity will it operate?
- which of the following types of system is it going to be?
    a) an automated payment system
    b) a front-office information reception system
    c) a front-office decision support system
    d) a back-office system?
- which staff will have to use the system and how will they use it?
- which customers will have to use the system and how will they use it?
- what are the specific tasks that the system will have to carry out?
- which financial instruments will it have to handle (if applicable)?
- in which financial markets will the system operate (if applicable)?
- in which currencies will it have to operate (if applicable)?

One very useful piece of advice at this crucial stage where the specifications of the system are being formulated is that, in those cases where the system is primarily targeted towards the general public, *it is usually far better – from the point of view of winning new business and establishing a competitive advantage – to make the system part of an entire new marketing initiative by basing a new product or service around it rather than simply making the new system part of an existing product or service.*

A good example of what this means in practical terms within the retail financial sector is the Halifax Building Society's 'Cardcash' account, launched in July 1983. This highly successful account, which attained more than 1,000,000 cardholders by January 1986 and which was to gain nearly a further 3,000,000 by the end of the 1990s – and which continues to flourish – is remarkable in that it was the first retail banking account in the UK which was conceived entirely from the outset as an ATM-based account.

The Halifax Building Society did not simply launch its ATM network as part of its existing service, but created an entirely new product and service based around ATMs. This is easily the best way to deploy a new retail financial system: to make it part of a new product and marketing initiative rather than to make the financial system an end in itself.

Similarly, when, in 1988, the UK investment bank Barclays de Zoete

Wedd (BZW) launched a PC-based automated trading system for small (ie 'retail') share transactions which gave brokers the option of installing the system in their offices and enjoying access to the technology as well as BZW's commitment to matching the 'best execution' price within the market for a particular size of transaction, BZW did not make the system an extension of their existing service. Instead, BZW created an entirely new product, branded 'TRADE', which enjoyed considerable success, even in the depressed share markets of the post-Crash period.

As far as assessing the likely suitability of the system is concerned, further research will most likely be required. This research should look into the following matters, at the least:

- if the system is designed to be used by the public, it will be necessary to obtain some *independent*, unbiased research on the likely acceptability, or otherwise, of the new system among the public
- if the system is designed to be used by the institution's staff, it will be necessary to obtain some objective input regarding the system's likely acceptability, or otherwise, among staff.

The discussion in the previous chapter on computers as tools and computer useability is particularly relevant to this phase.

STAGE THREE: PRODUCING A BUDGET ESTIMATE

It is best to set down an accurate estimate of the budget at an early stage. The budget is of course the cost of the system to the institution, but it must be viewed in the light of the expected impact on the institution's revenue and profitability. These matters are not always easy to assess. For example, it is widely recognised within the retail banking industry that telephone banking not only brings with it the prospect of more customers being drawn to the telephone banking service itself but also cost savings being eventually made from a smaller number of customers needing to visit branches and consequently fewer staff being needed to man those branches and fewer branches themselves being needed. Obviously, forecasting cost benefits that depend on so many variables is highly complex, and specialised advice may be needed.

Generally, the budget will need to cover costs of the following:

- hardware
- software

- communications
- design
- project management
- training
- promotion (eg cost of advertising, public relations, direct mail and other marketing-related costs associated with communicating the benefits of the proposed new system to the people who will actually use it). For systems that will purely be used by staff (eg administrative systems) there will be the need to look at the cost of in-house communication of the benefits of the system to staff
- costs of using all external suppliers (eg hardware suppliers, network engineers, software operators, computer security consultants, computer useability consultants, information technology consultants and vendors of peripherals such as plastic cards and cheque books.)
- cost of using the institution's own staff. Many institutions forget that even where they are using their own staff to help operate and manage the implementation of a new system, there is an *opportunity cost* of using these staff, with this cost being the lost profit which the staff would otherwise be generating for the institution.

Once the budget has been estimated it can be considered in conjunction with the likely benefits. There is now a major opportunity to decide whether the figures add up and whether or not to proceed with the system.

Again, it is far better to drop a proposal which looks unpromising at this stage rather than to press on in stubborn fashion and risk a much more costly abandonment at a later stage.

STAGE FOUR: INTERPRETING THE SYSTEM'S REQUIREMENTS IN TECHNOLOGICAL TERMS

This is where the actual technical means to realise the aims of the system are investigated.

Examples of the kinds of questions that must be addressed here are as follows:

- what hardware will the system run on?
- who will design the software?
- which modified/unmodified package shall we buy (if appropriate)?
- what operating system shall we use?
- what level of memory will the system require? (NB: this must include

memory that you envisage will be needed in the future, not merely memory which will be required when the system is first deployed)

- in broad terms, what kind of user interface will the system have?
- what kind of in-house (LAN) communications will feature in the system?
- what kind of external (WAN) communications will feature in the system?
- what kind of computer security should the system feature?

An important part of this stage is the decision regarding which method to use to construct the system. Unfortunately, it is not possible to provide a list of recommended technology for various different types of application and equally impractical to suggest methods of construction to tally with certain applications. The reason for this is that applying financial technology to a particular application need is a flexible, creative task that can only be completed with any chance of success if each particular application is assessed with all the unique characteristics of the individual case in mind.

Another reason is that the 'answer' to the question: *what technology should we use to build such a system as this*? clearly depends on what technology is available and how technology is progressing. To take a simple example, a financial application which could only have been carried out with a mainframe computer in the mid-1980s might now be capable of being discharged with a Midrange computer, so quickly have Midrange machines equalled – and even exceeded – the power of all but the very largest mainframes.

However, despite all of the above, there are certainly some useful practical rules to bear in mind when deciding how to use technology to meet the need of an application within the financial sector. These relate to whether the system is to be built on an entirely customised basis, whether it is to be a modified (ie partly customised) package or whether a completely off-the-shelf package will suffice. This crucial decision has already been discussed on pages 66–8.

As far as making the requisite *precise* match between application and technology, this can only be achieved by a specialist information technology manager – probably assisted by a team of specialists. These specialists may already work for your institution (you might be one) or they will work for an external organisation such as an information technology consultancy which is hired specifically to manage the technological aspects of the implementation.

In any event, by the end of this stage the institution should know what the system will, or should, do when it is complete and what technological means will be used to build the system.

The institution will sometimes wish to build a prototype. This usually occurs where the system is fully customised. Prototypes are on the face of it a good idea, but they cost money and may slow down the implementation process, thereby reducing the competitive advantage of the deployment. It is arguable that if preparatory planning has been thorough, a prototype will not be necessary.

STAGE FIVE: GATHERING THE TOOLS OF IMPLEMENTATION

This stage involves the institution finalising its plans for what it wants to do and assembling the different items of technology and other resources which it will use in order to achieve its objectives.

It is during this phase that the plan to build the system ceases to be a mere theoretical proposal and starts to solidify into a real-life sequence of activities that will result in the system being built.

Note that the process of 'gathering the tools of implementation' means much more than simply deciding which vendors are going to supply the technology which is used to build the system. The tools of implementation in fact cover all aspects of the system's construction, launch and continued existence. Typically, an institution will need to select vendors in some, or all, of the following categories, with the possibility always existing that the institution may select more than one vendor in each category:

- hardware supplier (ie suppliers of workstations as well as the principal computer)
- software designer
- systems house (if an entire system is being bought in, possibly prior to modification)
- project manager (see Stages One and Six)
- communications system supplier
- training organisation (particularly if the system is to be used mainly by staff)
- useability design consultancy
- financial information vendor
- decision support analytics vendor
- artificial intelligence vendor (for a rule-based or neural net system)
- plastic card vendor (for an ATM or EFTPOS initiative)
- telephone banking system vendor
- cheque book printing vendor

- advertising agency (for an automated payment system that will be promoted to the public)
- public relations consultancy (for an automated payment system that will be promoted to the public)
- direct mail agency (for an automated payment system that will be promoted to the public).

The institution will have to start making a serious financial commitment to the project at this stage, since contractual agreements will need to be entererd into by the institution and selected vendors. Naturally, this means that the institution should take considerable effort to ensure that the vendors selected are the right ones for it. As far as the vendor selection process is concerned, the case study on pages 132–7 takes you through this process by reference to the construction of a real-life system that was deployed in September 1992.

STAGE SIX: IMPLEMENTATION

The implementation stage concerns all the processes involved in bringing the new system to a stage where it can be used.

The first, and most important, issue to address is the relationship between the project manager and his team. The project manager will basically be responsible for the timely and on-budget progression of the project and should not hesitate to apply pressure if he feels that the project is falling behind schedule or that some members of the team (whether in-house or external members) are not pulling their weight.

Many institutions, while keeping the project manager within their own ranks, prefer to delegate much of the implementation process to an external consultancy. This is likely to be particularly the case if a modified or unmodified package is being used, when it is likely that the consultancy may have originally specified the package.

There are many good consultancies around and it is probably true that the recession has at least had the beneficial effect of weeding out many of the worst ones, but even the best consultancies need to be kept on a tight rein.

The point is that, ultimately, the only thing that one can say with any certainty about using a consultancy is that the consultancy's top priority will be to make as much money from your institution as it possibly can while retaining your goodwill. The consultancy may have other, nobler, priorities but this will be the top one.

Be assured that not only will the consultancy place its own interests before your institution's, but it will hardly give a moment's thought to any other approach. Consultancies can certainly provide excellent input towards solving one or more specific technological or logistical problems associated with your new system. However, there is little sense in allowing them to control every aspect of the system's implementation – which is precisely why institutions are well advised to appoint an in-house project manager.

Note, incidentally, that the project manager(s) – whether this be an individual or a team – does not necessarily require a detailed knowledge of the technology that is being deployed. What they do need is a very close acquaintanceship with the objectives of the system and in particular they should know exactly what the system should do when it is installed and what it should cost. Some external vendors are only too glad to try to bamboozle an institution with technological complexity and to inflate the budget through additional, noncontracted areas of activity which somehow become 'highly advisable' or even 'essential' once the project has started. Don't let them get away with it!

Naturally enough, the project manager really comes into his own during the implementation stage. In summary, the principal tasks of the project manager are as follows:

- select any additional or replacement vendors during the implementation phase (the project manager will already have selected the principal vendors)
- manage all the separate resources needed to complete the project. This includes technological resources (eg hardware and software) and peripherals (eg new customer literature, plastic cards and new cheque books)
- liaise with selected vendors and ensure that they stick to their contractural agreements
- ensure that the cost of the project stays within budget (or within a prearranged allowance over budget)
- arrange staff training in using the new system
- arrange for the marketing campaign (if applicable) for the system. As we have seen, a marketing campaign will be required in most cases where the new system is an automated banking system (eg ATM, EFTPOS or telephone banking deployment) which is designed to boost the institution's profile and quality or service to the general public
- monitor the installation of the prototype system (if applicable) and either make the final decision on whether (or when) to proceed to the final version of the system or refer this decision to a higher decision-making entity (eg the institution's Board).

STAGE SEVEN: POST-IMPLEMENTATION

The institution's involvement with a new type of system does not come to an end once the new system is in place. A concerted and consistent programme of post-implementation monitoring is essential in order to ensure that the benefits of the initiative to the institution – and to its customers – are maximised.

The institution should regard the post-implementation task as being part of the project management process and should undertake this task itself in most cases.

The main areas on which the post-implementation stage should focus are as follows:

- satisfactory technological operation of the system
- areas where technological modification is required
- general quality of useability of the system
- take-up of the new system among customers (where applicable)
- acceptability of the system to staff
- increased revenue and profits ascribable to the system
- impact of the system on the institution's overall profile.

The project manager should ensure that the correct resources are put in place to monitor all these areas. One particularly useful strategy here, if the institution's budget can stand it, is to appoint an entirely new consultancy to monitor the system post-implementation, since this approach is naturally more likely to reveal problems with the system and areas where further work is still required than if the system were monitored by the consultancy or systems house which initially installed it.

Finally, all contracts with suppliers should contain an element where the final part of the payment is only made once the system has been operating successfully for a certain period, say one month. This approach means that the consultancy or systems house is likely to jump to attention when teething problems are reported to it early on after implementation, whereas otherwise the institution might find that the external organisation is suddenly too busy to make a rapid response to the problem.

6 MANAGING COMPUTER SECURITY

Introduction

Let us begin with some definitions.

'Computer security' is here defined as *any implementation or activity directed at maintaining or improving the integrity, operation and resistance to internal or external unauthorised interference of a computer installation*, whilst a 'computer security breach' is considered to be *any actual breach in the integrity or security of the installation*. A 'hazard' or 'threat' is regarded as *any potential attack on the installation*, and a 'precautionary measure' is *any measure taken to prevent a threat to the installation from being realised*.

We also need a term for someone who wilfully seeks to cause, or actually causes, a computer security breach. It is tempting to refer to such a person as a 'computer criminal' but this term is not entirely accurate, since in many countries the enactment of computer security breaches is not illegal and even exploiting these breaches for personal gain is invariably not illegal. My preferred term, 'unauthorised person', is somewhat less glamorous than 'computer criminal', but more accurate. In particular, it acknowledges that an unauthorised person may well be someone working within the financial institution who is authorised to use a particular element of the installation but not the element that is the subject of the breach. Although no reliable statistics are available on the proportion of wilful computer security breaches which are 'inside' jobs, there is no doubt that the vast majority of such breaches are either entirely inside jobs or perpetrated with the connivance of an insider.

THE NEED FOR AN INTEGRATED APPROACH TOWARDS COMPUTER SECURITY

Computer security within financial institutions is a wide-ranging and often controversial subject, but one matter on which there is great unanimity is the need for an institution to adopt a unified approach towards hazard analysis and the implementation of precautionary measures. In other words, it is widely agreed that an institution ought to plan and deploy computer security-related precautionary measures simultaneously across all its range of functions.

There are three principal reasons for unanimity on the need for this integrated approach:

1 a financial institution benefits from economies of scale in having the same in-house staff or consultants working on a defence against the different hazards
2 management will benefit from better hazard control if all hazards are planned for and guarded against in a unified manner
3 an integrated and comprehensive programme of threat analysis will make the implementation of the necessary precautionary measures easier and more effective than would be the case if the implementation were carried out on a piecemeal basis.

THE EXTENT OF COMPUTER SECURITY BREACHES IN FINANCIAL INSTITUTIONS

It is not possible to obtain any reliable information for the extent to which financial institutions in any particular country and over any particular period of time suffer computer security breaches. The reason for this is that financial institutions which have suffered any kind of computer security breach are less than willing to publicise the fact. None the less, the following points can be made:

- minor computer security breaches, such as lost data due to physical damage or loss, frequently occur at most financial institutions
- major computer security breaches, such as computer fraud, the intro-duction of viruses and unauthorised persons obtaining access to data, probably occur with some regularity at financial institutions which take inadequate precautions to prevent these from happening
- retail financial institutions generally have more effective precautionary measures in place than do commercial financial institutions because they believe that any public perception that they are vulnerable to computer-related fraud or computer breakdown would be disastrous for business
- large financial institutions generally have more effective precautionary measures in place than small- to medium-sized financial institutions, which is usually because large institutions have greater computer security budgets than smaller institutions, and are able to benefit from the eco-nomies of scale which occur in implementing precautionary measures.

COMPUTER SECURITY HAZARDS

The major types of hazard

One problem facing anyone involved in computer security is that there is an over glamorised, largely inaccurate public perception of the nature of computer security hazards and the types of people who wilfully cause them. This perception is often shared by those senior executives of a financial institution who control the budget (if any) for implementing precautionary measures against computer security breaches.

This public perception is that computer fraudsters are cunning, gifted people who, from some safe haven, do clever things with a computer terminal in order to 'hack' into a computer system and wind up greatly enriched. In fact, the majority of breaches and their perpetrators are considerably less glamorous than this, even if equally dangerous. In reality, computer security for a financial institution is more than just a matter of stopping unauthorised persons from 'hacking' into the institution's computer system to obtain valuable information or to divert funds illicitly to a secret account in a Swiss bank. Computer security might well alternatively be termed computer hygiene, that is, it concerns all the knowledge and practice associated with maintaining the health of a computer system. Broadly speaking, the health of a financial institution's computer system will have been protected if it has implemented the maximum level of protection against the major types of hazard, namely:

- physical destruction or damage
- temporary or permanent loss of power
- interference with the computer system by an unauthorised person.

Examples of physical destruction or damage range from a catastrophic event such as a fire in the computer room or part of the building where a principal computer is housed to spilling coffee over a computer disk and thereby rendering it unusable. The extent of the damage caused will depend on the task being carried out by the damaged element of the institution's computer resources and the length of time during which the computer installation – or part of it – is out of action.

The great information processing power of computers means that even damage to a small element of a computer installation can be extremely costly to the financial institution which suffers the damage. For example, if the spilt coffee renders unusable a computer disk which contains a unique list of the names and addresses of a thousand arduously researched new business prospects then the impact of the damage within an institution will be great, despite the accident being relatively insignificant.

Examples of temporary or permanent loss of power range from the failure of a local mains electricity supply to a fuse being blown in a plug that powers a computer terminal. Again, the impact of the damage will depend on the loss of information (if any) and the loss of function.

The third type of hazard – interference with the computer system by an unauthorised person – is the one on which this chapter principally focuses. There are two main reasons.

1 Unauthorised interference (which, as we have seen, is much more likely to involve an existing member of staff than a complete stranger) takes many potential forms, from a major fraud to someone gaining illicit access, at a terminal level, to confidential information. As such, protecting against unauthorised interference requires far more ingenuity than protecting against physical destruction or damage and temporary or permanent loss of power.

2 The measures which need to be taken by a financial institution to protect its computer system against physical destruction or damage and temporary or permanent loss of power belong to the realm of common sense and good general management. There is, however, inevitably a chance element in such physical accidents which can never be completely eradicated. *However, an effective computer security strategy should be able either to eliminate the risk of unauthorised interference or else reduce it to an absolute minimum.*

Why computers are generally so vulnerable to security hazards

There are three main reasons why computers are particularly vulnerable to security hazards.

1 *Computers are made of relatively fragile components.* As tools, computers suffer from the great disadvantage that, unlike many less sophisticated tools (such as screwdrivers and hammers), they are extremely vulnerable to physical damage. Computers are generally built out of wire, plastic and glass (for the screens) and the more compact computer components become, the more likely it is that a relatively minor accident can cause substantial damage. Furthermore, although developments in computer technology since the mid-1980s have meant that powerful computers can often be located in ordinary office environments, many host computers, even now, make special demands in terms of physical location in that they must be accommodated in rooms with special air conditioning and provisions to

guard against electromagnetic interference if they are to work efficiently or at all.

2 *Modern computers are compact and powerful.* Whereas the earliest computers that were built in the 1940s or even earlier provided relatively little processing power despite being large and cumbersome, today's computers have a high power to size ratio. This means not only that damage to a relatively small component can have grave consequences in terms of lost data, but also that unauthorised interference which is directed at a small part of the entire system can none the less have a powerful influence over the entire system. Such power is attractive to an unauthorised user, who will hope to avoid detection by being involved illicitly with the system for the minimum time.

3 *Computers already have a great utility, and this is increasing.* As a result, computers are being increasingly widely used, which naturally creates a growing number of opportunities for unauthorised interference.

Why financial institutions' computers are particularly vulnerable to hazards

In addition to the general reasons why computers are vulnerable to hazards, there are also several important reasons why computers used by financial institutions are especially vulnerable to hazards.

1 *Financial institutions are increasingly heavy users of computer systems.* Not only are financial institutions already major users of computers, but the role which computers are now playing in institutions as a marketing tool and therefore a competitive weapon means that financial institutions are likely to be using computers even more in the future than they are at present.

2 *The information passing through financial institutions' computer systems relates directly to money.* Although obvious this is none the less an important point. The computer systems which financial institutions use are either transmitting that most desired of commodities, money, or else handling money-related information.

3 *Financial institutions' computer systems usually run in real-time.* Real-time processing (or 'online transaction processing') is a term used to describe the way in which data is communicated across a communications line within a computer system. When information is sent in real-time (or 'online') the information is transmitted the instant it becomes available and reaches the recipient with a speed limited only by the speed of electromagnetic waves (where radio communications are being used) or by the speed of electrons through a wire. Since these speeds are the speed of light and one-sixth of the

speed of light, respectively, real-time and online communications are considered to be instantaneous. Although, where the sender or recipient is many thousands of miles away, slight delays in switching and in transmission may result in a delay of a few seconds.

Real-time communications are used extensively within the financial sector. Typical examples of such applications are the link between a bank's automated teller machines (ATMs) and the bank's host computer; a credit transfer system for sending funds to external counterparties; and a foreign exchange trading system that allows dealing with external counterparties.

The widespread use of real-time processing within the financial sector has two major repercussions for computer security. Firstly, interfering with a real-time system is likely to be particularly attractive to people bent on fraud, since the real-time nature of the system means that by the time the fraud is detected the funds obtained illicitly may already have been diverted to the fraudster's own account. Secondly, there is a powerful momentum within any financial institution running a real-time processing system to *keep the system running*, at all costs, in order to avoid defaulting on obligations to clients and customers. A computer fraudster knows that this momentum exists and that many financial institutions will do their utmost to keep their real-time processing system running, even if they suspect that the system is being interfered with by an unauthorised person. Indeed, most financial institutions deploy *fault-tolerant* host computers to run their real-time processing systems, so that a fault in a component of the host computer does not lead to system failure – further evidence of institutions wishing to keep the system running at all costs.

4 *Financial institutions make extensive use of packaged computer software*. Packaged computer software, or 'packages' as they are known in the computer trade, are software modules which have usually been designed by a specialised external organisation. Packages are available for a wide range of financial sector applications. Because buying in a package is almost invariably cheaper than designing customised software from scratch, and also because many financial institutions may not have the in-house resources to design the software, therefore packages are popular in the financial sector. Unfortunately, they carry with them two major security hazards.

Firstly, the widespread use of packages means that someone bent on unauthorised interference may be able to acquire a knowledge of one popular package and use this knowledge in interfering with many institutions' computer systems.

Secondly, the simple act of loading the package into a financial institution's computer system is itself fraught with potential danger, since if the package contains a deliberately or inadvertently introduced rogue element such as a 'virus' or 'logic bomb', the financial institution's entire computer system might quickly be infected.

5 *Financial institutions increasingly use open architectures.* Open architectures are computer system protocols which allow a financial institution to make use of any software which has been written to conform to the open architecture in question. Examples of open architectures are UNIX and DOS. Financial institutions use open architectures because these give them great flexibility to deploy a wide range of customised and packaged software. However, the increasingly widespread use of open architectures gives more scope to those who wish to interfere with a computer system, since greater standardisation of computer systems means that an illicit approach can be developed to attack the open architecture and can then be tried on any financial institution which does not have adequate computer security precautions in place.

6 *Increasing competition between financial institutions may tempt management to cut costs by skimping on computer security.* The days when financial institutions, retail or commercial, could count on retaining a secure client or customer base for years on end are past. Today, even the longest-established institutions must fight for market share and profitability, which means that they must pay as strict attention to costs as they do to making an impact in the marketplace. All too often, the result of this strict attention to costs is that computer security provisions are cut back or not implemented.

MANAGEMENT RESPONSIBILITY FOR COMPUTER SECURITY

Ideally, a financial institution should have a computer security officer or team of such officers. In practice, only larger institutions can afford to employ a computer security officer or team. Small- to medium-sized institutions usually include the computer security function as part of the duties of an information technology manager, a security manager (ie the manager of all the institution's security) or an operations manager.

Whatever the job title of the person or persons responsible for computer security, the nature of the management responsibility for computer security must be recognised from the outset. Above all, *the work of the computer security officer and his team must principally be directed at preventing computer security breaches. Locking the stable door after the horse has bolted is a poor substitute for keeping the horse under lock and key.*

As might be expected, there is a direct link between time, effort and money spent on computer security activity and the effectiveness of that activity. It is important that the computer security function should have sufficient staff time devoted to it, but even more important that the computer security officer and his team should be able to report directly to senior management. Figure 6.1 below shows the ideal position of the computer security officer in the institution's hierarchy.

THE PROBLEM OF WHETHER OR NOT TO REPORT A COMPUTER SECURITY BREACH

Is it in the interests of a financial institution which suffers a breach in its computer security to publicise the fact? Even if the institution decides (as many do) to keep the matter confidential, what is the likelihood that details of the breach will in any event eventually reach the media?

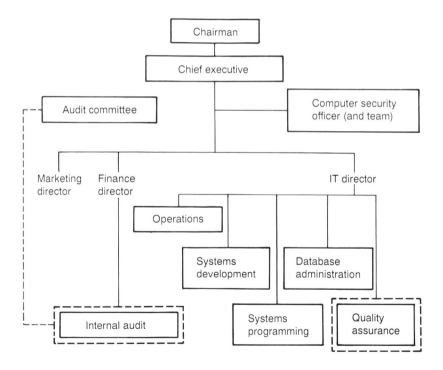

Figure 6.1   The ideal position of the computer security officer in the hierarchy of a financial institution

A strong desire on the part of many institutions to avoid the embarrassment which they believe (with good reason, in some cases) would occur if they were to publicise a computer security breach is one reason why many institutions prefer to call in a private organisation to investigate a computer security breach by an unauthorised person rather than refer the matter to the police.

Although no financial institution is likely to take specific measures to publicise a computer security breach that it has suffered, institutions often do face the choice between allowing information (however unspecific) to become public in the normal course of events and taking deliberate steps to minimise the likelihood of such publicity occurring. This is a difficult choice and it is not easy to offer any specific guidance on how to deal with the matter beyond observing that, *if the rumour persists, then releasing to the media a concise and truthful statement of the facts may well head off much media interest, whereas trying to keep the matter under wraps once the story has broken will only whet journalists' appetites.*

Of course, an even better solution is not to suffer a computer security breach in the first place!

GUARDING AGAINST COMPUTER MISUSE

Introduction

In computer security for financial institutions, prevention is infinitely more important than cure: this principle is fundamental to any computer security considerations. An examination of how financial institutions should undertake to maximise the security of their computer systems and terminal systems follows.

Six key elements in the computer security process can be isolated. The basic contention of this report is that if due and continuing attention is paid to all these elements, a financial institution will have a very high level of protection against loss or damage due to computer security breaches.

The six key elements are:

- insurance
- managing the role of the computer security officer
- the computer security review
- personnel management
- procedural controls
- technical controls.

Insurance

Insurance can play an important role in minimising losses arising from damage to any part of a computer installation and losses due to wilfully illicit use by an unauthorised person, but insurance must not be seen as a substitute for the kind of precautionary measures that are discussed further on.

Insurance for computer systems is available from many large insurers, but as the terms of these policies are complex, insurance brokers can advise on what type of cover is available. As a rule, cover for damage to a computer installation is more readily available than cover for loss due to illicit use. Even where this cover is available, premiums can be so high that a financial institution may conclude that premiums would be better spent on implementing effective precautionary measures. However, as the majority of insurers now expect such precautionary measures to be in place before they grant coverage for loss due to wilful misuse, in practice a financial institution is unlikely to be able to choose between spending money on precautionary measures or on insurance premiums. Any claims made under such policies will not be accepted unless the insured institution can prove that the precautionary measures were in place.

Specifically, insurance policies relating to a financial institution's computer systems are likely to cover the following hazards:

- material damage
- consequential loss (business interruption) including the cost of recreating lost data
- legal liability to third parties due to negligence or fraud
- employee liability.

Wilful misuse by employees is covered by what are known as 'fidelity guarantee' policies. In the UK, for example, the familiar 'Bankers' Blanket Bond' for frauds by bank employees was extended during the 1980s to cover loss due to fraudulent input of electronic data or computer instructions by means of:

- unauthorised access to a terminal
- fraudulent preparation of data tapes
- fraudulent preparation of computer programs
- obtaining access to a bank's communications lines
- fraudulent use of electronic communications systems by the alteration of messages or the misuse of authorisation.

This type of policy only covers the wilful misuse of a computer or terminal system by a bank's employees. Different policies are available from insurers to cover wilful misuse by ex-employees, consultants, contractors and suppliers.

In most cases a computer security review has to be completed by external risk assessors before an insurance policy can be agreed.

MANAGING THE ROLE OF THE COMPUTER SECURITY OFFICER

The need for the computer security officer – whether working alone or with the help of a team – to have the ear of senior management has been discussed. The role of the computer security officer is now considered in more depth.

Although all employees of a financial institution ought to be made to feel that maintaining computer security is part of their job responsibility – and should be encouraged to report suspicious matters accordingly – an institution must identify a specific officer (and a team, too, if the size of the institution warrants this) who will be primarily responsible for all aspects of its computer security. The level of authority needed means that a relatively senior officer is required (probably someone no younger than forty, while the varied range of expertise needed necessarily requires someone with a wide knowledge both of computer security procedures and the institution's business.

As someone concerned above all with the security of the financial institution's computer installations and the integrity of the employees who come into contact with it, the *computer security officer*'s role is different from that of the *security officer*, who will be mainly concerned with physical security (particularly entry to the institution's premises) and theft prevention. However, these two officers should work together where necessary, particularly since – as is seen later in this chapter – good computer security begins with good physical security.

The computer security officer's activities will typically include the security aspects of the following areas of the institution's business:

- general structure and organisation of computer resources
- computer systems personnel (NB. This does not only mean professionals who program the institution's computers, but anybody who comes into contact with computers during the course of their work)
- availability of computer systems
- security and integrity of stored data

- systems development and maintenance
- communications systems (ie voice, data, electronic mail)
- computer system and terminal system operations
- analysis and scheduling of jobs which require computer assistance.

The need to formulate a computer security policy

On appointment, the computer security officer's first task – assuming that there is no major computer security breach which requires immediate investigation – is almost invariably to compile a comprehensive computer security policy and ensure that the principles and guidelines which it embodies are notified to all personnel. The policy need not necessarily be long or detailed, but must contain the following sections.

1 A clear and concise introduction explaining why computer security is so important for the institution.

2 Details of the objectives and scope of the policy.

3 Guidance regarding the role which individual members of staff are expected to play in computer security.

4 A description of the assets and functions to be protected.

5 A general description of the computer security measures (procedural and technical) to be employed (NB: for obvious reasons of security, the precise nature of these measures should not be revealed to anybody except on a 'need-to-know' basis.)

6 A general description of the methods by which compliance will be monitored. Again, there is no need to be too precise over the exact nature of this monitoring. It is sufficient for personnel to know that not only will they be expected to comply with the policy, but that they will be watched on occasion to make sure that they do indeed comply with it.

The computer security officer's tasks focus on the computer security policy. A typical step-by-step activity plan for a computer security officer would be as follows:

- draft a version of the computer security policy and submit this to the Board for approval
- once the computer security policy has been approved, circulate and publicise it among all employees
- discuss and agree computer security procedures for all departments
- compile computer security checklists for each department based on these discussions
- using each checklist, perform computer security reviews for each department

- report to the Board on the results of the departmental reviews
- promptly investigate all reported breaches of security
- continue to liaise with all departments on computer security matters
- update the computer security policy in accordance with any relevant changes in circumstances
- liaise with internal and external auditors.

For the computer security officer to carry out these functions with maximum efficiency, the officer has to hold – and arrange for the regular completion of – the following documents. These will all need to be updated regularly and revised. Examples of the most important documents here are:

- register of computer uses and applications
- detailed log of computer security breaches and responses
- details (probably confidential) of precautionary measures taken by all departments
- computer security checklist.

To perform his job effectively, the computer security officer will require a regular inflow of data to include particular details.

1 New hardware, application systems, operating software and communications equipment.

2 Technical developments relating to the institution's computer systems.

3 Changes in the nature of the institution's business.

4 Significant external developments in the institution's operating environment.

5 Details of computer security breaches which the institution has suffered.

6 Any available details of computer security breaches which rival institutions have suffered. Within the financial sector, computer security officers of financial institutions often exchange – on a highly confidential basis – information about breaches which they have suffered or about threats which they believe to be targeted towards the financial sector (eg relating to particular computer viruses or certain hackers).

The computer security review

The computer security review is a comprehensive and – ideally – exhaustive analysis of an organisation's computer security. It will usually consist of two parts, the first being an analysis of computer security of the organisation at present and the second part explaining what the weak areas are (ie areas that seem particularly vulnerable to computer loss) and how they can be strengthened.

The review is often carried out by external consultants, although a highly skilled in-house computer security officer or team may be able to undertake it.

Computer security reviews must be made on a regular basis if the effectiveness of the overhaul which they represent is to be maximised. In the financial sector, most institutions would be content with an annual review, although where a computer installation is highly sensitive and where the precautionary measures deployed within are complex, a more regular review – perhaps every six months – would seem advisable.

The compilation of the first computer security review will require a great deal of work and also considerable reserves of patience from the staff involved to obtain the fullest picture of computer security at the institution in question. Subsequent reviews, however, can usually be compiled with less effort and will typically be restricted to two processes:

1 updating computer security requirements (eg new business areas, new hardware and software and different working methods)
2 confirming that new computer security precautionary measures recommended as a result of the previous computer security review are in place.

Researching and putting a computer security review together usually involves the following stages.

Familiarisation
This first step is directed at understanding the overall applications of computers in the institution under scrutiny.

Identification of threats
Next, establish what needs to be protected (eg financial assets, confidential data and the institution's reputation: specific computer-related threats to the institution must be carefully identified.

Risk evaluation
A list of priorities for protection should be agreed by experienced managers and the staff of the relevant departments, based on which of the following types of risk are regarded as most serious. Precautionary measures to reduce the risk involved should be taken accordingly:

- loss of business (to whatever degree seems most likely)
- loss of assets

- loss of reputation
- loss of public confidence
- loss from legal suits.

Evaluation of existing precautionary measures

The next phase is to identify any existing computer security precautionary measures, assess their effectiveness and make recommendations for increasing it.

A common mistake at this stage is to assume that the precautionary measure under scrutiny is totally effective and so ignore the need for back-up controls and recovery procedures. Few precautionary measures can be relied upon absolutely. *The ideal approach to computer security is the 'onion skin' approach, in which the failure of any one particular security measure will not leave an asset completely unprotected (ie another aspect of security will take the strain.* Figure 6.2 (see overleaf) illustrates the onion-skin approach, an important concept in computer security which will be met later in this chapter, when looking at the different types of technical precautionary measures available.

Recommendation of new precautionary measures

The review process now moves towards recommending new precautionary measures to be deployed within the institution. It is important to note that precautionary measures for computer security fall into five main categories, although some measures may fall into more than one category. Thus, precautionary measures should perform at least one of the following functions:

- completely prevent a breach from taking place
- reduce the likelihood of a breach taking place
- enable the detection of a breach
- enable the institution to recover from a computer security breach
- mitigate the effect of the breach on the institution.

Within most financial institutions, there will usually be a certain amount of discussion – even controversy – regarding whether recommended precautionary measures should be implemented. Budgetary considerations have to be taken into account and it should be stressed that even senior managers may have difficulty in understanding exactly how potent a threat to their institution's activities computer security breaches can represent.

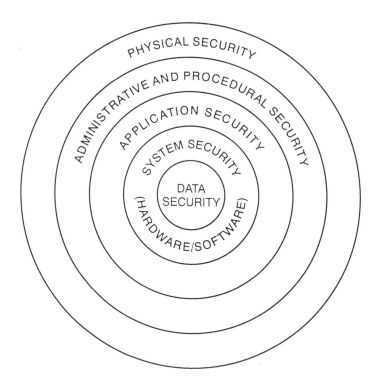

Figure 6.2   The 'onion skin' approach to computer security

This is where the interpersonal skills of the computer security officer who commissioned the review (or who carried it out) are of great importance in overcoming the inertia and indifference which senior managers have towards spending money on what are essentially defensive measures. These skills become paramount in persuading the institution's senior management to deploy the necessary precautionary measures.

Fortunately, in recent years there has been ample coverage of computer crime and computer fraud in the media (although, as we have seen, media coverage has often suggested that breaches are perpetrated by sophisticated outsiders and given insufficient coverage to the role played by insiders). This should mean that senior management is more aware of the gravity of the threat posed by computer security breaches than would have been the case even five years ago.

All recommendations for new precautionary measures must focus on measures which are likely to be as follows.

1 *Effective*. The new measures must pass the criteria used for existing measures, and be:

- designed to deal with the vulnerability
- adequate to seal the vulnerability entirely if properly enforced
- enforceable (ie it is possible to know whether the measure has been implemented and is being carried out, particularly if it requires active participation from staff to carry it out, which it may not do)
- reliable
- formally adopted by the institution and implemented with the full support of senior management.

A measure which does not have the full support of senior management is unlikely to be effective, either because staff, detecting the dissension that exists among senior management, will not have the requisite morale which would lead them to ensure that it is deployed comprehensively and vigorously or because where an initiative to control computer security is not supported by senior managers, the very people whose responsibility it is to deploy it may be half-hearted about the deployment. It follows that, where computer security is concerned, senior management must 'close ranks' and make it clear that they are completely behind the initiative.

2 *Efficient*. The new precautionary measure must ultimately be capable of justification in cost terms. Before a final decision is taken on implementation, a reasonably accurate estimation must be made of the total cost of the solution, including any additional maintenance costs, labour costs and so on.

Implementation of new precautionary measures

Implementation of the new measures recommended by the computer security review must be decisive, wide-ranging and technically accurate, with a full back-up process being put in place which communicates the benefits of the system to staff and urges them to comply with the measure and generally maintain a high level of vigilance regarding the institution's computer security. Generally, once staff realise that a threat to its computer system constitutes a threat to the institution's profits and thus to their own livelihoods, they will realise that complying with the new measure in full is to their advantage.

Several risk analysis software packages are available which can simplify and standardise computer security reviews. The software will often be founded upon a database of rules drawn from experience in the field of computer security, and will enable risks and vulnerabilities to be listed in order of priority, and will suggest remedies for apparent security weaknesses. Such software does not, of course, replace experienced computer security staff, but it can both provide a structure for computer security reviews and perform the calculations necessary to furnish an objective assessment of risks and countermeasures. Examples of such software packages are Riskpac, SRA, MARION and CRAMM.

PERSONNEL MANAGEMENT

Experience has shown that the majority of serious cases of computer misuse are 'inside' jobs, with the perpetrator being a trusted member of the institution's staff, sometimes working in league with more experienced criminals (who will have no compunction about leaving the insider to take the blame and face retribution if the heist starts to go wrong) and sometimes being a 'sleeper' who establishes a record of trust before striking.

An institution's overall computer security policy must take into account the dangers posed by staff – particularly staff working in the computer systems department – who are dishonest, disgruntled or merely incompetent.

Good personnel management is an essential part of good computer security. In particular, the personnel management policy should cover the following areas.

1 In every computer systems installation there are key staff whose activities are of critical importance. They should be identified, given special attention by management and, as soon as practicable, back-up staff should be trained to reduce the organisation's dependence on these key people. They should be left in place but periodically switched to other tasks so that they do not become too closely involved with a particular task for too long.

2 Recruitment procedures should be designed to ensure, as far as possible, that staff are competent and honest. References should be obtained and always checked and a probation period should be used in appropriate cases to verify competence.

3 Facilities should exist within the personnel department for staff with personal difficulties, such as financial, family or psychological problems, to obtain counselling or referral to an outside counsellor. Where insiders have played a major role in perpetrating a computer crime, the fundamental source of the deviation from normal honest behaviour has often been the

onset of a personal problem to which the employee could see no possible resolution.

4 Staff should be encouraged to report, confidentially, on colleagues who seem to be displaying abnormal degrees of stress or behaving in a manner which suggests that they might constitute a security risk.

5 Salary and incentives should be appropriate to the responsibilities of the staff concerned to ensure that the interests and objectives of employers and employees coincide. A comprehensive, practical training programme will encourage employees to consider career development within the institution and avoid the demoralisation caused by lack of achievement.

6 Dismissal and resignation procedures should take into account the damage which can be caused by a dishonest or disgruntled employee while serving a period of notice. If an employee with access to the computer network is allowed to serve out his notice (which may not be advisable), logging on procedures should be changed to prevent the employee in question from using the network during this time.

7 Staff – particularly those with 'hands-on' responsibilities – should be obliged to take their annual holidays. Failure to take any leave usually displays a need to be continually near the system. It is often when a perpetrator is away that a fraud is detected.

PROCEDURAL CONTROLS

The following procedures and policies tend to increase computer security.

Segregation of duties
This is the policy, adopted by most of the world's leading financial institutions, of taking steps to prevent one individual member of staff from having access to, or being in charge of, every element in a particular computing function. For example, one major UK clearing bank does not allow computer programmers to undertake program analysis work. Similarly, the bank has a policy of spreading encryption keys and other security components among a number of people, to ensure that at any one time no single person has access to all the keys.

Four eyes' principle
This policy, related to segregation of duties, means that an institution takes steps to ensure that, where a computing function offers the potential for fraud and theft, wherever possible two people will be needed to access that

function, such as the need for two separate passwords to be keyed into a system or two separate cards to be swiped through a cardswipe, before the function can be accessed. Similarly, computer programs themselves should be independently checked and approved before being entered into the computer.

A good example of the 'four eyes' principle in action is the procedure, followed by most institutions, of customers' deposits into deposit boxes or automated teller machines being checked by two members of staff. As well as removing temptation from a member of staff, this procedure also gives the institution enhanced credibility in the event of a dispute with a customer over a deposit.

Maintaining audit trails

Audit trails (computer-based records containing information relating to who used a computer system or terminal system, when they used it, how long they used it for and related information) are an essential part of computer security because they greatly facilitate investigations into where misplaced funds have gone and who might be responsible for taking them.

TECHNICAL CONTROLS

Introduction

Technical controls are those precautionary measures which are located in the high-tech infrastructure of the computer system itself.

Computers being high-technology tools, the range of technological controls to which an institution must pay attention when seeking to maximise its computer security, are extensive and complex. Examining these controls, and the particular hazards against which they are most adept at defending, occupies the remainder of this chapter.

The microchip has permitted the construction of computer security technology that is compact, powerful, reasonably priced and, therefore, far more widely available. Indeed, it could be argued that computer security technology in the 1990s is able to meet all the challenges that face it and that, consequently, computer security is in essence not a technical problem but a management one: the technology is readily available; what matters is whether the institution has a budget for deploying computer security technology and, if so, how the institution intends to spend it. This is why so much attention focuses on management attitudes rather than simply on the practical solutions which are available to maximise computer security.

Current research and development in the field of computer security technology lies in refining existing technologies rather than in developing new ones. The emphasis is on consolidating existing innovations and convincing an increasing number of users that they need the technology, rather than on hastening to break new technological ground.

Technical precautionary measures are best analysed in conjunction with their associated threats:

- the physical access threat
- the electronic access threat
- the communications security threat
- the systems shutdown threat
- the electromagnetic induction threat.

The physical access threat

This is the threat of an unauthorised person gaining access to the physical proximity of any computer terminal or any other part of the computer system. Precautionary measures to deal with this threat are straightforward. The control system should be based around an entry control method which uses both an electronic token and a password or code so that:

- access to specific rooms as well as to specific buildings can be controlled
- access can be immediately and instantly revoked if an individual ceases to be authorised (eg due to resignation or dismissal). There is therefore no need to try to obtain keys back
- an accurate audit trail can be composed, showing who entered which room and when, and how long they remained there.

Figure 6.3 (see overleaf) shows a ten-point summary of principal physical access controls.

However, not even the most state-of-the-art physical access control system will be of use if entry to the front lobby is not sufficiently monitored. A major element of vulnerability remains the essential need to accommodate visitors. They should always be shown to the office where they are going and escorted back down to the lobby. They should always be relieved of their entry passes when they leave the building (many otherwise highly security-conscious institutions often forget to ask visitors for their entry passes when they leave with the obvious result that many of these passes go astray). *Above all, someone must be in charge of front-lobby security who is not prepared to allow security procedures to slacken.*

---

1 Control access and exit points to and from a building, paying particular attention to tradesmen's entrances 'round the back' of the building.

2 Restrict access to computer rooms and other high-security areas.

3 Make extensive use of staff identification procedures (eg passes, cards, photographs and biometric identification procedures). Ensure that habitual use of these procedures does not lead to complacency and reduced attentiveness.

4 Take particular care with access control procedures for visitors.

5 Take particular care with procedures relating to night shifts.

6 Make extensive use of security staff and surveillance equipment.

7 Locate computer facility in a secure part of the building.

8 Ensure that physical security procedures cover physical transport of data or software between sites.

9 Arrange alternative suppliers of critical components.

10 Ensure that faulty physical access control mechanisms default to 'prevent access' mode.

Figure 6.3   Ten-point summary of physical access controls

The electronic access threat

This is the threat of an unauthorised person being able to gain access to a computer terminal.

Again, the relevant precautionary measures are straightforward. As with the physical access threat, by far the most effective control is to implement an 'electronic token plus codeword' system of personalised access control, restricting access to specific terminals to authorised staff. Modern systems not only allow the restriction to be imposed on certain staff using certain terminals, but even allow it to be imposed at certain times of the day. Such a system is a powerful weapon in the battle against unauthorised use of terminals and provides an invaluable audit trail for the use of any specific terminal.

The communications security threat

This is the threat of an unauthorised person being able to interfere with any computer data communications which an institution sends from one point to another, whether internally, between branches or to an external counterparty.

Communications security, or network security, has been the focus of considerable media attention during the past few years, even though much of the furore about 'hacking', 'viruses' and other threats to communications security may be because they make good newspaper copy rather than because they are particularly difficult threats to counter.

All the same, financial institutions must pay attention to guarding against would-be misusers of their communications systems. A particular danger would be the threat posed to communications systems which pass data from an institution's office to an external counterparty. These external links carry payment instructions relating to billions of pounds every day from financial institutions to counterparties, as well as confidential information which could potentially be worth an equivalent amount. The consequences of this data being deliberately corrupted, altered or lost would be disastrous.

The technical controls for maximising the security of a financial institution's data communications are straightforward and relatively inexpensive to deploy; so straightforward that potential breaches in data communications should not represent such a real threat to so many institutions. The reason why they do is that many institutions do not give the implementation of precautionary measures against this type of computer security threat the attention which they ought.

Due to the particular nature of the data communications process, a precautionary measure for a communications security system must not slow messages down nor, if possible, require the temporary suspension of the system for the precautionary measure to be implemented. This last requirement is even more important if the computer system in question is operating in real-time.

The need to deter unauthorised access

Where possible, an institution ought to consider making its system unattractive to unauthorised users, which is of course easier said than done, since after all the entire emphasis of this book has been to urge institutions to regard their financial technology as a key factor in their bid for competitive advantage, which means making the systems relevant to users' needs and also making them easy and enjoyable to use. However, there is not really a paradox here, since it is clearly one thing to make a system appealing to authorised users, and quite another to make it unattractive to unauthorised users.

In practice, however, retail institutions have little scope for making a system unattractive to unauthorised users other than deploying authorisation procedures which should restrict the user to the owner of the account. In wholesale banking there is more scope for making the system unattractive to the unauthorised, although here, too, it is essential not to alienate bona fide counterparties and clients.

In wholesale banking, one useful technique is to make the 'welcome' message say something which leads unauthorised persons to conclude that the system is not worth interfering with, since they rarely spend more than a few minutes trying to get into a system if it does not interest them. If, for example, the name of the operator of a computer system is given as a well-known financial institution, would-be unauthorised persons might get together and spend the time it takes to break into the system.

A simple solution, if at all practicable, might be to change the name of the system to something uninteresting, such as 'Janitorial Supplies'. Another useful method is to ask for a great deal of information when someone wants to gain entry to a system: the system might request the employee's name, date of birth, department name, supervisor's name and so on; the authorised user is instructed to disregard the requested information and merely enter his name, insert three spaces and enter the password. The request for all the other information should be designed to make the intruder believe it will be impossible to get into the system and discourage any attempt.

Encryption and message authentication

Techniques for maximising the security of communications between computer systems are of two kinds. The first type of technique, *encryption*, aims to encode the communicated message and thus prevent an unauthorised person from finding out what it says. The second type, *message authentication*, seeks to prevent an unauthorised person from tampering with the communicated message, which would otherwise be possible even if the message were in encrypted form. For maximum security of the communicated message, both encryption and message authentication are required, although few organisations go to these lengths; most rely on encryption only.

Encryption is an encoding procedure which takes place at the point of entry of the message to be communicated; it uses software that can be incorporated into the home network via the entry terminal. The message is sent to the external destination, where it is decoded by the same encryption process. The software governing the point of data entry process and the delivery of data process must use the same encryption key, ie a number which is used as the basis for generating the encrypted form of the message.

Encryption relies for its effectiveness on the fact that the encrypted form of the message is generated by a highly complex algorithm which would take so long to break through random trial and error, even if a powerful computer were used for this purpose, that the code is for all practical purposes unbreakable (at least with the reservations below). Since an encryption algorithm is only used in conjunction with a specific key, it is possible for a proprietary algorithm to be supplied, with the algorithm then being 'customised' by the use of a key.

The two most common current encryption standards are Data Encryption Standard (DES) and Rivest, Shamir and Adleman (RSA), named after its inventors. The DES, also known as the Data Encryption Algorithm (DEA), is a standard developed in the 1970s by the US National Bureau of Standards and is extensively used in commerce and finance. In view of its widespread use in international banking networks it is likely to be generally employed throughout the world for some time to come. The DES is a symmetric block cipher employing 64-bit blocks of plain text which are transformed in 64 bits of ciphertext using a 64-bit key. DES may be implemented on microchips so that the encryption/decryption process can be performed at high speed. DES has a number of modes of implementation and can be used with a block, cipher block chaining or stream cipher.

RSA is an assymetric block cipher, and is regarded as the most popular algorithm for public key cryptography. The keys in RSA are several hundred bits in length and the block size varies with the parameters chosen. A user requires some assistance in the mathemetically demanding process of setting up the block size, encryption and decryption keys; moreover the algorithm is more computationally demanding than DES. However, micro-chips are now available for the RSA algorithm and some form of key generation service will normally be provided to users.

For all practical purposes, the use of encryption means that a message communicated between a financial institution's computer and a counter-party should be safe from anyone reading it, this does not necessarily mean that it will be safe from being tampered with. For example, a malevolent hacker might, on seeing that his efforts to read the message must end in frustration, decide to swap elements of the message around, still in its encrypted form, thereby giving the recipient a different message from that originally intended. In order to prevent this from happening, message authentication must be used.

Message authentication helps to protect a user against his data being tampered with by enabling him to check when such tampering has occurred. The message authentication technique involves a special code being put into the data at the point of entry and only allows the data to reach the recipient if the code has been transmitted along with the message, unimpaired. If anyone tries to tamper with the message, the message authentication system will alert the bona fide recipient that this has occurred.

A standard for message authentication encoding has been set down by the American National Standard Institute. This standard is known as 'ANSI Standard X9.9'.

The ideal situation for a institution, as far as its communications security requirements are concerned, is to deploy both encryption and message authentication. In due course, such precautions may be seen as essential.

Where financial institutions are communicating with each other via a data communications system, the techniques of 'nonrepudiation' and 'sender authentication' are important.

'Nonrepudiation' is required where it is in the interests of either counter-party to be able to prove that a particular message was sent. Nonrepudiation is a communications security technique which involves making use of a 'digital signature', in essence a piece of code which an institution may choose to attach to all messages which it receives from or sends to counterparties. Since it is conveyed in encrypted form, the digital signature cannot be accessed or deleted by any party and enables either counterparty to prove that a particular message (such as to buy or sell stock) was sent. The evidence would be strong enough to use in court, if necessary.

Digital signatures are also important for 'sender authentication'. This technique is used where the recipient wishes for proof that the sender is who he says he is. This technique usually involves both counterparties agreeing in advance to a particular password, the use of which by the sender will constitute the proof of his identity. Sender authentication is a potent tech-nique to prevent an institution being defrauded by acting on a bogus instruc-tion, such as a fraudulent order to transfer funds.

Some of the breaches in computer communications security which organ-isations most fear are summarised in two terms: *hacking* and the computer *virus*.

Hacking

In the 1970s the expression 'hacker' was merely used to denote someone who was enthusiastic about computers and liked using them. It is only since the late 1980s that the term has started to denote a more sinister figure: one who practises hacking – the process whereby an unauthorised user tries to gain entry to a computer network by defeating the system's access controls. A hacker might work in his victim's office but is more likely to operate via an external communications system.

The computer virus

A computer *virus* is a rogue software element which typically gains access to a computer system via legitimate or apparently legitimate software and then, much in the manner of a pathological virus, sets to work to damage its host by a variety of means that usually include continual self-replication. Some viruses are essentially benign, in that they cause no damage to stored data, but have an effect which is usually limited to some device such as flashing a message on the computer screen. Other viruses are malevolent, in that they destroy data or interfere with the workings of a program. The most dangerous type of virus – unfortunately becoming more common – is designed to conceal its own tracks, with the result that many pieces of software incorporating the virus may be copied by an institution from the original, contaminated software before the fact of the contamination is known.

Viruses which are designed to activate when the computer program reaches a certain stage are often known as 'logic bombs' or 'time bombs'.

Controlling hackers and viruses

The remedies available to the problem of hackers and viruses are relatively straightforward. A good way to deal with hackers is to install a specialised type of access control system for all external parties who wish to enter the communications network. This system is usually known as a 'dial-back' modem and requires any would-be user to be called back by the system before the user can access it. This simple technique is widely used by national telephone organisations in order to verify that a person using a particular service, such as operator dialling, is actually calling from the telephone number which he quotes.

Some dial-back systems are programmed so that they can only call certain prearranged bona fide numbers. Where this is the case, a hacker who is not calling from these numbers is unable to access the system. In theory, it is hard for any hacker to fake his own telephone number and the vast majority of hackers, confronted with such a system, would probably move on to some less secure system operated by another organisation.

Viruses can be combated in two principal ways. Firstly, if an institution constantly makes back-ups of its data (at least on a daily basis), the risk of a virus damaging an entire databank is minimised. Secondly, the best method of preventing a virus from entering the institution's computer system is to make regular (ie daily) use of a 'checksum' program which is able to detect whether a piece of software has been altered in any way. By making regular back-up copies of data and software, and deploying checksum programs, it should be possible for an institution to prevent virus access to his system.

The systems shutdown threat

Systems shutdown occurs when an entire computer system ceases to be operative. The causes are numerous and include power failure, fire, major physical accident or major software or hardware failure.

Any financial institution which is making heavy use of computers should deploy the latest methods for protecting the environment where the computers are housed and have a workable contingency plan in place in case a power failure occurs. Most institutions deal with this difficulty by having a fire control system in place (often incorporating halon gas, which drives combustible oxygen away from the environment) and an array of batteries for short-term power replacement and an externally-situated generator for longer-term power replacement.

However, this still leaves a problem if the installation meets with a catastrophe such as a physical accident or a devastating fire. In this eventuality, what the institution ideally needs is an alternative site, with computers already in place, where it can transfer its existing computing requirements. This is where *disaster recovery facilities* come in. They are essentially facilities which are available in an emergency to the institutions which have paid for them. Because the likelihood of an individual institution requiring disaster recovery facilities is small and the chances of two or more institutions requiring the service simultaneously are negligible (if this happened, the agreement covering the facility should provide for the other participating institutions to help with the spare capacity in their own computer systems) it is quite feasible for several of them to band together and fund a disaster recovery facility.

The electromagnetic induction threat

In broad terms, this is the threat of an unauthorised person gaining access to, or interfering with, a computer system without any direct online interference, but by deploying a variety of techniques which exploit the fact that all elements of a computer system emit electromagnetic radiation which can be 'read' by an inductive process even some distance away from the physical siting of the hardware.

The precautionary methods to guard against this threat are:

- if feasible, install all terminals as far away as possible from exterior walls
- where the threat is very grave, a powerful defensive measure is to place a copper screen between the source of the electromagnetic radiation and the possible siting of an illicit detection device.

A proprietary standard exists for office cabinets which are designed to house a computer or terminal system and thereby prevent, or greatly reduce, the emission of electromagnetic radiation. These cabinets are manufactured to the 'Tempest' standard, which originated at the UK Ministry of Defence.

7 THE FUTURE OF FINANCIAL TECHNOLOGY

I began this book with a tribute to financial technology; I end it with an attempt to peer into a somewhat murky crystal ball and suggest how the world of financial technology is likely to develop in the future and thus indicate how financial technology will need to be managed in time to come.

For the purposes of this chapter I limit my forecasts of the future to what remains of the 1990s. Attempting to make predictions beyond that would give the forecasts the air of mere speculation. On the face of it there is no harm in making such speculations, but the entire thrust of this book has been on detailing the practical realities of financial technology in today's financial arena and there seems to me no sense in abandoning this main objective, even at this stage.

The following, then, are my suggestions for how financial technology will develop during the remainder of the 1990s. I have listed the topics in order of probable importance.

1 Increasing processing and data storage power

There seems no doubt at all that processing and storage power will continue to increase, with technological developments reaching the point where even the very largest real-time applications can be run on a Midrange computer and where PC LANs will be increasingly useful for all but the very largest in-house applications. Personal computers themselves will become powerful enough for individual users to have access to extreme levels of processing and storage power.

2 Increasing sophistication of financial packages

With processing and storage power becoming increasingly widely available at a fairly modest cost, financial institutions will be able to give the widest range of users access to the most sophisticated front- and back-office packages.

3 Increasing systems integration between front and back office

The Dubin & Swieca system discussed in detail on pages 132–7 is an example of a system that features the integration in one technological resource of a variety of front- and back-office functions. Such systems integration will become increasingly important in the future, as institutions come to realise that it offers considerable opportunities to gain competitive advantage by allowing front and back offices to benefit from each other's information and thereby improve the general efficiency of the institution as well as its customer service. Systems integration also helps to facilitate more rapid development and implementation of a financial system.

4 Increasing sophistication of decision support systems

It seems inevitable that systems for providing decision support in the front office by handling a wide range of data feeds and representing this information in a format most useful to the decision maker will become increasingly powerful and increasingly widely used. One principal effect of this will be to make markets more efficient, since everybody will tend to have access to the same information. This phenomenon is already clearly happening in many US markets. Where markets are highly efficient, opportunities for gaining a competitive edge are, by definition, very rare, since no single participant can expect to have the opportunity to gain consistent exceptional profits.

In this scenario, indexation will probably become even more popular than it is already and active, 'stock-picking' types of decision-making may become increasingly regarded as old-fashioned and doomed to failure. Also, traders and investors will become ever more dependent on the entire risk of the market (ie the systematic risk) in which they are operating and macro-economic factors will tend to become vastly more important than they are today. Specific factors relating to the business activities of individual corporations (which issue financial instruments) will be communicated to the market so quickly by means of technology and accommodated in the price of these institutions' shares that in-depth research on these organisations' activities will become less important as a means of influencing trading and investment decisions.

5 Increased use of data communications

This is such an obvious trend that it hardly needs stating, but none the less it is worth pointing out that data communications, already so all-pervasive within most financial institutions, can only continue to proliferate within the financial sector. As the 1990s proceed, an increasing number of negotiations which currently take place via the telephone will take place via computer screen and across a data communications line, as this method is not only faster, less expensive and more accurate, but it also easily lends itself to the recording of the transaction.

6 Increased use of outsourcing for certain 'commodity'-type technology services

Outsourcing involves a particular service being supplied by an external organisation to a user. Many types of technology are initially supplied on an outsourced basis, usually because the cost of the technology is too high for an organisation to buy in the technology itself. Examples of technologies that were once supplied mainly on an outsourced basis are telex, fax (tele-copier), photocopier and data processing. The demand for outsourcing these technologies reduce once the technologies became less expensive. However, now that the 'commodity' nature of many services which are delivered through financial technology has become apparent, and with increasingly sophisticated data communications meaning that links between the outsourcer and the customer can be extremely rapid and efficient, outsourcing has again become an important force in the financial technology industry. The following types of services are most usually the subject of outsourcing:

- ATM network operation
- client accounting
- clearance and settlement.

In time, however, many other types of services that have a high degree of technological input may become the subject of outsourcing. Given that the institution has complete control over which of its facilities are outsourced and when and by which organisation, there is a good deal to be said in favour of outsourcing. Not only does it allow the facility to be handled by specialists who may be expected to make savings due to bulk operation (and ought to pass at least some of these savings on to the institution) but outsourcing allows the institution to focus on its day-to-day business while knowing that if the outsourcer does not discharge its responsibilities properly the institution has some comeback.

7 Increased status of information technology staff within the institution

Whatever else this book may have shown, it should at least have suggested that, for a financial institution seeking to maximise its competitive advantage from the use of technology, simply regarding technology as 'data processing' is no good at all. As institutions place a proper regard on the role of the information technology department, they will have the wisdom to start increasing the seniority of information technology staff, thereby acknowledging the essential role which financial technology managers play in ensuring the current and future health of an institution.

8 Increased recognition of the importance of useability

I have already discussed this matter in detail in Chapter Four, and at this point would only say that many institutions have plenty to learn on the subject of making their systems more attractive and enjoyable to use by customers and staff.

And what of the other, more glamorous trends in financial technology? What role will artificial intelligence play in the financial sector of the future? How will the probable inevitable development of advanced forms of virtual reality affect the financial sector? Rather than speculate too openly here, I prefer to set down a single guideline to cover the role which all types of advanced technology play in the financial sector: *other things being equal, any technology which has the realistic potential to offer a financial institution a competitive advantage in some area of its activity, will be explored in detail by that institution.* For financial technology managers, what this means, above all, is that they can look forward, both now and in the future, to working with technologies which are at the forefront of what human ingenuity can devise.

GLOSSARY

Application One of the tasks (or the only task) which a computer is designed to carry out.

Audit trail A record of the activities of a computer system that enables a transaction to be traced through the system from start to finish, with the precise level of information that is available throughout the tracing process depending on how thorough and comprehensive the audit trail has been designed to be.

Artificial intelligence (AI) A term used in a general way to denote the attribute of a computer system that attempts to simulate a human thought process involving some degree of subjective judgement.

Computer security Any implementation or activity directed at maintaining or improving the integrity, operation and resistance to external unauthorised interference of a computer installation.

Computer A configuration of computer hardware and software which can undertake a useful task.

Decision support system A computer system that supplies information which can help a human with formulating a financial decision.

Disaster recovery A branch of computer security that involves creating a contingency plan in the event that a major accident, fire or prolonged loss of power shuts down a computer centre.

Electromagnetic induction A phenomena whereby electromagnetic radiation can be detected and 'read' by suitably placed devices, usually installed illicitly.

Encryption A technique for coding data to prevent unauthorised persons from reading it.

Hardware Computer machinery.

Hacker Someone who attempts, whether successfully or not, to obtain illicit access to a database along a communications link. In the US, a criminally disposed hacker is sometimes known as a 'cracker'.

Icon In computer useability, a symbol (usually screen-based), which helps the user to gain access to a useful icon (q.v.).

Inference engine A computer system component which searches a knowledge base in order to provide judgements relating to a particular case.

Local area network (LAN) An internal network of computer terminals.

Knowledge base An organised body of information in computer memory, designed to amount as far as possible to a replication of that knowledge 'held' in a human expert's brain and which relates to a particular field of expertise.

Logic bomb A type of virus which is automatically triggered when a computer program or type of application reaches a certain stage.

Mainframe The largest type of computer.

Message authentication An encryption technique which enables the recipient of data along a network to detect whether the data has been illicitly modified or otherwise tampered with.

Metaphor In computer useability, a method used within the user interface to enable the user to carry out an action by referring the action to some activity with which the user will be familiar.

Minicomputer A medium-sized computer; smaller than a mainframe but not small enough to sit on the user's desk.

Neural net A simple computerised simulation of the neurone/synapsis connective process of the human brain.

Object-oriented programming A computer programming technique that involves tackling a problem (typically a problem relating to an application) by breaking it down into a sequence of intermediate steps of individual 'objects'.

Password A unique identifying name or number which gives its holder access to a computer system.

Personal computer (PC) A computer which is compact enough to sit on the user's desk.

PIN A personal identification number: this is a number, usually of four digits in length, which is used widely in conjunction with an electronic token such as a card, to gain access to a computer terminal or system.

Program trading This term is now most usually taken to mean trading an entire block or portfolio of shares in a single transaction, or series of transactions, with the computer usually being employed to keep a record of the transaction or transactions.

RSA Rivest, Shamir Adlemann: a widely used encryption code.

Rule-based system A type of computer system that involves using a knowledge base (q.v.) and an inference engine (q.v.) to arrive at certain conclusions. Also known as a knowledge-based system.

Software Computer programming media.

Unauthorised person Someone who does not have authorisation to carry out a particular computer application. Note that an unauthorised person may well be authorised to carry out other applications within the institution.

Virus A 'rogue' computer program – often introduced via otherwise legitimate software – which interferes (whether on a benign or malicious basis) with a legitimate computer function or application.

Virtual reality A computerised simulation of real sense data which is designed to give the user the illusion that the simulated sense data came from the real world.

Wide area network (WAN) A network of computer terminals that reaches out to external offices, whether of the institution that runs the network or of a counterparty.

Workstation A general term for a desktop computer with access to enough memory and processing power for the user to be able to use the workstation to complete useful work. A workstation is typically a PC or a terminal networked to a minicomputer or mainframe computer.

BIBLIOGRAPHY

Arkin, S. (Ed.). *Prevention and Prosecution of Computer and High Technology Crime*. New York: Matthew Bender, 1989.

Albrecht, W. Steve; Howe, Keith R; Romey, Marshall B. 'Deterring Fraud: The Internal Auditor's Perspective'. *The Institute of Internal Auditors Research Foundation, Altamonte Springs*, Florida: 1984.

Baker, Richard H. *The Computer Security Handbook*. Pennsylvania: Tab Professional and Reference Books, 1985.

Bologna, G. Jacks; Lindquist, Robert J. *Fraud Auditing and Forensic Accounting*. New York: John Wiley & Sons, 1987.

Brand, S. *The Media Lab – Inventing the Future at MIT*. London: Viking, 1987.

Comer, Michael J. *Corporate Fraud*. Maidenhead, UK: McGraw-Hill, 1977 (Second edition 1985).

Comer, Michael J.; Ardis, Patrick M.; Price, David H. *Bad Lies in Business*. Maidenhead, UK: McGraw-Hill, 1988.

Diaper, Dan (Ed.). *Knowledge Elicitation*. New York: Ellis Horwood, 1987.

Dreyfus, H. L.; Dreyfus, S. E. *Mind Over Machine*. Oxford, UK: Basil Blackwell, 1986.

Feigenbaum, McCormack, Nii. *The Rise of the Expert Company*. London: Macmillan, 1987.

Kerr, Philip, *A Philosophical Investigation*, Chatto & Windus, London, 1992.

Longley, D. and Shain, J. *Data and Computer Security*. London: Macmillan, 1987.

Nettler, Gwynn. *Lying, Cheating and Stealing*. Cincinatti: Anderson Publishing Company, 1982.

Norman, D. A. *The Psychology of Everyday Things*. New York: Basic Books, 1987.

Polanyi, M. *The Tacit Dimension*. London: Routledge & Kegan Paul, 1987.

Price, David. *Fraudbusting*. London: Mercury, 1991.

Reed, Alan; Watt, Steve. *The Computer Security Manager*. Amsterdam: Elsevier, 1990 (Second edition).

Schneiderman, B. *Designing the User Interface – Strategies for Effective Human-Computer Interaction*. New York: Addison-Wesley, 1987.

Turing, Alan. 'On Computable Numbers, with an Application to the Entscheidungsproblem'. *Proceedings of the London Mathematical Society*, Series 2, Volume 42, 1937, (pages 230–265).

INDEX

CK303

全书.

大结构